WELCOME TO TRANQUILITY

ONE FOOT IN THE GRAVE

WELCOME TO TRANQUILITY

ONE FOOT IN THE GRAVE

GAIL SIMONE
Writer

HORACIO DOMINGUES
Artist

JONNY RENCH
CARRIE STRACHAN
Colorists

TRAVIS LANHAM
Letterer

NEIL GOOGE
JOHNNY RENCH
Cover Artists

ETHAN VAN SCIVER
MOOSE BAUMANN
Variant Cover Artists

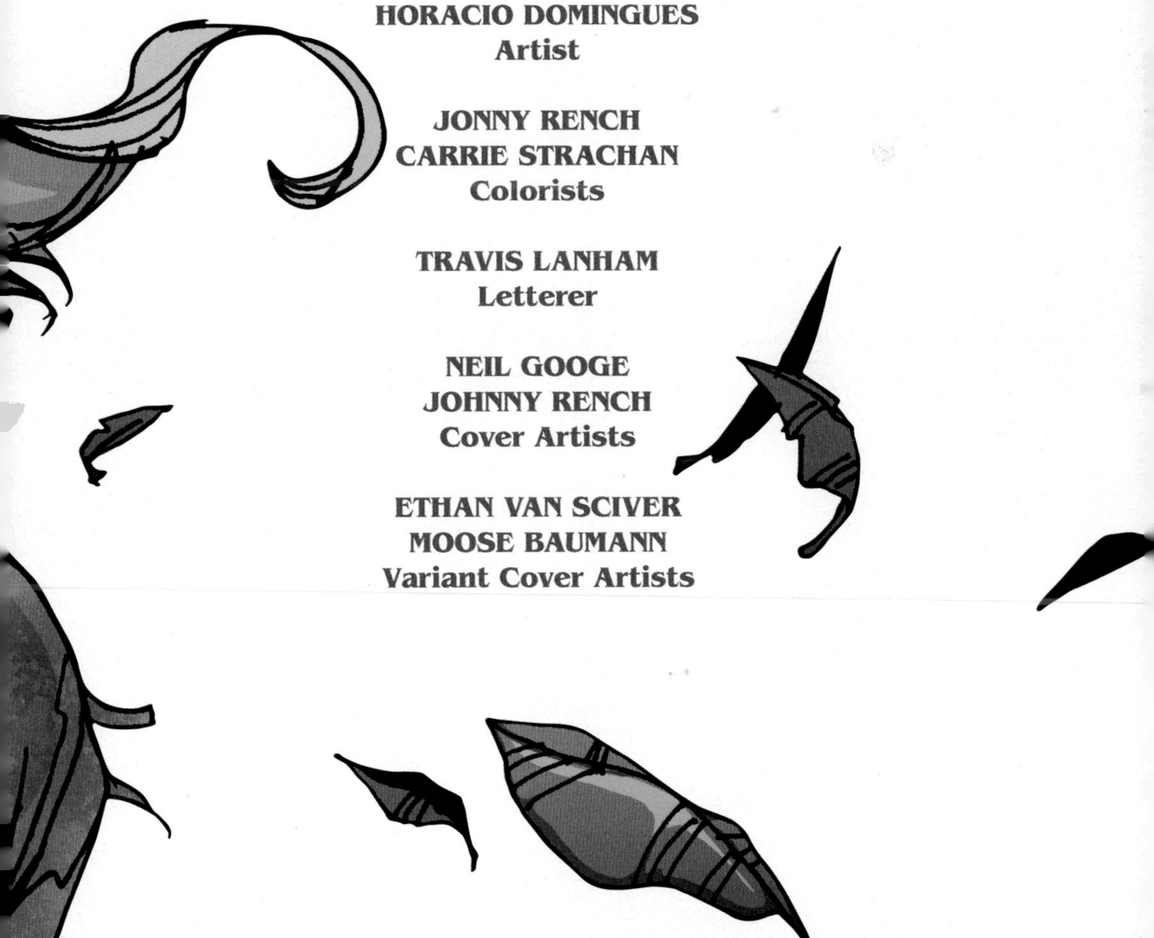

Ben Abernathy
Editor – Original Series

Kristy Quinn
Assistant Editor – Original Series

Ian Sattler
Director Editorial, Special Projects and
Archival Editions

Robbin Brosterman
Design Director – Books

Eddie Berganza
Executive Editor

Bob Harras
VP – Editor in Chief

Diane Nelson
President

Dan DiDio and Jim Lee
Co-Publishers

Geoff Johns
Chief Creative Officer

John Rood
Executive VP – Sales, Marketing and
Business Development

Amy Genkins
Senior VP – Business and Legal Affairs

Nairi Gardiner
Senior VP – Finance

Jeff Boison
VP – Publishing Operations

Mark Chiarello
VP – Art Direction and Design

John Cunningham
VP – Marketing

Terri Cunningham
VP – Talent Relations and Services

Alison Gill
Senior VP – Manufacturing and Operations

David Hyde
VP – Publicity

Hank Kanalz
Senior VP – Digital

Jay Kogan
VP – Business and Legal Affairs, Publishing

Jack Mahan
VP – Business Affairs, Talent

Nick Napolitano
VP – Manufacturing Administration

Ron Perazza
VP – Online

Sue Pohja
VP – Book Sales

Courtney Simmons
Senior VP – Publicity

Bob Wayne
Senior VP – Sales

WELCOME TO TRANQUILITY:
ONE FOOT IN THE GRAVE

Published by DC Comics. Cover and compilation
Copyright © 2011 DC Comics. All Rights Reserved.

Originally published by WildStorm Productions in
single magazine form in WELCOME TO TRANQUILITY:
ONE FOOT IN THE GRAVE 1-6. Copyright © 2010,
2011 DC Comics. All Rights Reserved. All characters
featured in this issue, the distinctive likenesses thereof
and related elements are trademarks of DC Comics.
The stories, characters and incidents mentioned in
this publication are entirely fictional.
DC Comics does not read or accept unsolicited
submissions of ideas, stories or artwork.

DC Comics, 1700 Broadway, New York, NY 10019
A Warner Bros. Entertainment Company
Printed by Quad/Graphics, Dubuque, IA, USA.
6/17/11. First Printing.
ISBN: 978-1-4012-3175-0

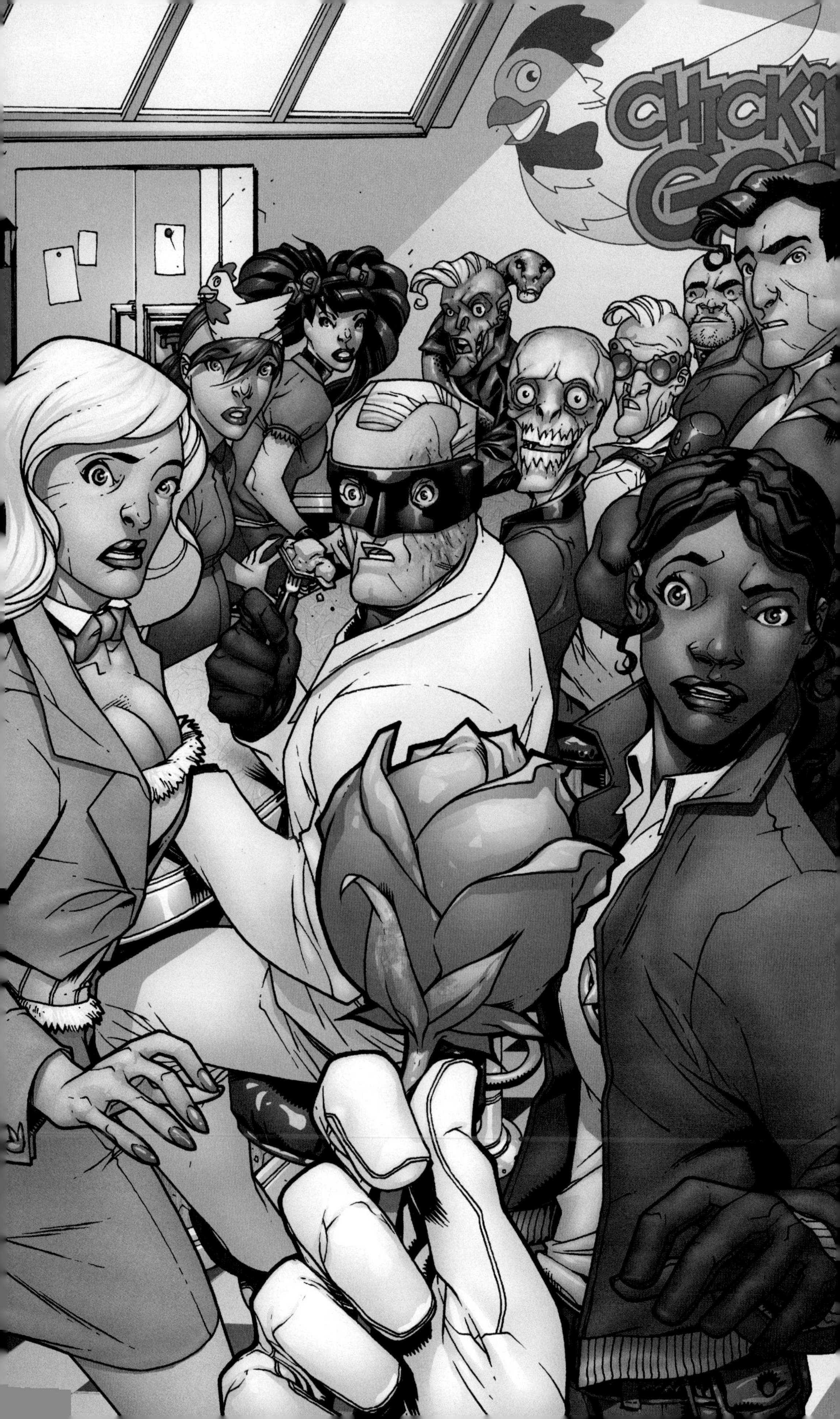

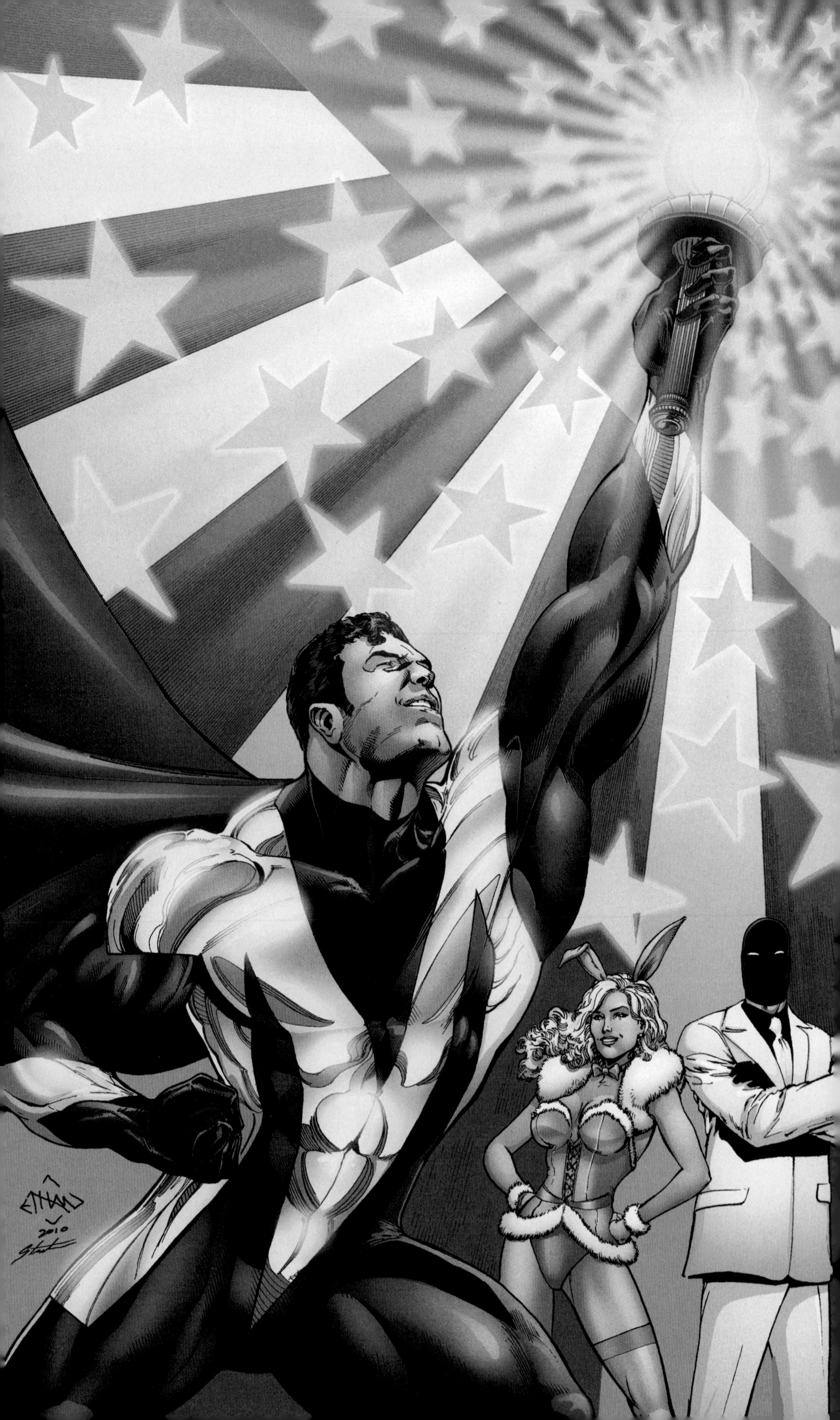

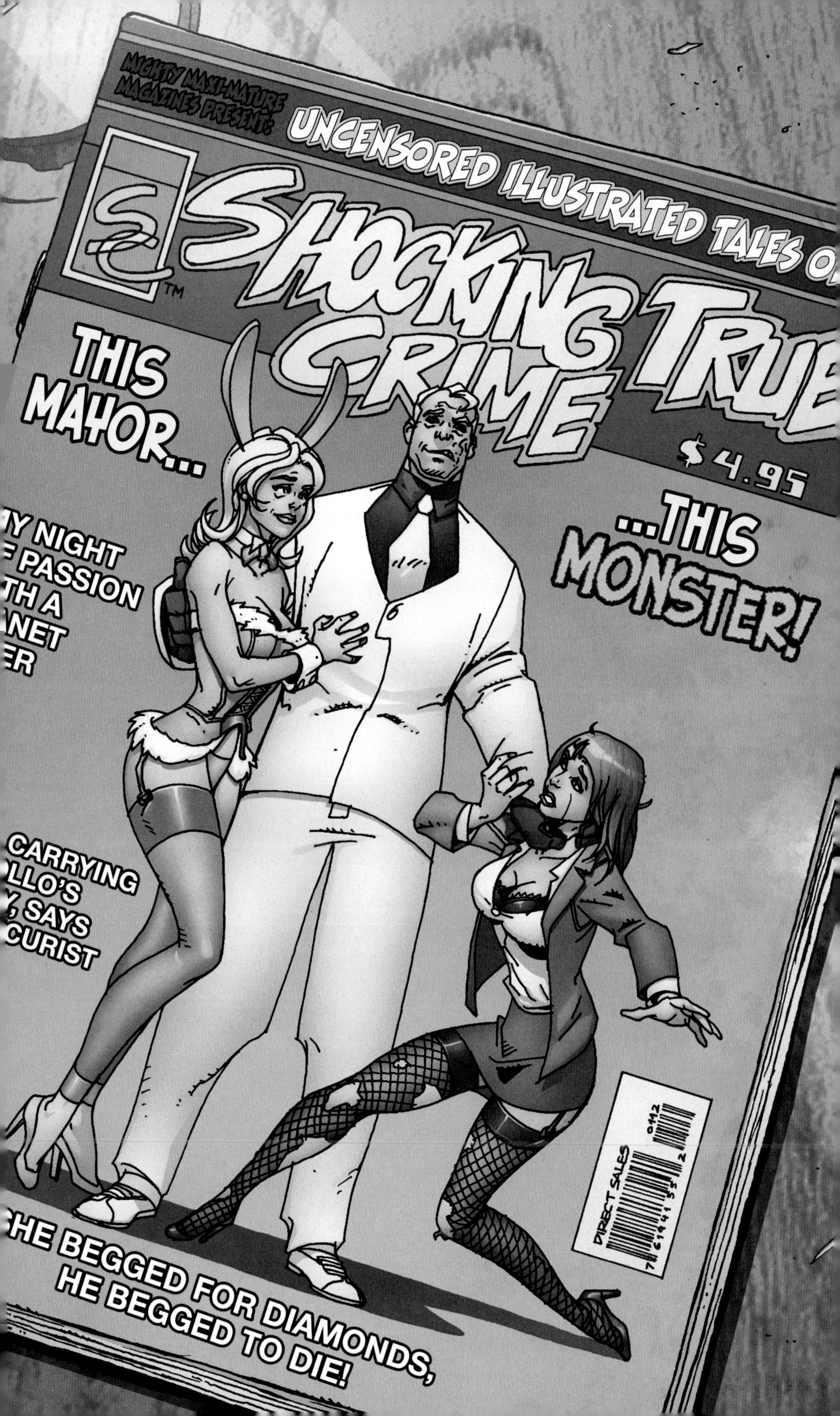
MIGHTY MAXI-MATURE MAGAZINES PRESENT:
UNCENSORED ILLUSTRATED TALES O
SHOCKING TRU
CRIME
$4.95
THIS MAYOR...
...THIS MONSTER!
Y NIGHT
F PASSION
TH A
NET
ER
CARRYING
LLO'S
Y, SAYS
CURIST
HE BEGGED FOR DIAMONDS,
HE BEGGED TO DIE!
DIRECT SALES

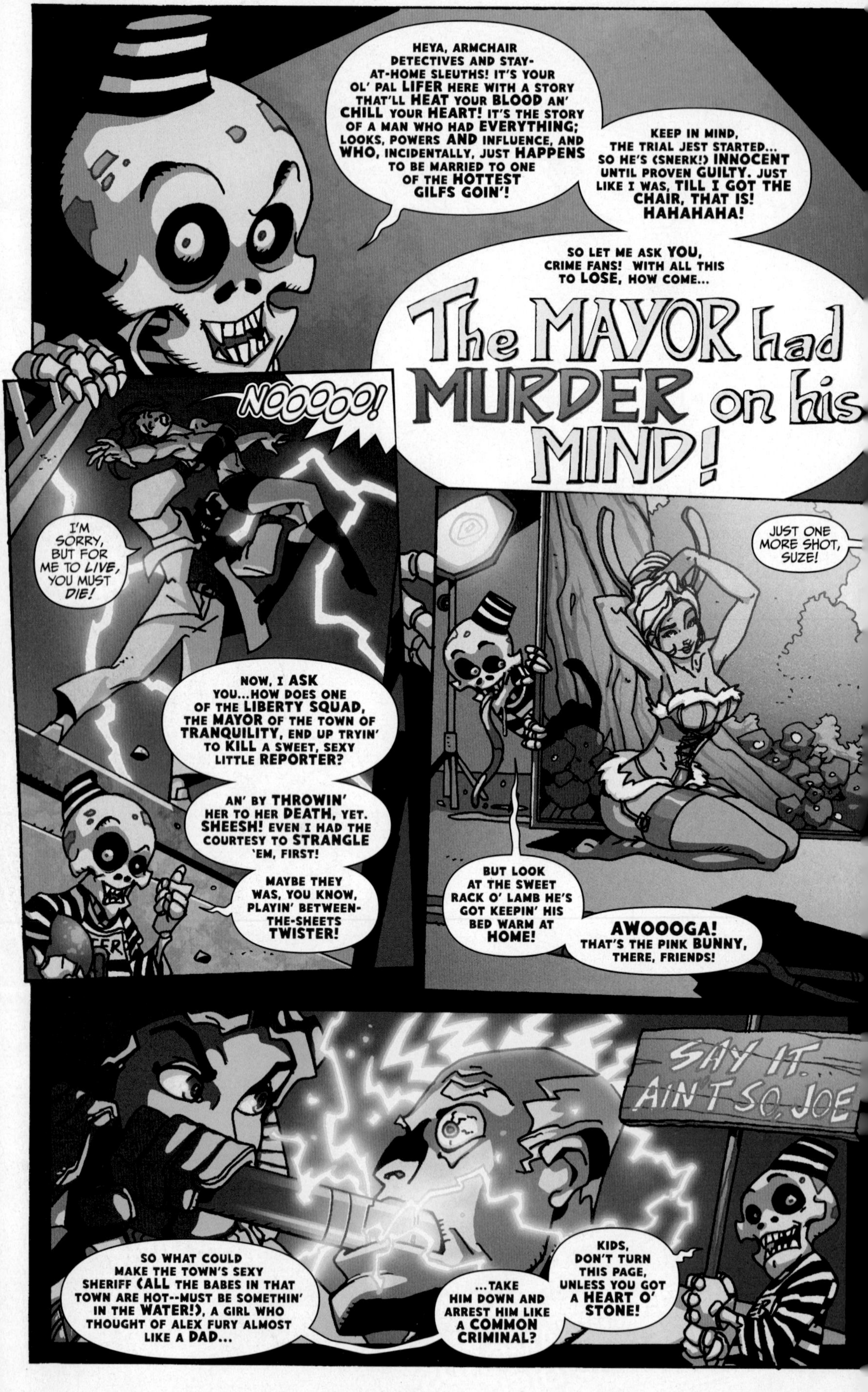
HEYA, ARMCHAIR DETECTIVES AND STAY-AT-HOME SLEUTHS! IT'S YOUR OL' PAL LIFER HERE WITH A STORY THAT'LL HEAT YOUR BLOOD AN' CHILL YOUR HEART! IT'S THE STORY OF A MAN WHO HAD EVERYTHING; LOOKS, POWERS AND INFLUENCE, AND WHO, INCIDENTALLY, JUST HAPPENS TO BE MARRIED TO ONE OF THE HOTTEST GILFS GOIN'!
KEEP IN MIND, THE TRIAL JEST STARTED... SO HE'S (SNERK!) INNOCENT UNTIL PROVEN GUILTY. JUST LIKE I WAS, TILL I GOT THE CHAIR, THAT IS! HAHAHAHA!
SO LET ME ASK YOU, CRIME FANS! WITH ALL THIS TO LOSE, HOW COME...
The MAYOR had MURDER on his MIND!
NOOOOOO!
I'M SORRY, BUT FOR ME TO LIVE, YOU MUST DIE!
NOW, I ASK YOU...HOW DOES ONE OF THE LIBERTY SQUAD, THE MAYOR OF THE TOWN OF TRANQUILITY, END UP TRYIN' TO KILL A SWEET, SEXY LITTLE REPORTER?
AN' BY THROWIN' HER TO HER DEATH, YET. SHEESH! EVEN I HAD THE COURTESY TO STRANGLE 'EM, FIRST!
MAYBE THEY WAS, YOU KNOW, PLAYIN' BETWEEN-THE-SHEETS TWISTER!
JUST ONE MORE SHOT, SUZE!
BUT LOOK AT THE SWEET RACK O' LAMB HE'S GOT KEEPIN' HIS BED WARM AT HOME!
AWOOOGA! THAT'S THE PINK BUNNY, THERE, FRIENDS!
SAY IT AIN'T SO, JOE
SO WHAT COULD MAKE THE TOWN'S SEXY SHERIFF (ALL THE BABES IN THAT TOWN ARE HOT--MUST BE SOMETHIN' IN THE WATER!), A GIRL WHO THOUGHT OF ALEX FURY ALMOST LIKE A DAD...
...TAKE HIM DOWN AND ARREST HIM LIKE A COMMON CRIMINAL?
KIDS, DON'T TURN THIS PAGE, UNLESS YOU GOT A HEART O' STONE!

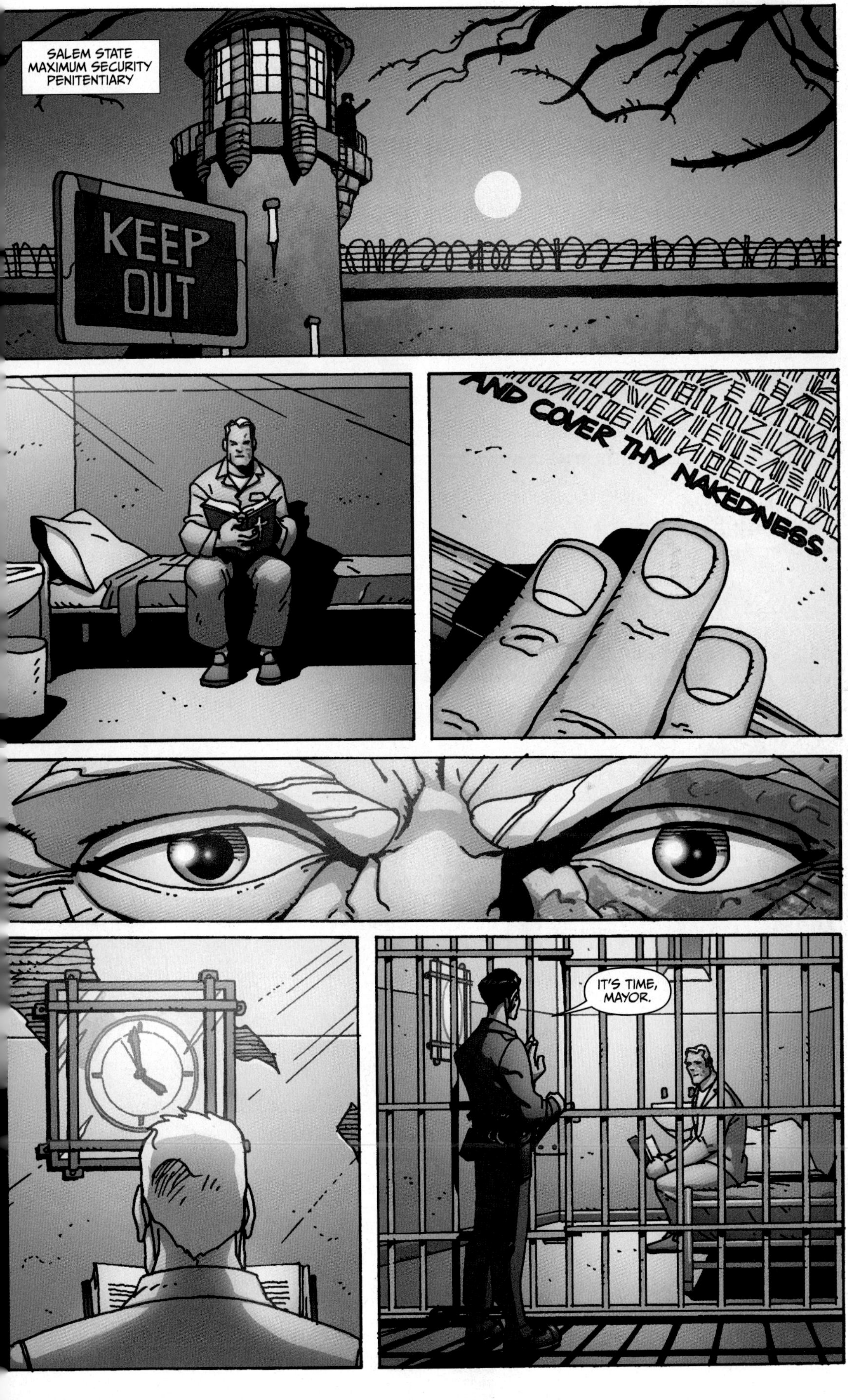
SALEM STATE MAXIMUM SECURITY PENITENTIARY
KEEP OUT
AND COVER THY NAKEDNESS.
IT'S TIME, MAYOR.

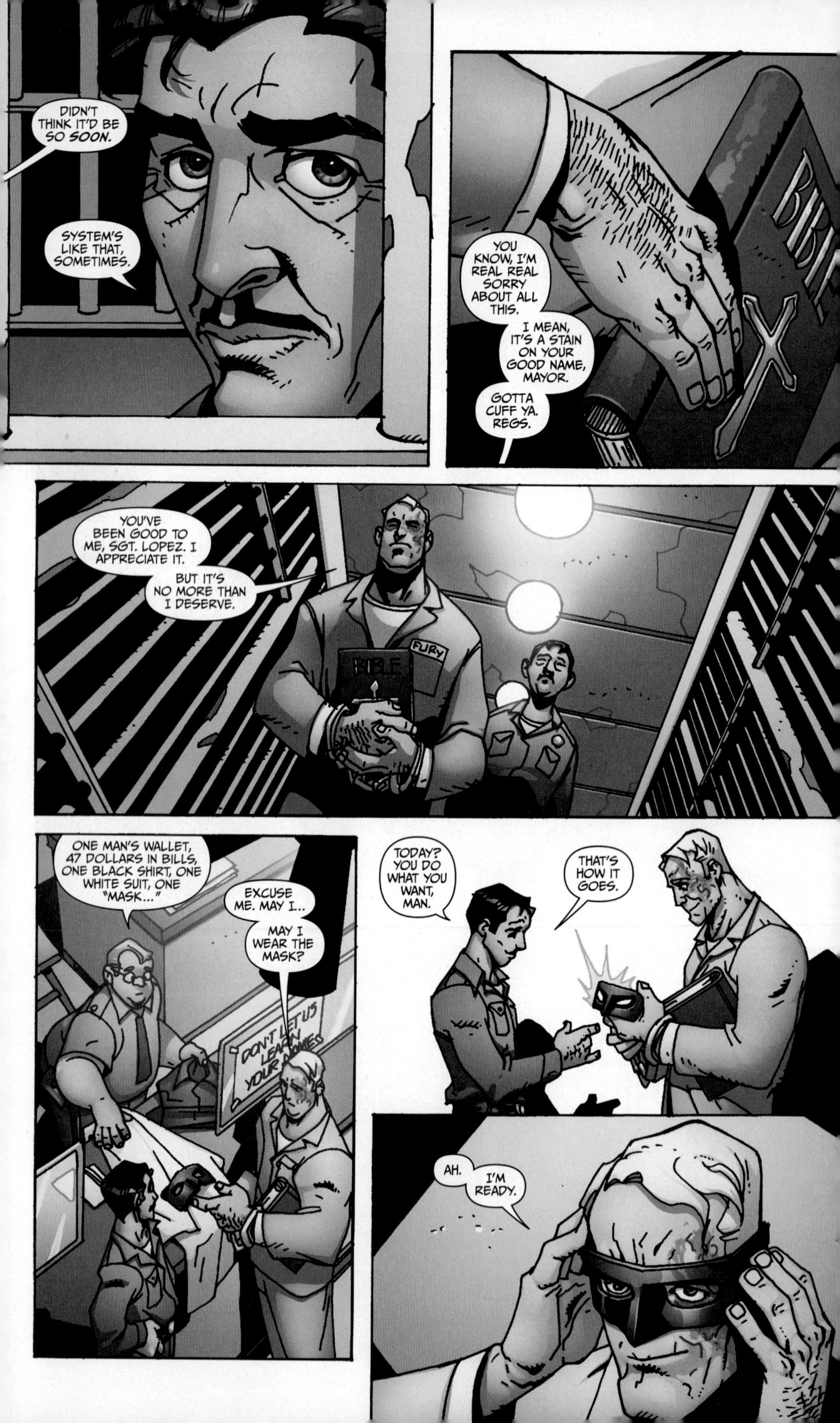
DIDN'T THINK IT'D BE SO SOON.
SYSTEM'S LIKE THAT, SOMETIMES.
BIBLE
YOU KNOW, I'M REAL REAL SORRY ABOUT ALL THIS.
I MEAN, IT'S A STAIN ON YOUR GOOD NAME, MAYOR.
GOTTA CUFF YA. REGS.
YOU'VE BEEN GOOD TO ME, SGT. LOPEZ. I APPRECIATE IT.
BUT IT'S NO MORE THAN I DESERVE.
BIBLE
FURY
ONE MAN'S WALLET, 47 DOLLARS IN BILLS, ONE BLACK SHIRT, ONE WHITE SUIT, ONE "MASK..."
EXCUSE ME. MAY I...
MAY I WEAR THE MASK?
DON'T LET US LEARN YOUR NAMES
TODAY? YOU DO WHAT YOU WANT, MAN.
THAT'S HOW IT GOES.
AH.
I'M READY.

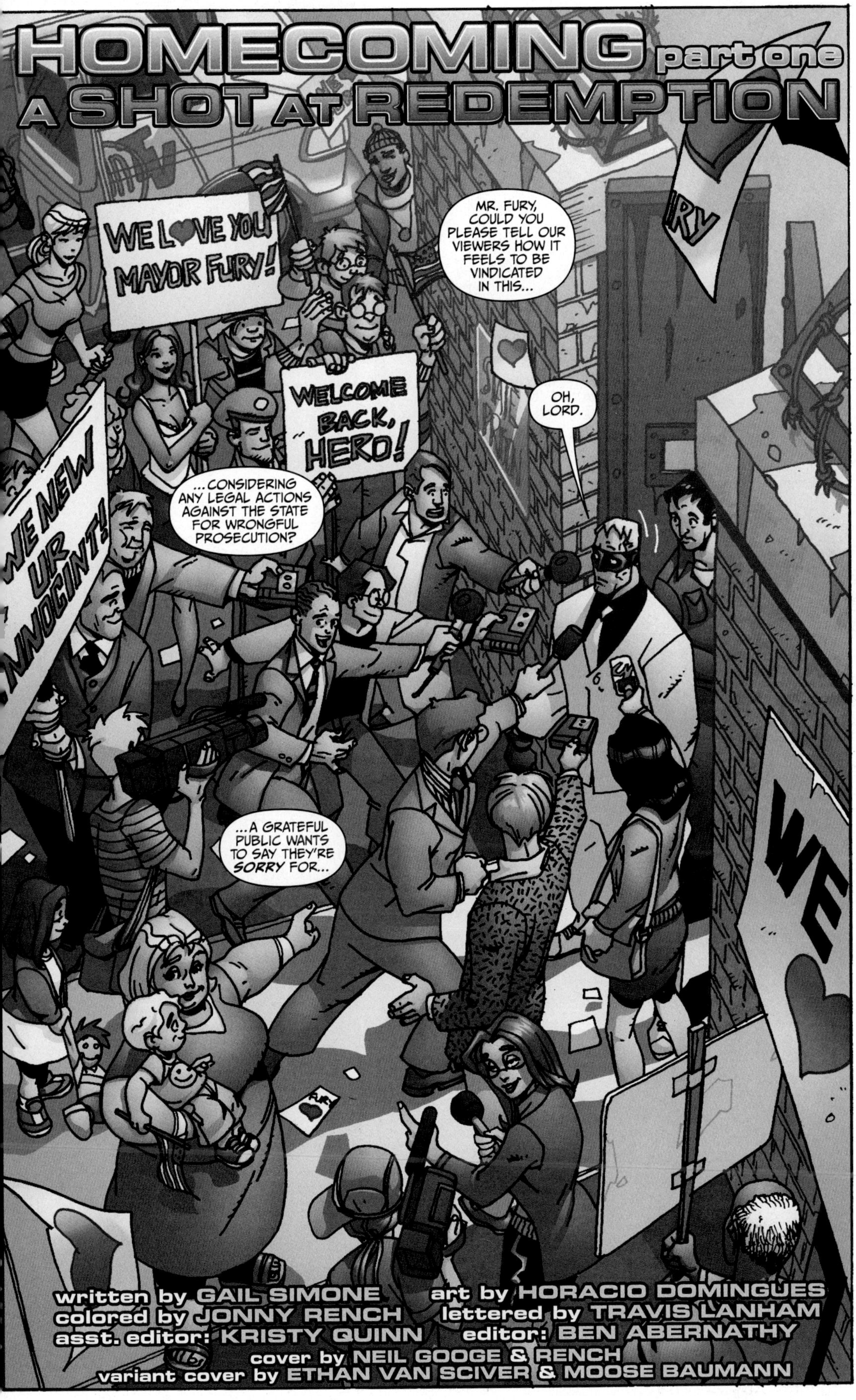
HOMECOMING part one
A SHOT AT REDEMPTION
WE LOVE YOU MAYOR FURY!
MR. FURY, COULD YOU PLEASE TELL OUR VIEWERS HOW IT FEELS TO BE VINDICATED IN THIS...
WELCOME BACK, HERO!
OH, LORD.
WE NEW UR INNOCINT!
...CONSIDERING ANY LEGAL ACTIONS AGAINST THE STATE FOR WRONGFUL PROSECUTION?
...A GRATEFUL PUBLIC WANTS TO SAY THEY'RE SORRY FOR...
written by GAIL SIMONE art by HORACIO DOMINGUES
colored by JONNY RENCH lettered by TRAVIS LANHAM
asst. editor: KRISTY QUINN editor: BEN ABERNATHY
cover by NEIL GOOGE & RENCH
variant cover by ETHAN VAN SCIVER & MOOSE BAUMANN

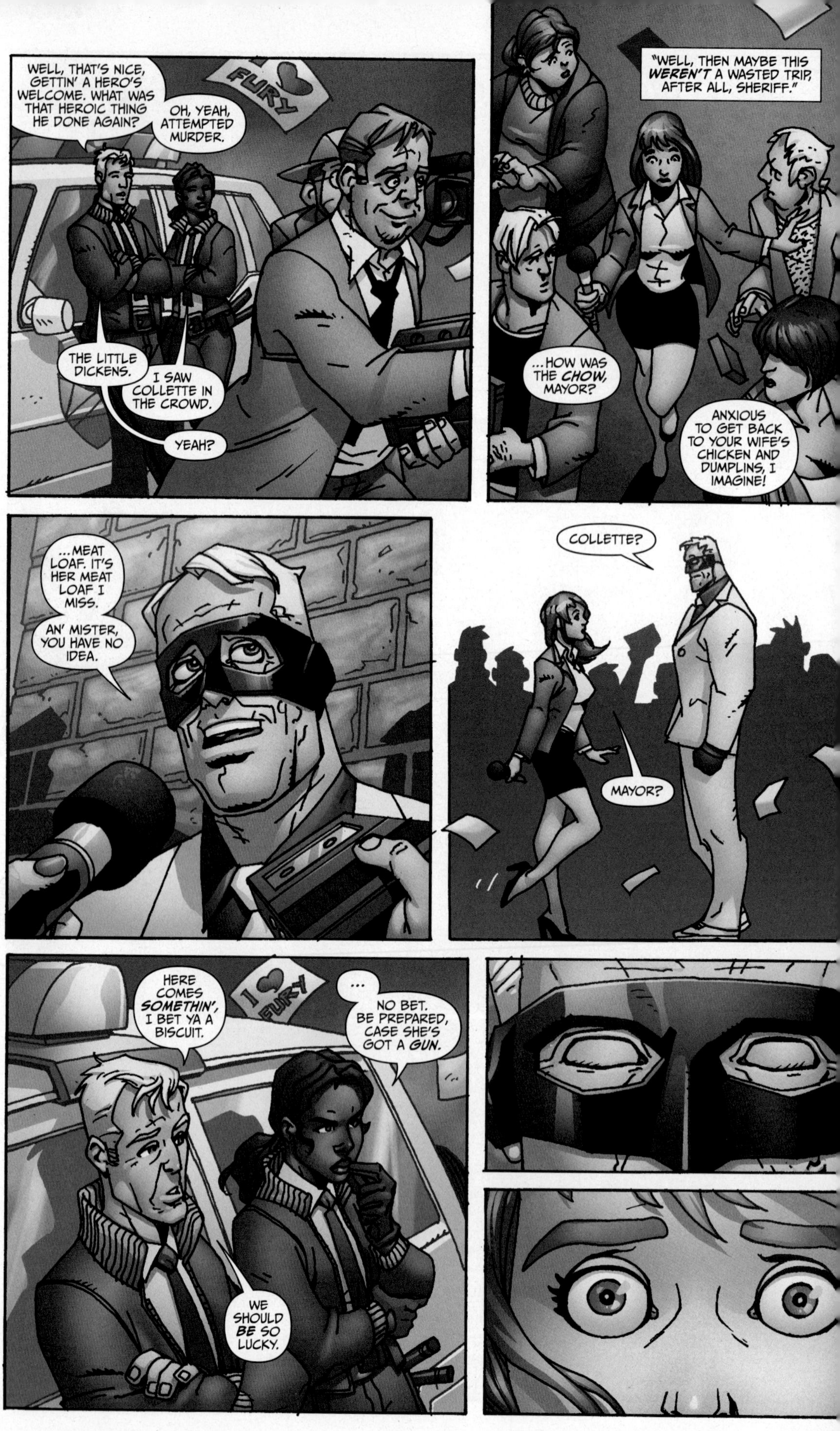
WELL, THAT'S NICE, GETTIN' A HERO'S WELCOME. WHAT WAS THAT HEROIC THING HE DONE AGAIN?
OH, YEAH, ATTEMPTED MURDER.
I ♥ FURY
THE LITTLE DICKENS.
I SAW COLLETTE IN THE CROWD.
YEAH?
"WELL, THEN MAYBE THIS WEREN'T A WASTED TRIP, AFTER ALL, SHERIFF."
...HOW WAS THE CHOW, MAYOR?
ANXIOUS TO GET BACK TO YOUR WIFE'S CHICKEN AND DUMPLINS, I IMAGINE!
...MEAT LOAF. IT'S HER MEAT LOAF I MISS.
AN' MISTER, YOU HAVE NO IDEA.
COLLETTE?
MAYOR?
HERE COMES SOMETHIN', I BET YA A BISCUIT.
I ♥ FURY
...
NO BET. BE PREPARED, CASE SHE'S GOT A GUN.
WE SHOULD BE SO LUCKY.

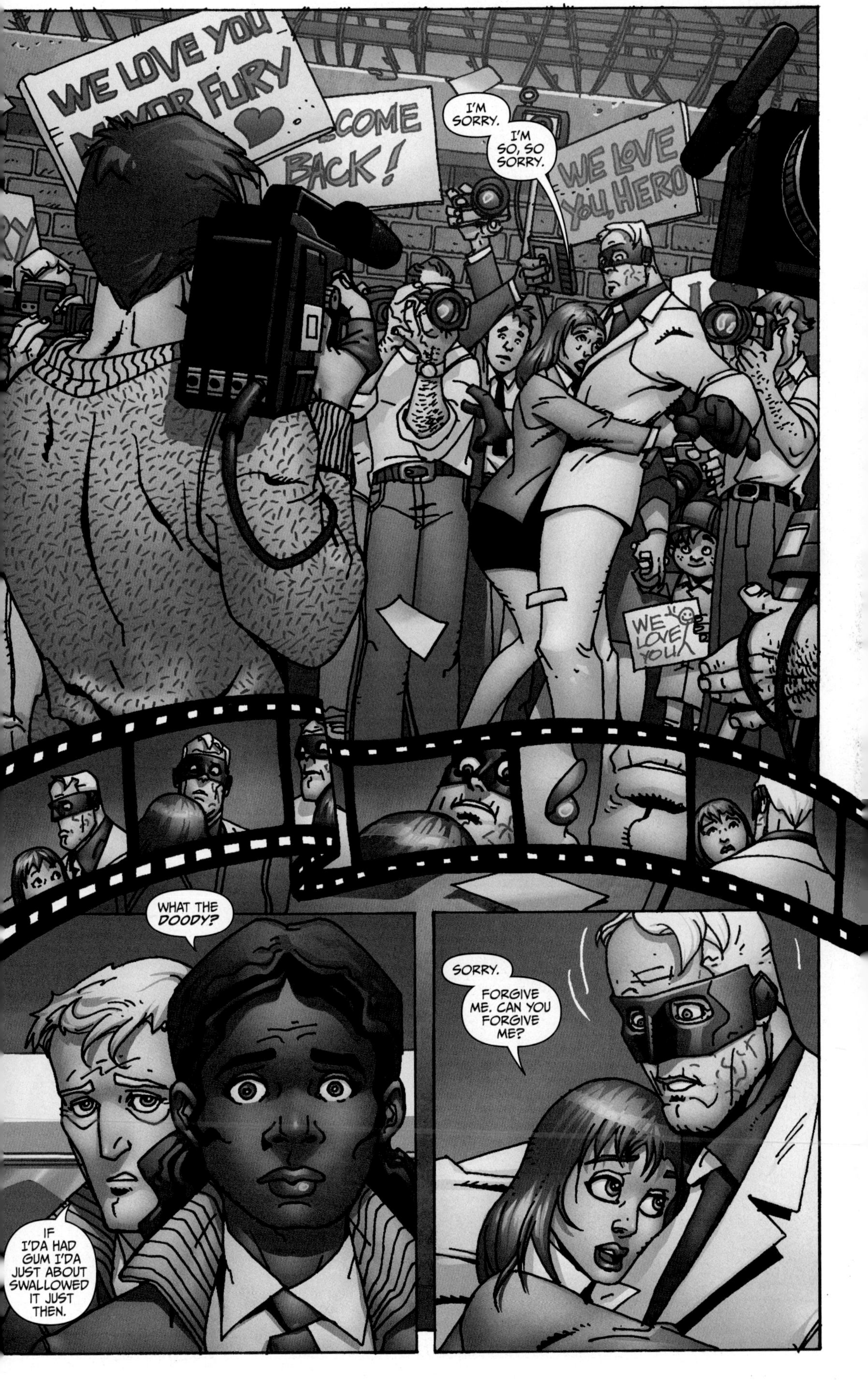
WE LOVE YOU MAYOR FURY
COME BACK!
I'M SORRY.
I'M SO, SO SORRY.
WE LOVE YOU, HERO
WE LOVE YOU
WHAT THE DOODY?
IF I'DA HAD GUM I'DA JUST ABOUT SWALLOWED IT JUST THEN.
SORRY.
FORGIVE ME. CAN YOU FORGIVE ME?

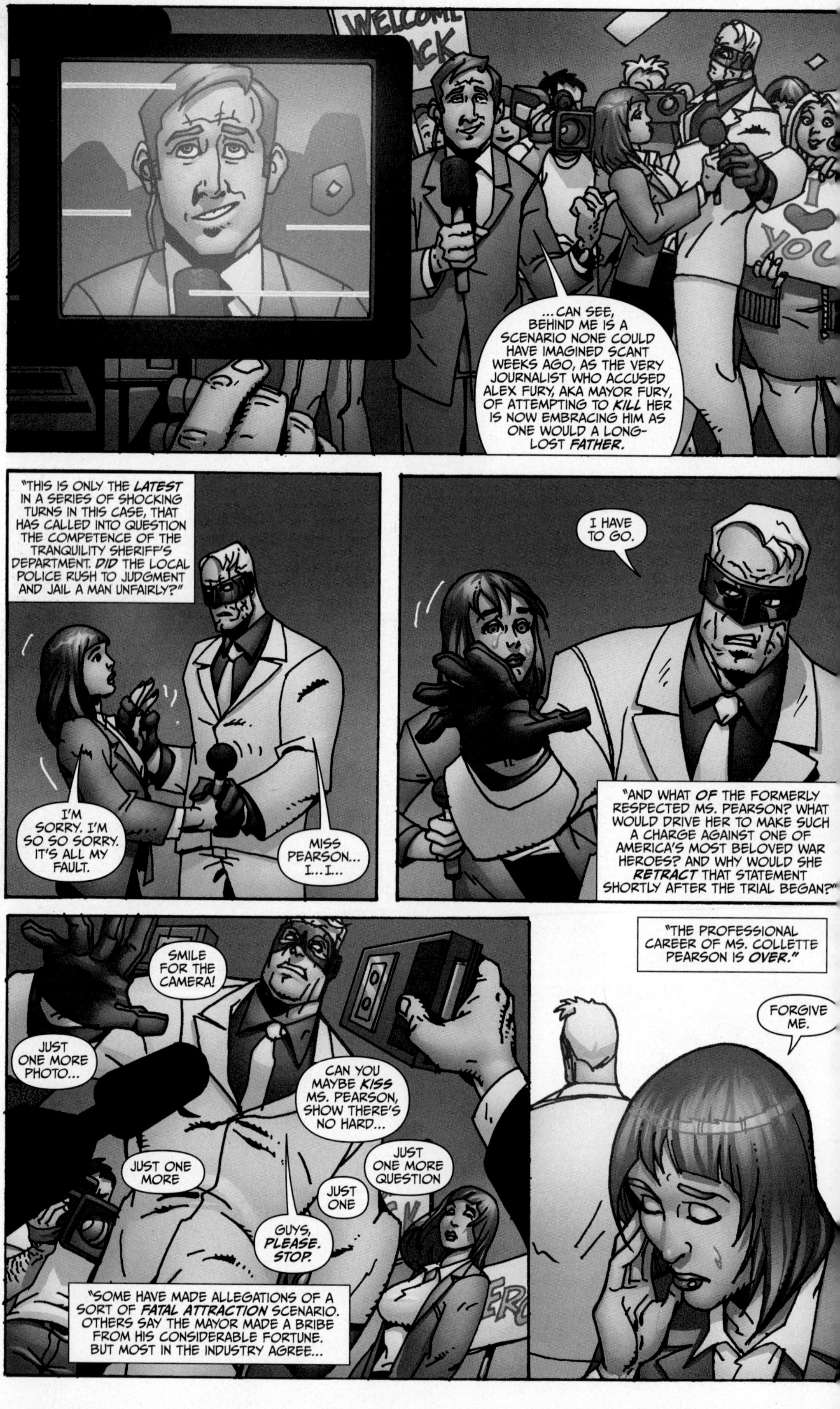

WELCOME
...CAN SEE, BEHIND ME IS A SCENARIO NONE COULD HAVE IMAGINED SCANT WEEKS AGO, AS THE VERY JOURNALIST WHO ACCUSED ALEX FURY, AKA MAYOR FURY, OF ATTEMPTING TO *KILL* HER IS NOW EMBRACING HIM AS ONE WOULD A LONG-LOST *FATHER.*
"THIS IS ONLY THE *LATEST* IN A SERIES OF SHOCKING TURNS IN THIS CASE, THAT HAS CALLED INTO QUESTION THE COMPETENCE OF THE TRANQUILITY SHERIFF'S DEPARTMENT. *DID* THE LOCAL POLICE RUSH TO JUDGMENT AND JAIL A MAN UNFAIRLY?"
I'M SORRY. I'M SO SO SORRY. IT'S ALL MY FAULT.
MISS PEARSON... I...I...
I HAVE TO GO.
"AND WHAT *OF* THE FORMERLY RESPECTED MS. PEARSON? WHAT WOULD DRIVE HER TO MAKE SUCH A CHARGE AGAINST ONE OF AMERICA'S MOST BELOVED WAR HEROES? AND WHY WOULD SHE *RETRACT* THAT STATEMENT SHORTLY AFTER THE TRIAL BEGAN?"
SMILE FOR THE CAMERA!
JUST ONE MORE PHOTO...
CAN YOU MAYBE *KISS* MS. PEARSON, SHOW THERE'S NO HARD...
JUST ONE MORE
JUST ONE MORE QUESTION
JUST ONE
GUYS, *PLEASE. STOP.*
"SOME HAVE MADE ALLEGATIONS OF A SORT OF *FATAL ATTRACTION* SCENARIO. OTHERS SAY THE MAYOR MADE A BRIBE FROM HIS CONSIDERABLE FORTUNE. BUT MOST IN THE INDUSTRY AGREE...
"THE PROFESSIONAL CAREER OF MS. COLLETTE PEARSON IS *OVER.*"
FORGIVE ME.

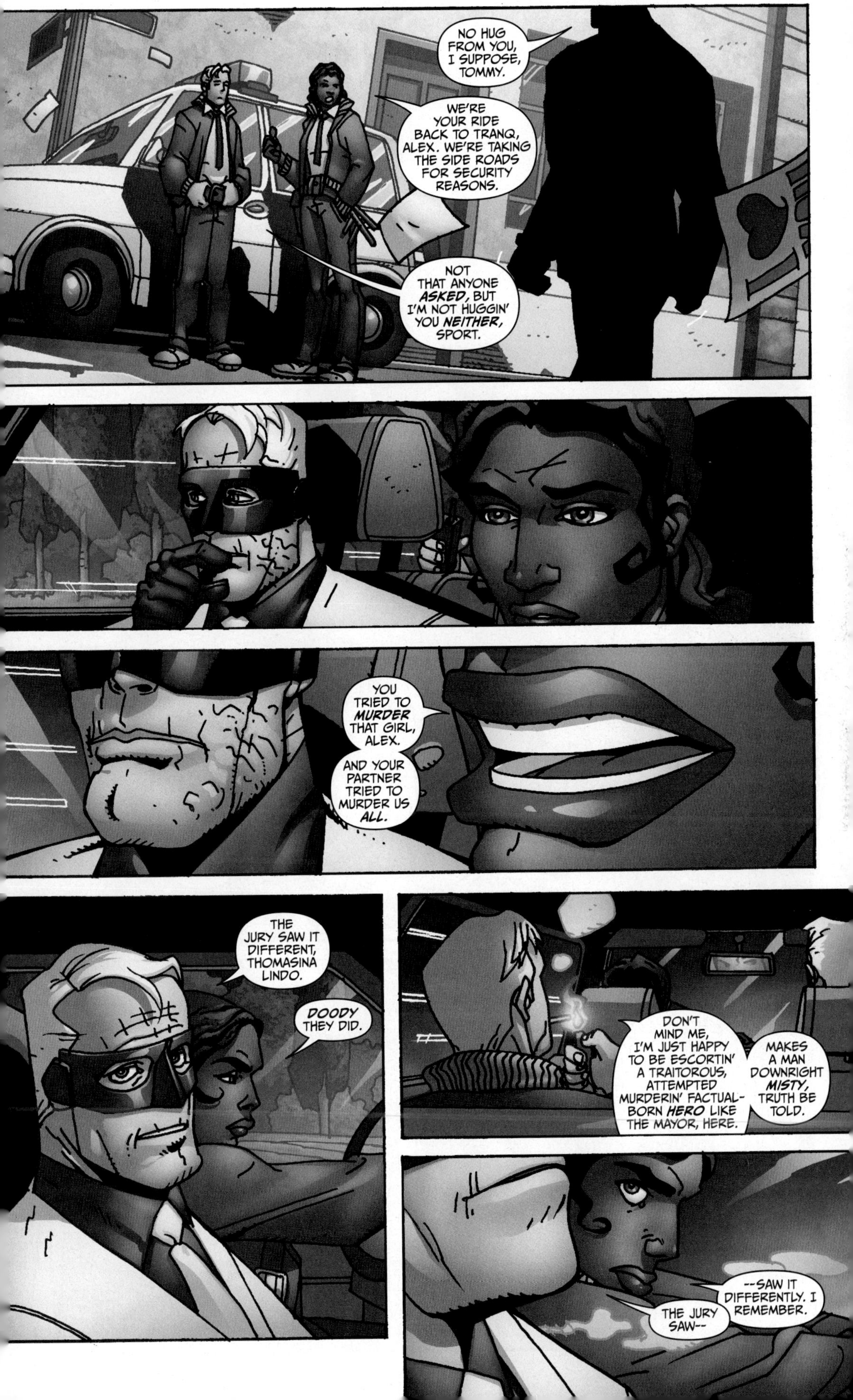
NO HUG FROM YOU, I SUPPOSE, TOMMY.
WE'RE YOUR RIDE BACK TO TRANQ, ALEX. WE'RE TAKING THE SIDE ROADS FOR SECURITY REASONS.
NOT THAT ANYONE ASKED, BUT I'M NOT HUGGIN' YOU NEITHER, SPORT.
YOU TRIED TO MURDER THAT GIRL, ALEX.
AND YOUR PARTNER TRIED TO MURDER US ALL.
THE JURY SAW IT DIFFERENT, THOMASINA LINDO.
DOODY THEY DID.
DON'T MIND ME, I'M JUST HAPPY TO BE ESCORTIN' A TRAITOROUS, ATTEMPTED MURDERIN' FACTUAL-BORN HERO LIKE THE MAYOR, HERE.
MAKES A MAN DOWNRIGHT MISTY, TRUTH BE TOLD.
THE JURY SAW--
--SAW IT DIFFERENTLY. I REMEMBER.

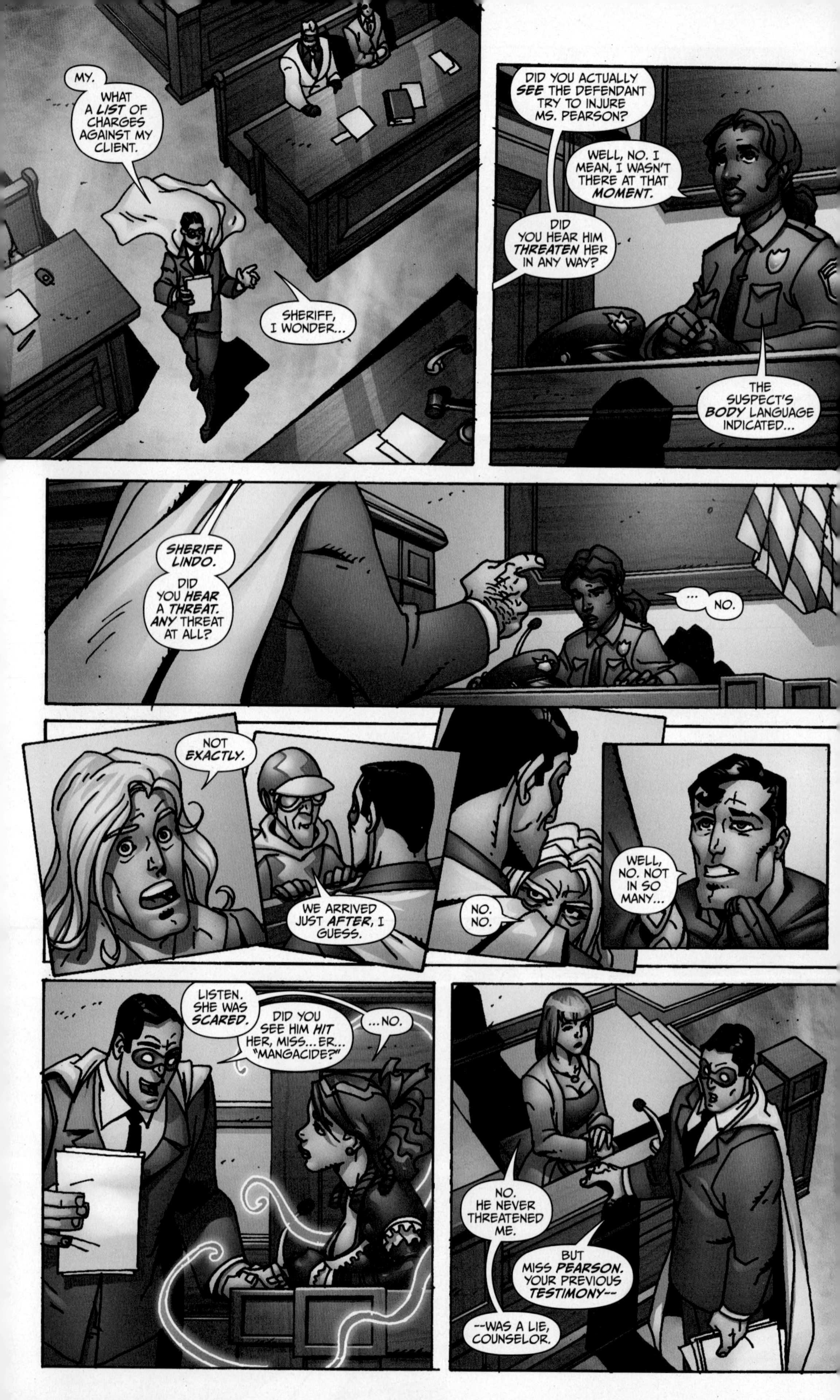
MY.
WHAT A LIST OF CHARGES AGAINST MY CLIENT.
SHERIFF, I WONDER...
DID YOU ACTUALLY SEE THE DEFENDANT TRY TO INJURE MS. PEARSON?
WELL, NO. I MEAN, I WASN'T THERE AT THAT MOMENT.
DID YOU HEAR HIM THREATEN HER IN ANY WAY?
THE SUSPECT'S BODY LANGUAGE INDICATED...
SHERIFF LINDO.
DID YOU HEAR A THREAT. ANY THREAT AT ALL?
...
NO.
NOT EXACTLY.
WE ARRIVED JUST AFTER, I GUESS.
NO. NO.
WELL, NO. NOT IN SO MANY...
LISTEN. SHE WAS SCARED.
DID YOU SEE HIM HIT HER, MISS...ER... "MANGACIDE?"
...NO.
NO. HE NEVER THREATENED ME.
BUT MISS PEARSON. YOUR PREVIOUS TESTIMONY--
--WAS A LIE, COUNSELOR.

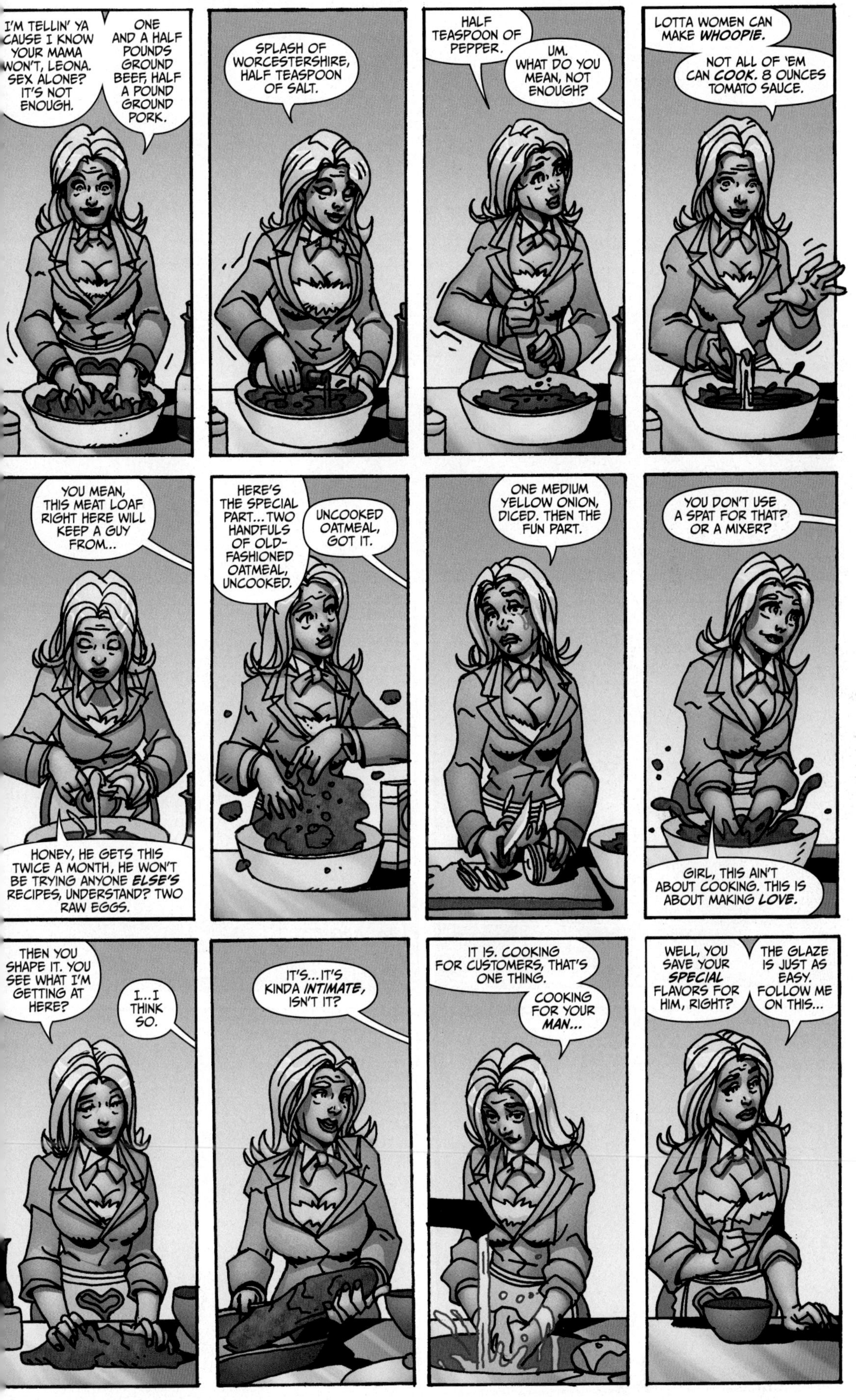

I'M TELLIN' YA CAUSE I KNOW YOUR MAMA WON'T, LEONA. SEX ALONE? IT'S NOT ENOUGH.
ONE AND A HALF POUNDS GROUND BEEF, HALF A POUND GROUND PORK.
SPLASH OF WORCESTERSHIRE, HALF TEASPOON OF SALT.
HALF TEASPOON OF PEPPER.
UM. WHAT DO YOU MEAN, NOT ENOUGH?
LOTTA WOMEN CAN MAKE *WHOOPIE.*
NOT ALL OF 'EM CAN *COOK.* 8 OUNCES TOMATO SAUCE.
YOU MEAN, THIS MEAT LOAF RIGHT HERE WILL KEEP A GUY FROM...
HONEY, HE GETS THIS TWICE A MONTH, HE WON'T BE TRYING ANYONE *ELSE'S* RECIPES, UNDERSTAND? TWO RAW EGGS.
HERE'S THE SPECIAL PART...TWO HANDFULS OF OLD-FASHIONED OATMEAL, UNCOOKED.
UNCOOKED OATMEAL, GOT IT.
ONE MEDIUM YELLOW ONION, DICED. THEN THE FUN PART.
YOU DON'T USE A SPAT FOR THAT? OR A MIXER?
GIRL, THIS AIN'T ABOUT COOKING. THIS IS ABOUT MAKING *LOVE.*
THEN YOU SHAPE IT. YOU SEE WHAT I'M GETTING AT HERE?
I...I THINK SO.
IT'S...IT'S KINDA *INTIMATE,* ISN'T IT?
IT IS. COOKING FOR CUSTOMERS, THAT'S ONE THING.
COOKING FOR YOUR *MAN...*
WELL, YOU SAVE YOUR *SPECIAL* FLAVORS FOR HIM, RIGHT?
THE GLAZE IS JUST AS EASY. FOLLOW ME ON THIS...

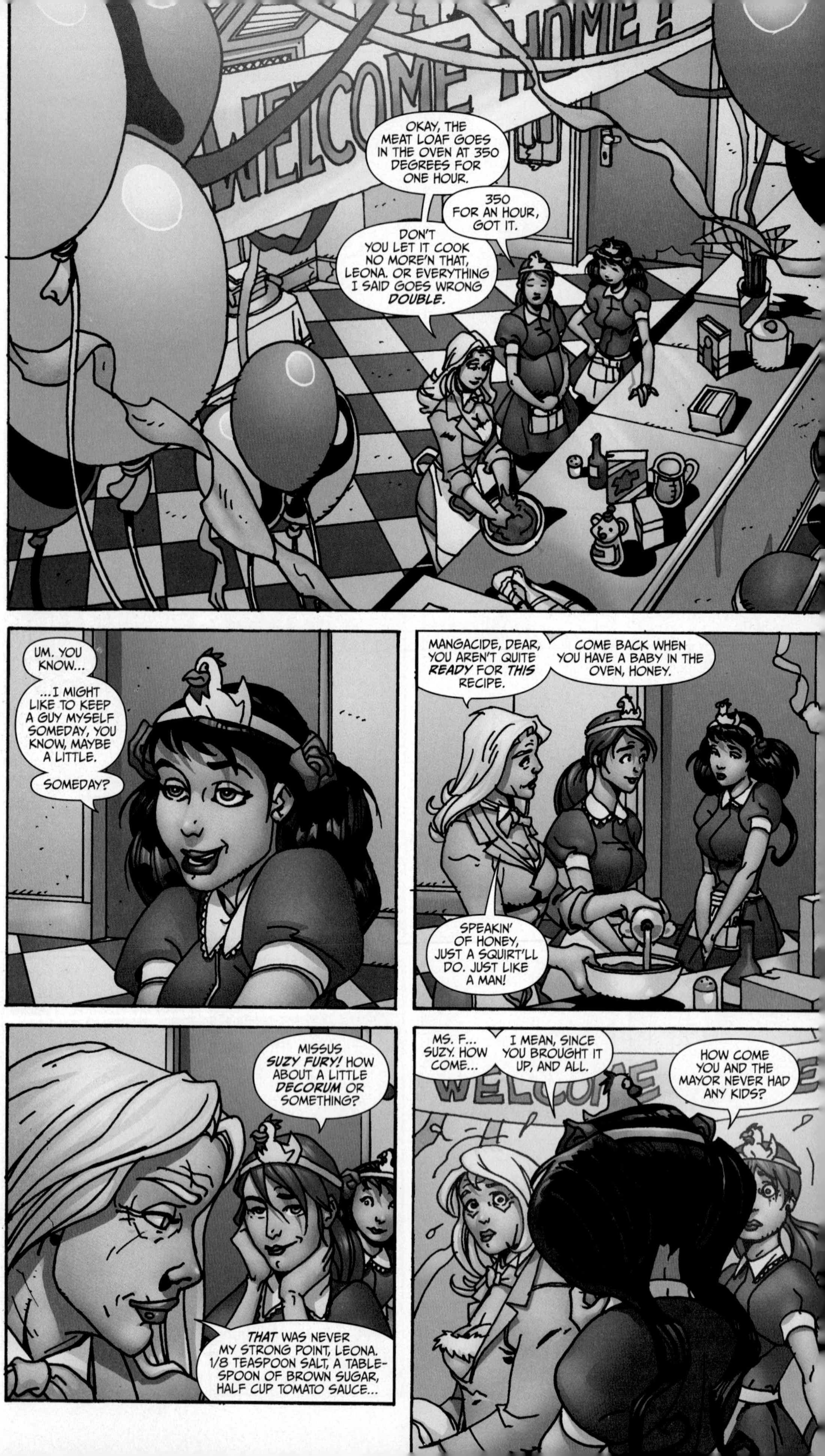
WELCOME HOME!
OKAY, THE MEAT LOAF GOES IN THE OVEN AT 350 DEGREES FOR ONE HOUR.
350 FOR AN HOUR, GOT IT.
DON'T YOU LET IT COOK NO MORE'N THAT, LEONA. OR EVERYTHING I SAID GOES WRONG *DOUBLE.*
UM. YOU KNOW...
...I MIGHT LIKE TO KEEP A GUY MYSELF SOMEDAY, YOU KNOW, MAYBE A LITTLE.
SOMEDAY?
MANGACIDE, DEAR, YOU AREN'T QUITE *READY* FOR *THIS* RECIPE.
COME BACK WHEN YOU HAVE A BABY IN THE OVEN, HONEY.
SPEAKIN' OF HONEY, JUST A SQUIRT'LL DO. JUST LIKE A MAN!
MISSUS *SUZY FURY!* HOW ABOUT A LITTLE *DECORUM* OR SOMETHING?
THAT WAS NEVER MY STRONG POINT, LEONA. 1/8 TEASPOON SALT, A TABLE-SPOON OF BROWN SUGAR, HALF CUP TOMATO SAUCE...
MS. F... SUZY. HOW COME...
I MEAN, SINCE YOU BROUGHT IT UP, AND ALL.
HOW COME YOU AND THE MAYOR NEVER HAD ANY KIDS?

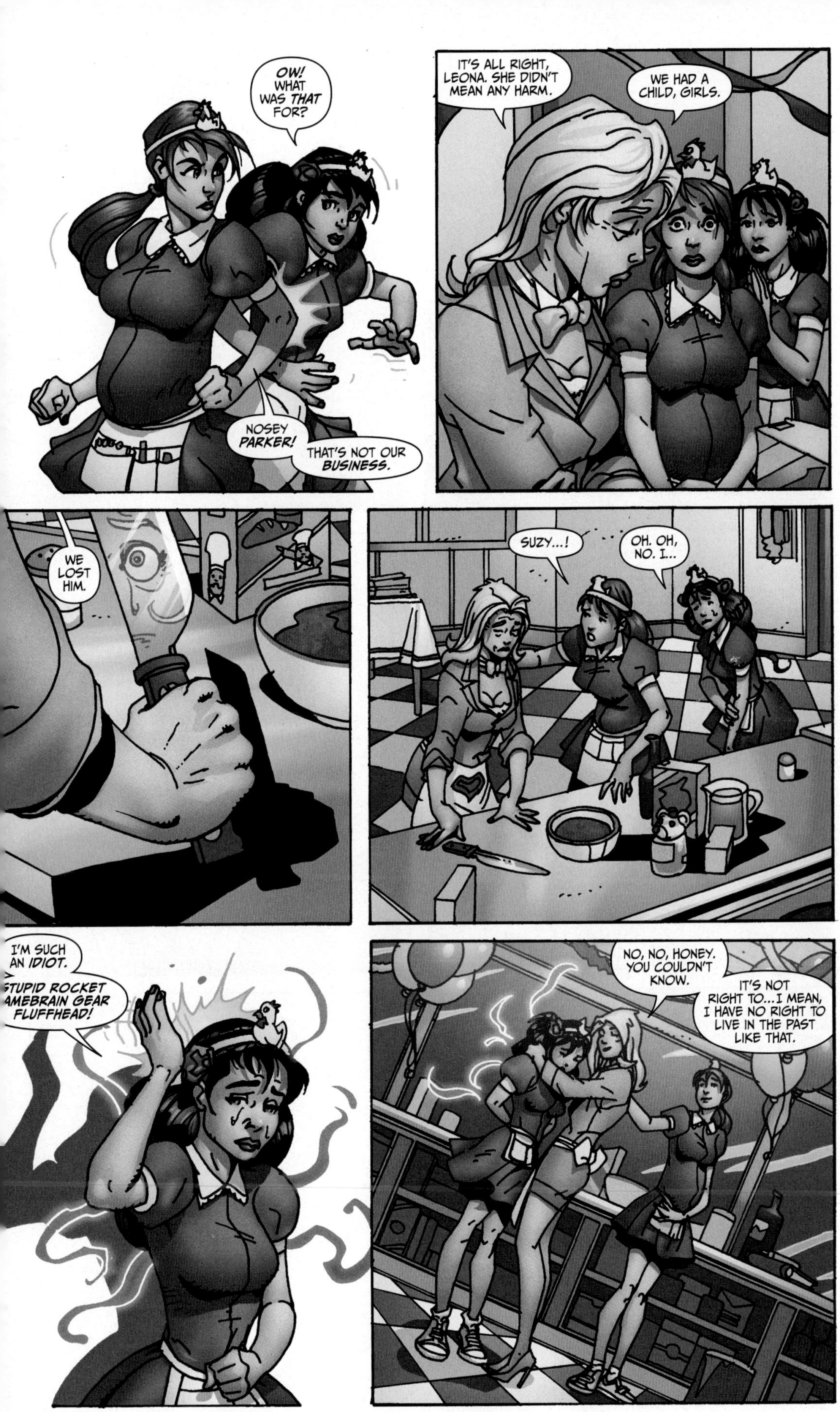
OW! WHAT WAS THAT FOR?
NOSEY PARKER!
THAT'S NOT OUR BUSINESS.
IT'S ALL RIGHT, LEONA. SHE DIDN'T MEAN ANY HARM.
WE HAD A CHILD, GIRLS.
WE LOST HIM.
SUZY...!
OH. OH, NO. I...
I'M SUCH AN IDIOT.
STUPID ROCKET LAMEBRAIN GEAR FLUFFHEAD!
NO, NO, HONEY. YOU COULDN'T KNOW.
IT'S NOT RIGHT TO...I MEAN, I HAVE NO RIGHT TO LIVE IN THE PAST LIKE THAT.

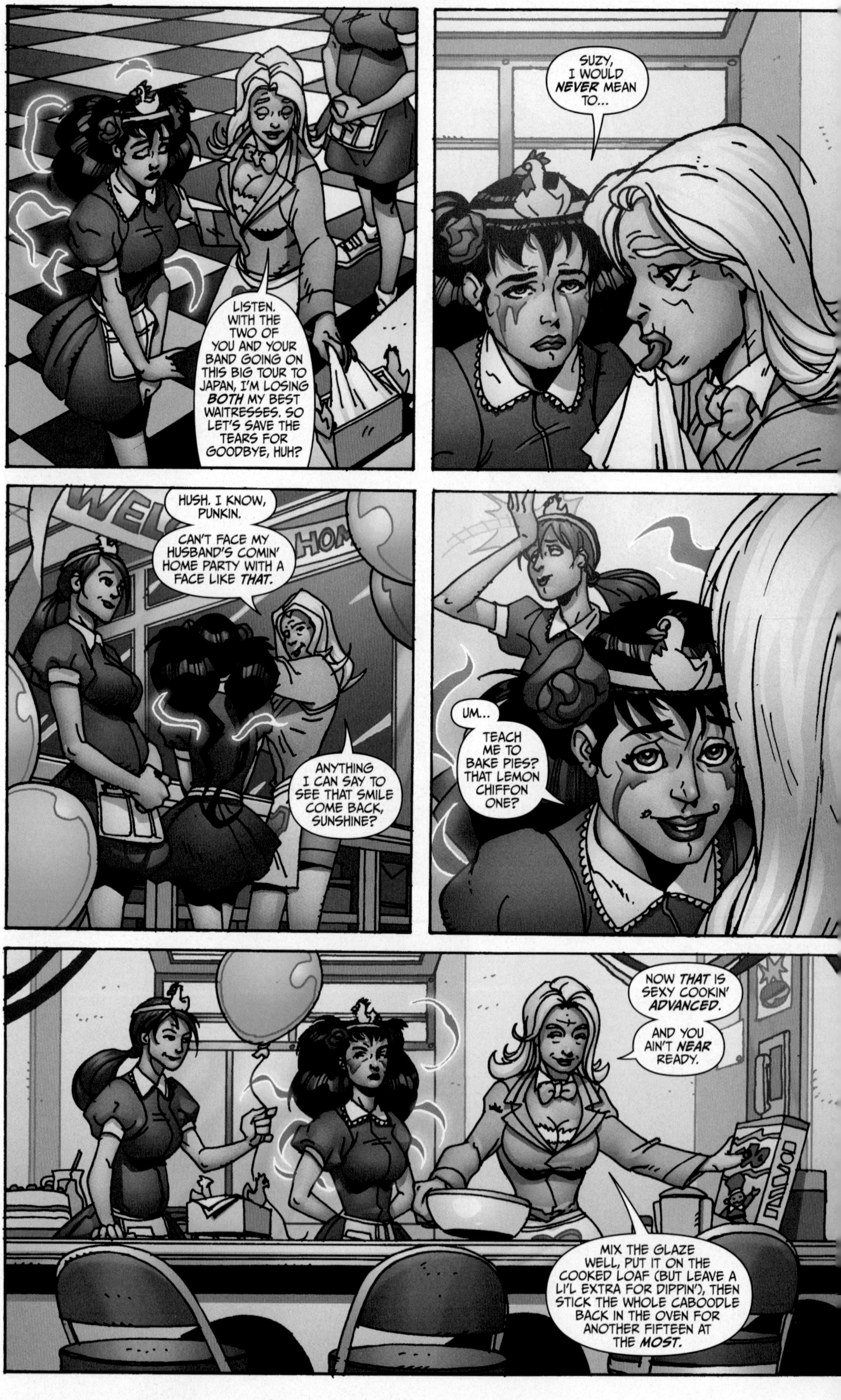
LISTEN. WITH THE TWO OF YOU AND YOUR BAND GOING ON THIS BIG TOUR TO JAPAN, I'M LOSING BOTH MY BEST WAITRESSES. SO LET'S SAVE THE TEARS FOR GOODBYE, HUH?
SUZY, I WOULD NEVER MEAN TO...
HUSH. I KNOW, PUNKIN.
CAN'T FACE MY HUSBAND'S COMIN' HOME PARTY WITH A FACE LIKE THAT.
ANYTHING I CAN SAY TO SEE THAT SMILE COME BACK, SUNSHINE?
UM...
TEACH ME TO BAKE PIES? THAT LEMON CHIFFON ONE?
NOW THAT IS SEXY COOKIN' ADVANCED.
AND YOU AIN'T NEAR READY.
MIX THE GLAZE WELL, PUT IT ON THE COOKED LOAF (BUT LEAVE A LI'L EXTRA FOR DIPPIN'), THEN STICK THE WHOLE CABOODLE BACK IN THE OVEN FOR ANOTHER FIFTEEN AT THE MOST.

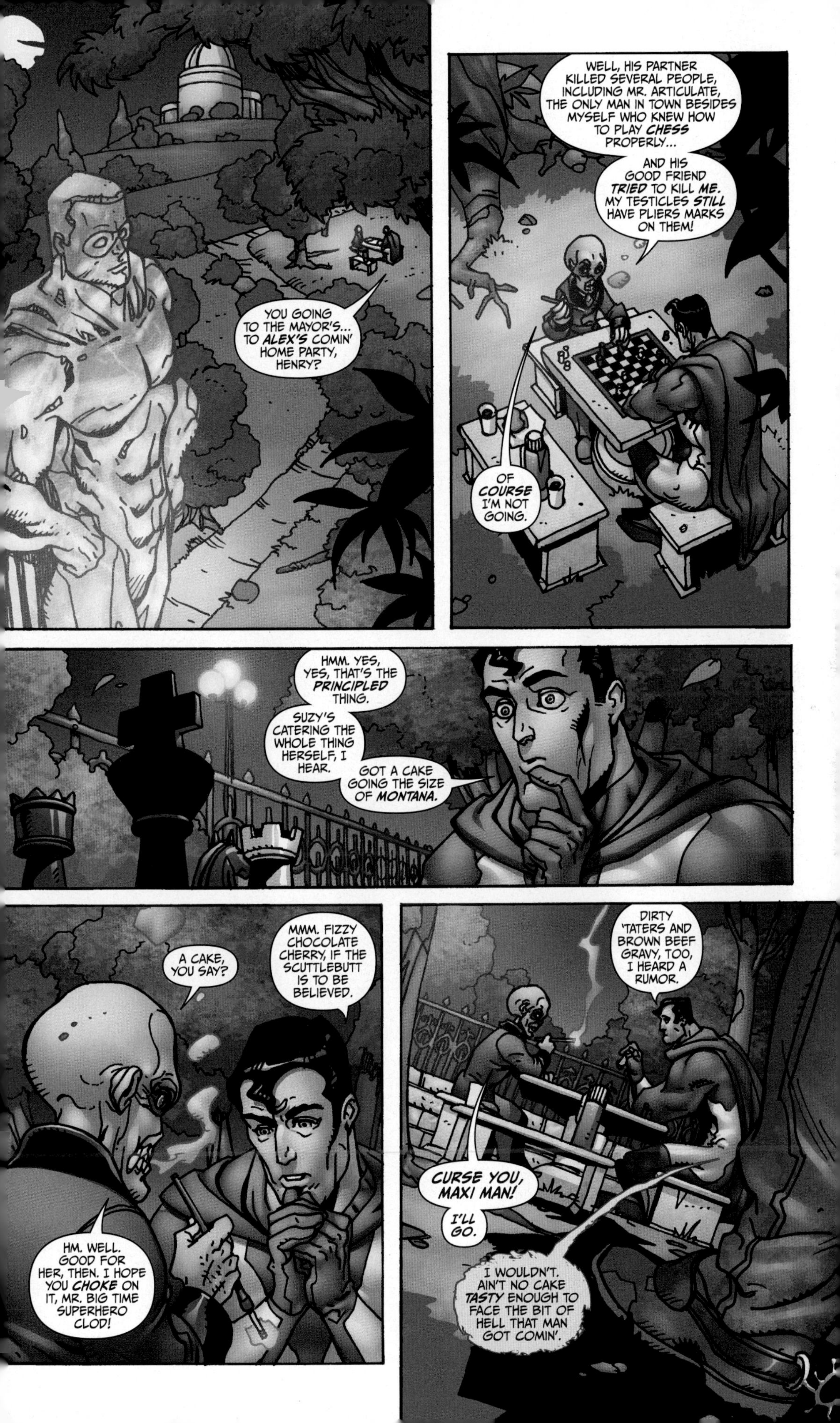
YOU GOING TO THE MAYOR'S... TO ALEX'S COMIN' HOME PARTY, HENRY?
WELL, HIS PARTNER KILLED SEVERAL PEOPLE, INCLUDING MR. ARTICULATE, THE ONLY MAN IN TOWN BESIDES MYSELF WHO KNEW HOW TO PLAY CHESS PROPERLY...
AND HIS GOOD FRIEND TRIED TO KILL ME. MY TESTICLES STILL HAVE PLIERS MARKS ON THEM!
OF COURSE I'M NOT GOING.
HMM. YES, YES, THAT'S THE PRINCIPLED THING.
SUZY'S CATERING THE WHOLE THING HERSELF, I HEAR.
GOT A CAKE GOING THE SIZE OF MONTANA.
A CAKE, YOU SAY?
MMM. FIZZY CHOCOLATE CHERRY, IF THE SCUTTLEBUTT IS TO BE BELIEVED.
HM. WELL. GOOD FOR HER, THEN. I HOPE YOU CHOKE ON IT, MR. BIG TIME SUPERHERO CLOD!
DIRTY 'TATERS AND BROWN BEEF GRAVY, TOO, I HEARD A RUMOR.
CURSE YOU, MAXI MAN!
I'LL GO.
I WOULDN'T. AIN'T NO CAKE TASTY ENOUGH TO FACE THE BIT OF HELL THAT MAN GOT COMIN'.

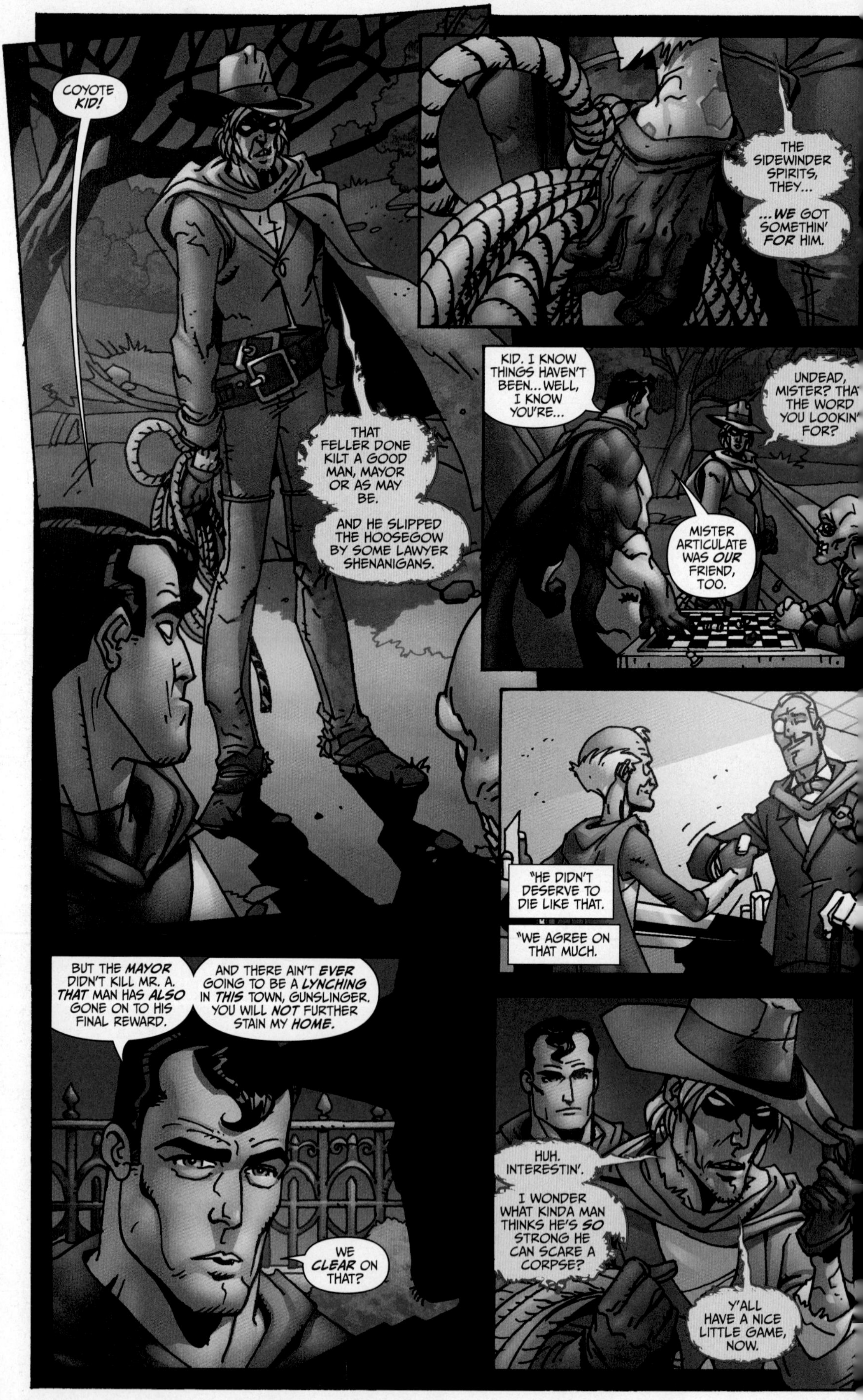
COYOTE KID!
THE SIDEWINDER SPIRITS, THEY...
...WE GOT SOMETHIN' FOR HIM.
THAT FELLER DONE KILT A GOOD MAN, MAYOR OR AS MAY BE.
AND HE SLIPPED THE HOOSEGOW BY SOME LAWYER SHENANIGANS.
KID. I KNOW THINGS HAVEN'T BEEN... WELL, I KNOW YOU'RE...
UNDEAD, MISTER? THA THE WORD YOU LOOKIN' FOR?
MISTER ARTICULATE WAS OUR FRIEND, TOO.
"HE DIDN'T DESERVE TO DIE LIKE THAT.
"WE AGREE ON THAT MUCH.
BUT THE MAYOR DIDN'T KILL MR. A. THAT MAN HAS ALSO GONE ON TO HIS FINAL REWARD.
AND THERE AIN'T EVER GOING TO BE A LYNCHING IN THIS TOWN, GUNSLINGER. YOU WILL NOT FURTHER STAIN MY HOME.
WE CLEAR ON THAT?
HUH. INTERESTIN'.
I WONDER WHAT KINDA MAN THINKS HE'S SO STRONG HE CAN SCARE A CORPSE?
Y'ALL HAVE A NICE LITTLE GAME, NOW.

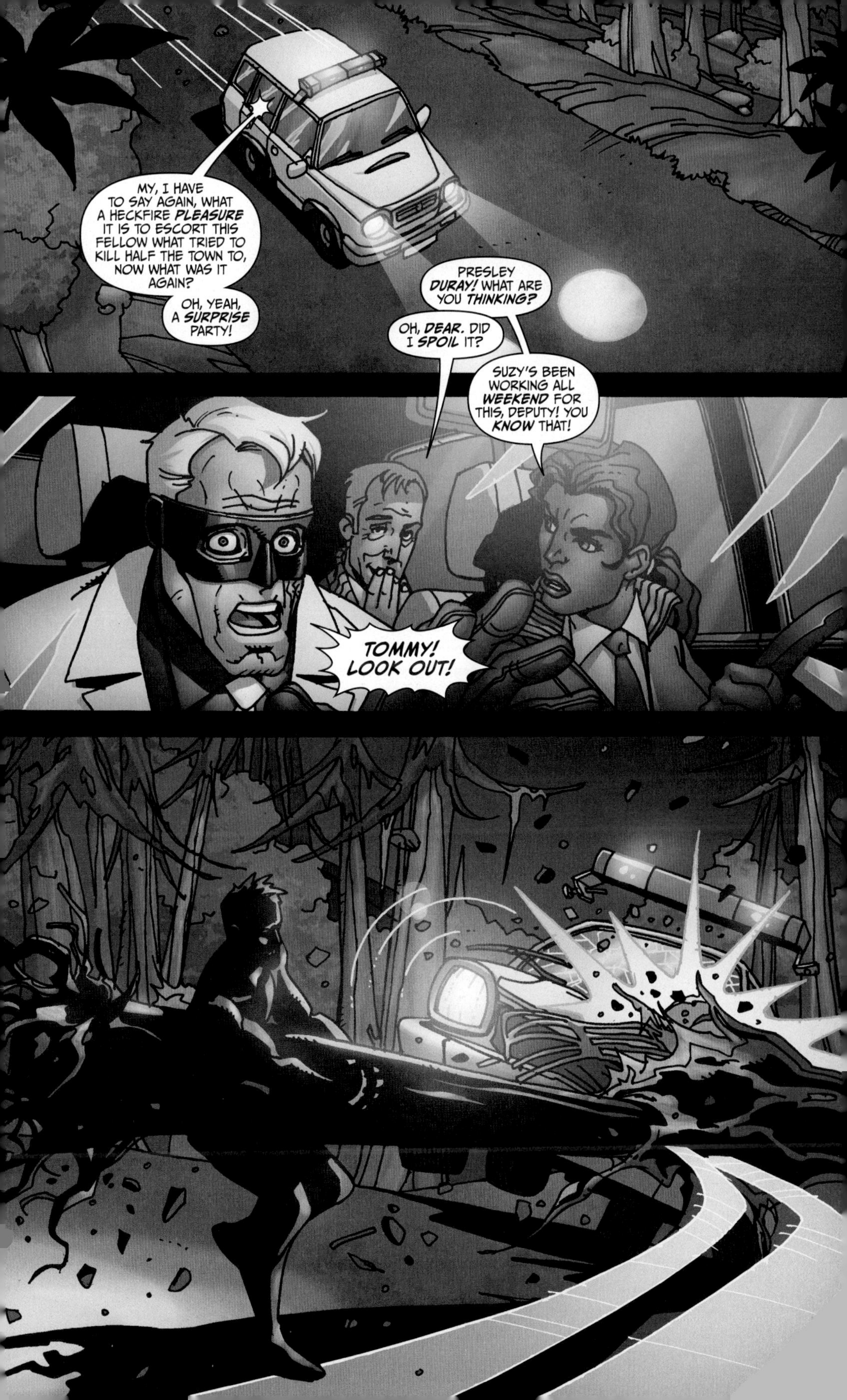
MY, I HAVE TO SAY AGAIN, WHAT A HECKFIRE PLEASURE IT IS TO ESCORT THIS FELLOW WHAT TRIED TO KILL HALF THE TOWN TO, NOW WHAT WAS IT AGAIN?
OH, YEAH, A SURPRISE PARTY!
PRESLEY DURAY! WHAT ARE YOU THINKING?
OH, DEAR. DID I SPOIL IT?
SUZY'S BEEN WORKING ALL WEEKEND FOR THIS, DEPUTY! YOU KNOW THAT!
TOMMY! LOOK OUT!

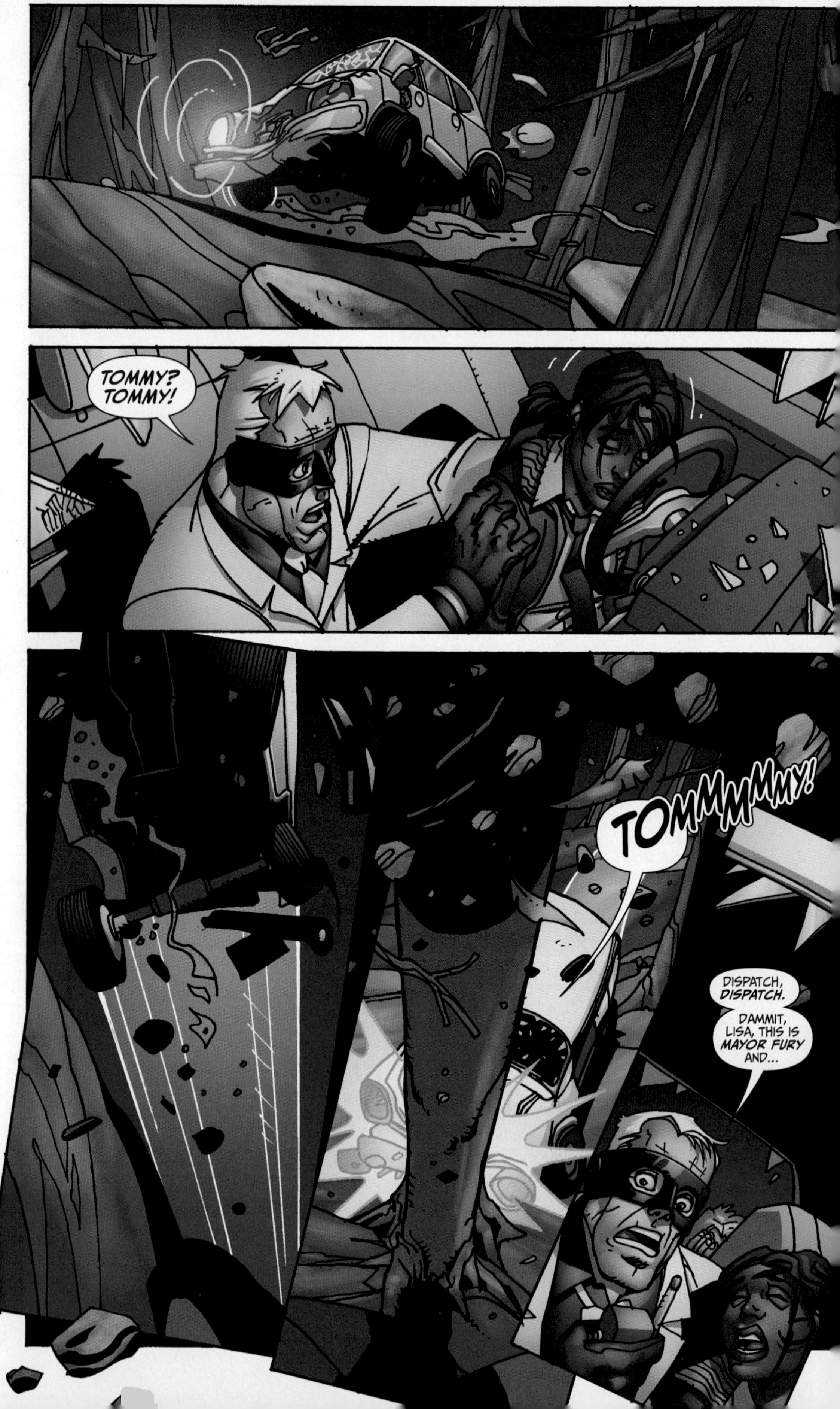
TOMMY? TOMMY!
TOMMMMMY!
DISPATCH, DISPATCH.
DAMMIT, LISA, THIS IS MAYOR FURY AND...

WHAT THE HELL?

COME WITH ME. THERE'S NO TIME.

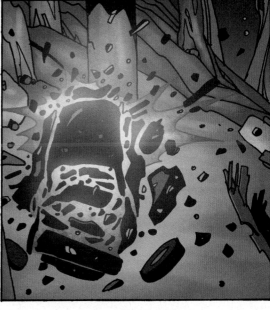

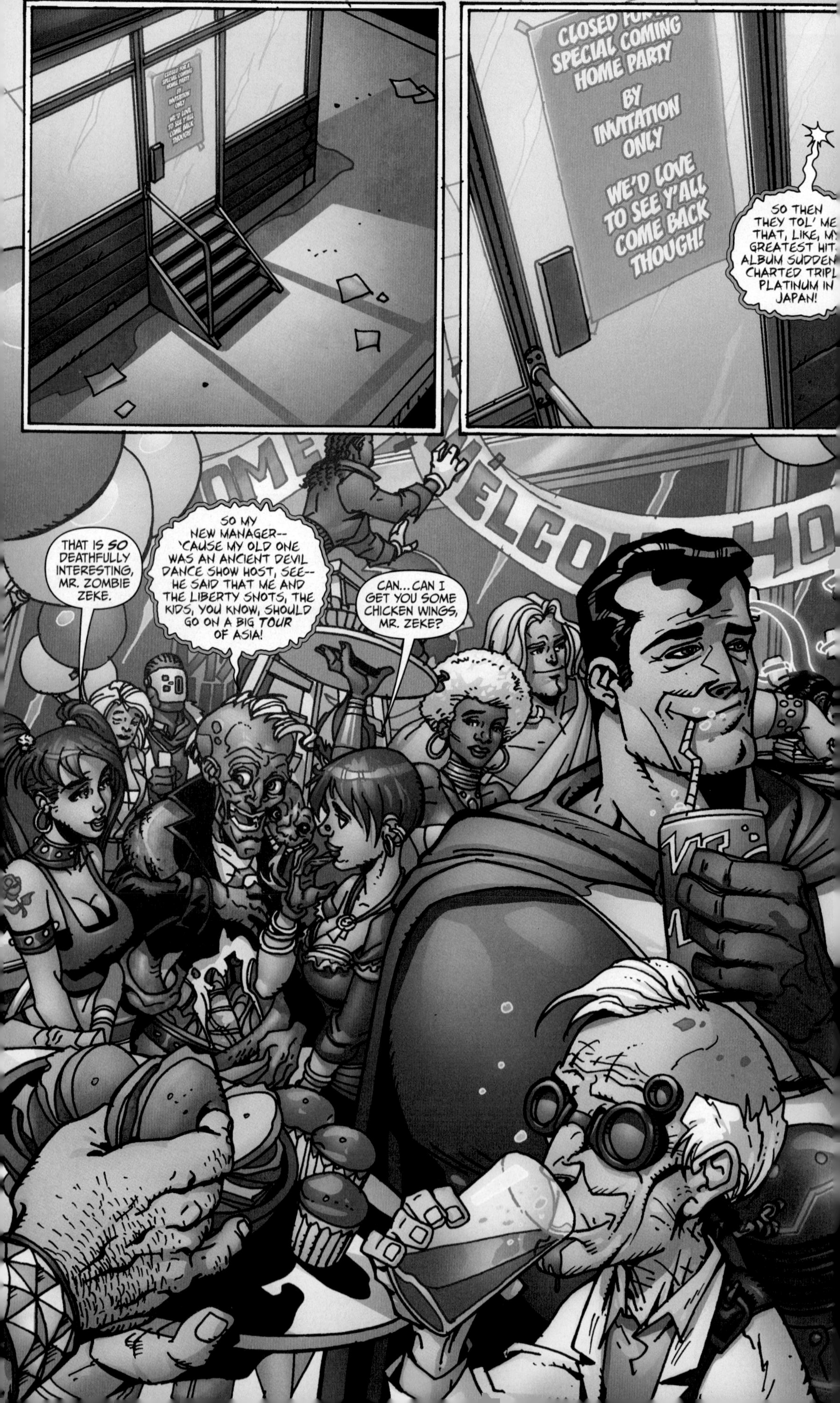
CLOSED FOR A SPECIAL COMING HOME PARTY BY INVITATION ONLY WE'D LOVE TO SEE Y'ALL COME BACK THOUGH!
CLOSED FOR SPECIAL COMING HOME PARTY BY INVITATION ONLY WE'D LOVE TO SEE Y'ALL COME BACK THOUGH!
SO THEN THEY TOL' ME THAT, LIKE, MY GREATEST HIT ALBUM SUDDEN CHARTED TRIPL PLATINUM IN JAPAN!
THAT IS SO DEATHFULLY INTERESTING, MR. ZOMBIE ZEKE.
SO MY NEW MANAGER-- 'CAUSE MY OLD ONE WAS AN ANCIENT DEVIL DANCE SHOW HOST, SEE-- HE SAID THAT ME AND THE LIBERTY SNOTS, THE KIDS, YOU KNOW, SHOULD GO ON A BIG TOUR OF ASIA!
CAN...CAN I GET YOU SOME CHICKEN WINGS, MR. ZEKE?

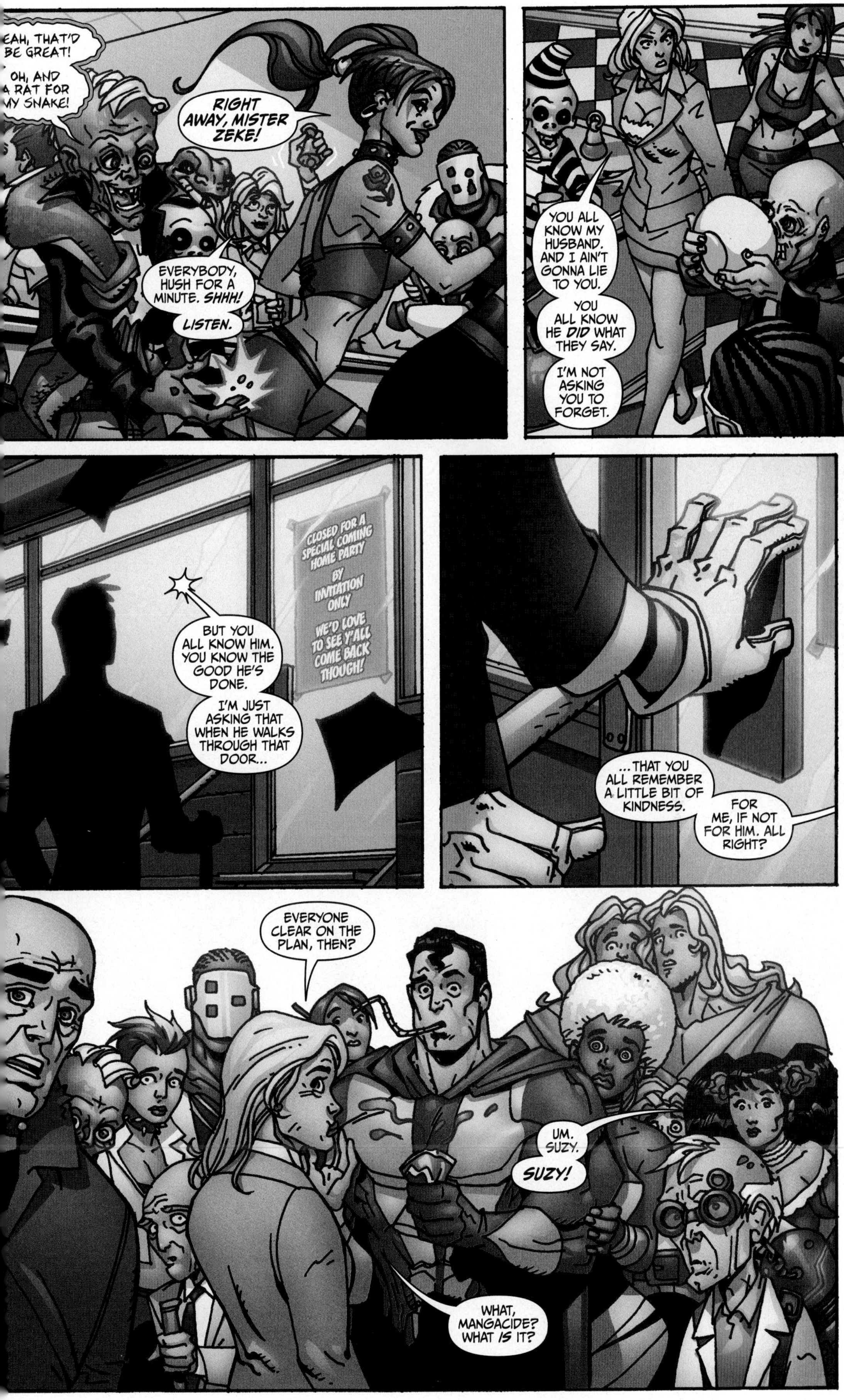

EAH, THAT'D BE GREAT!
OH, AND A RAT FOR MY SNAKE!
RIGHT AWAY, MISTER ZEKE!
EVERYBODY, HUSH FOR A MINUTE. SHHH!
LISTEN.
YOU ALL KNOW MY HUSBAND. AND I AIN'T GONNA LIE TO YOU.
YOU ALL KNOW HE DID WHAT THEY SAY.
I'M NOT ASKING YOU TO FORGET.
CLOSED FOR A SPECIAL COMING HOME PARTY BY INVITATION ONLY WE'D LOVE TO SEE Y'ALL COME BACK THOUGH!
BUT YOU ALL KNOW HIM. YOU KNOW THE GOOD HE'S DONE.
I'M JUST ASKING THAT WHEN HE WALKS THROUGH THAT DOOR...
...THAT YOU ALL REMEMBER A LITTLE BIT OF KINDNESS.
FOR ME, IF NOT FOR HIM. ALL RIGHT?
EVERYONE CLEAR ON THE PLAN, THEN?
UM. SUZY.
SUZY!
WHAT, MANGACIDE? WHAT IS IT?

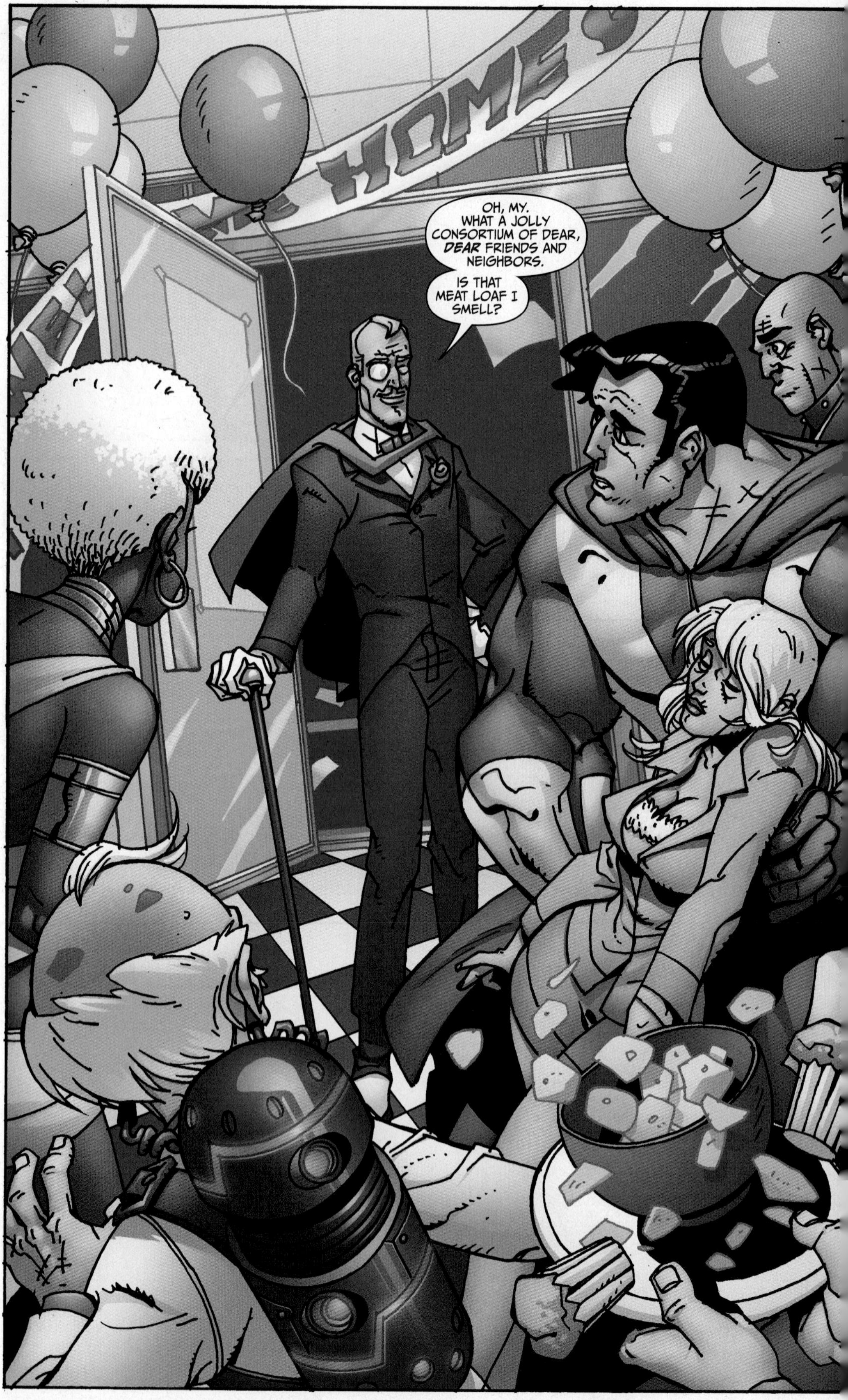
HOME
OH, MY. WHAT A JOLLY CONSORTIUM OF DEAR, *DEAR* FRIENDS AND NEIGHBORS.
IS THAT MEAT LOAF I SMELL?

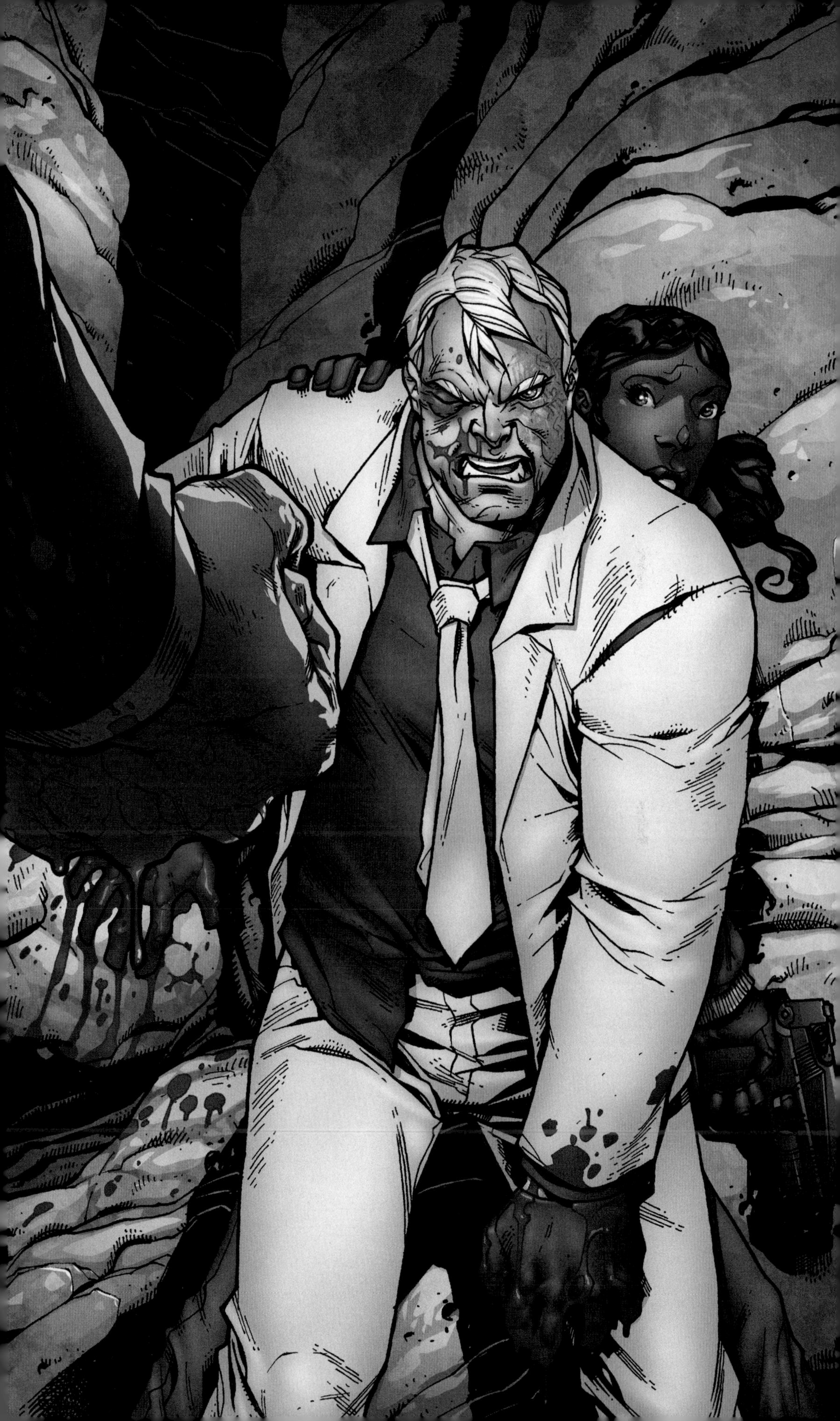

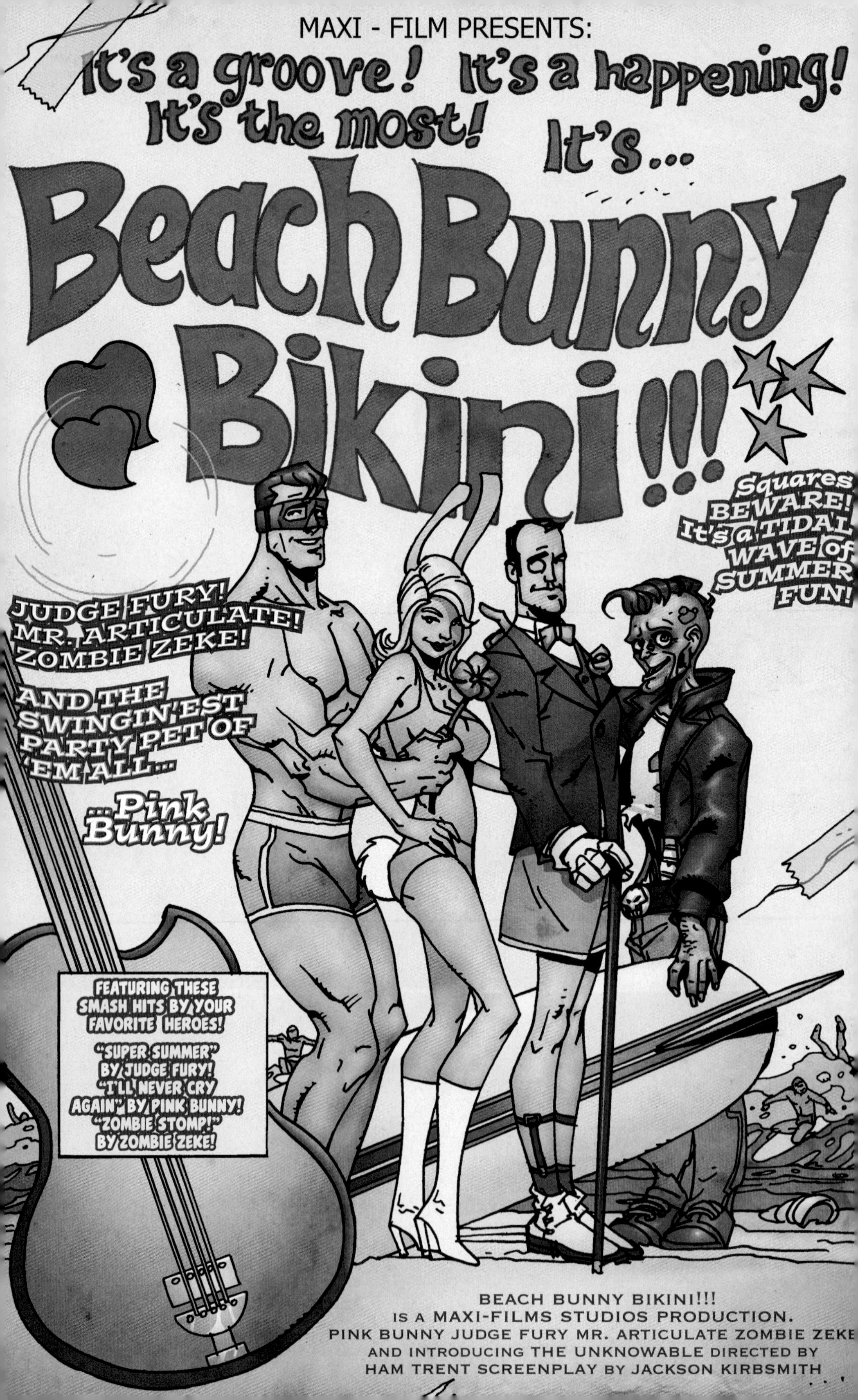

MAXI - FILM PRESENTS:
It's a groove! It's a happening!
It's the most! It's...
Beach Bunny Bikini!!!
Squares BEWARE! It's a TIDAL WAVE of SUMMER FUN!
JUDGE FURY! MR. ARTICULATE! ZOMBIE ZEKE!
AND THE SWINGIN'EST PARTY PET OF 'EM ALL...
...Pink Bunny!
FEATURING THESE SMASH HITS BY YOUR FAVORITE HEROES!
"SUPER SUMMER" BY JUDGE FURY!
"I'LL NEVER CRY AGAIN" BY PINK BUNNY!
"ZOMBIE STOMP!" BY ZOMBIE ZEKE!
BEACH BUNNY BIKINI!!!
IS A MAXI-FILMS STUDIOS PRODUCTION.
PINK BUNNY JUDGE FURY MR. ARTICULATE ZOMBIE ZEKE
AND INTRODUCING THE UNKNOWABLE DIRECTED BY
HAM TRENT SCREENPLAY BY JACKSON KIRBSMITH

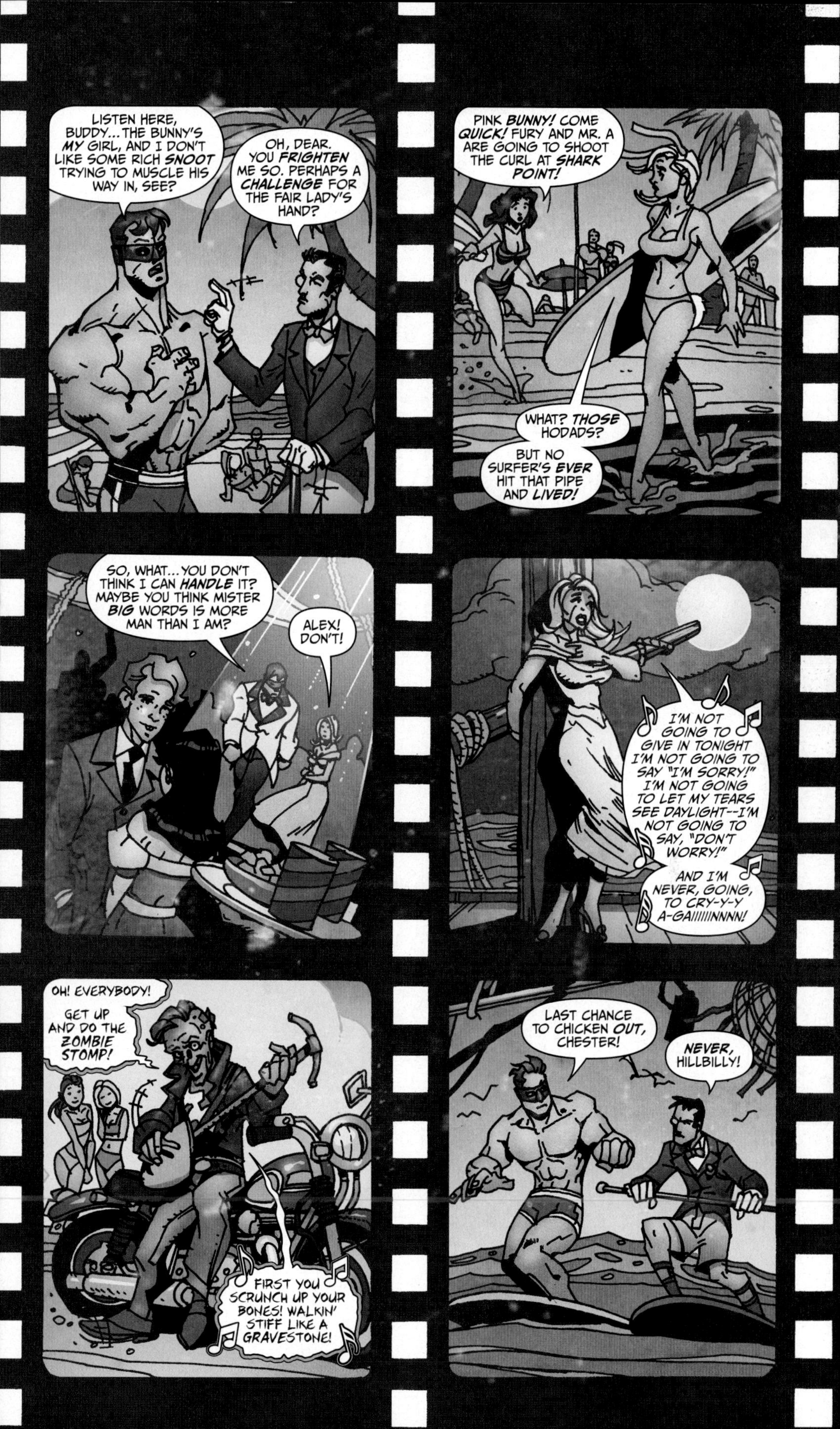
LISTEN HERE, BUDDY... THE BUNNY'S MY GIRL, AND I DON'T LIKE SOME RICH SNOOT TRYING TO MUSCLE HIS WAY IN, SEE?
OH, DEAR. YOU FRIGHTEN ME SO. PERHAPS A CHALLENGE FOR THE FAIR LADY'S HAND?
PINK BUNNY! COME QUICK! FURY AND MR. A ARE GOING TO SHOOT THE CURL AT SHARK POINT!
WHAT? THOSE HODADS?
BUT NO SURFER'S EVER HIT THAT PIPE AND LIVED!
SO, WHAT... YOU DON'T THINK I CAN HANDLE IT? MAYBE YOU THINK MISTER BIG WORDS IS MORE MAN THAN I AM?
ALEX! DON'T!
I'M NOT GOING TO GIVE IN TONIGHT I'M NOT GOING TO SAY "I'M SORRY!" I'M NOT GOING TO LET MY TEARS SEE DAYLIGHT--I'M NOT GOING TO SAY, "DON'T WORRY!"
AND I'M NEVER, GOING, TO CRY-Y-Y A-GAIIIIIINNNN!
OH! EVERYBODY!
GET UP AND DO THE ZOMBIE STOMP!
FIRST YOU SCRUNCH UP YOUR BONES! WALKIN' STIFF LIKE A GRAVESTONE!
LAST CHANCE TO CHICKEN OUT, CHESTER!
NEVER, HILLBILLY!

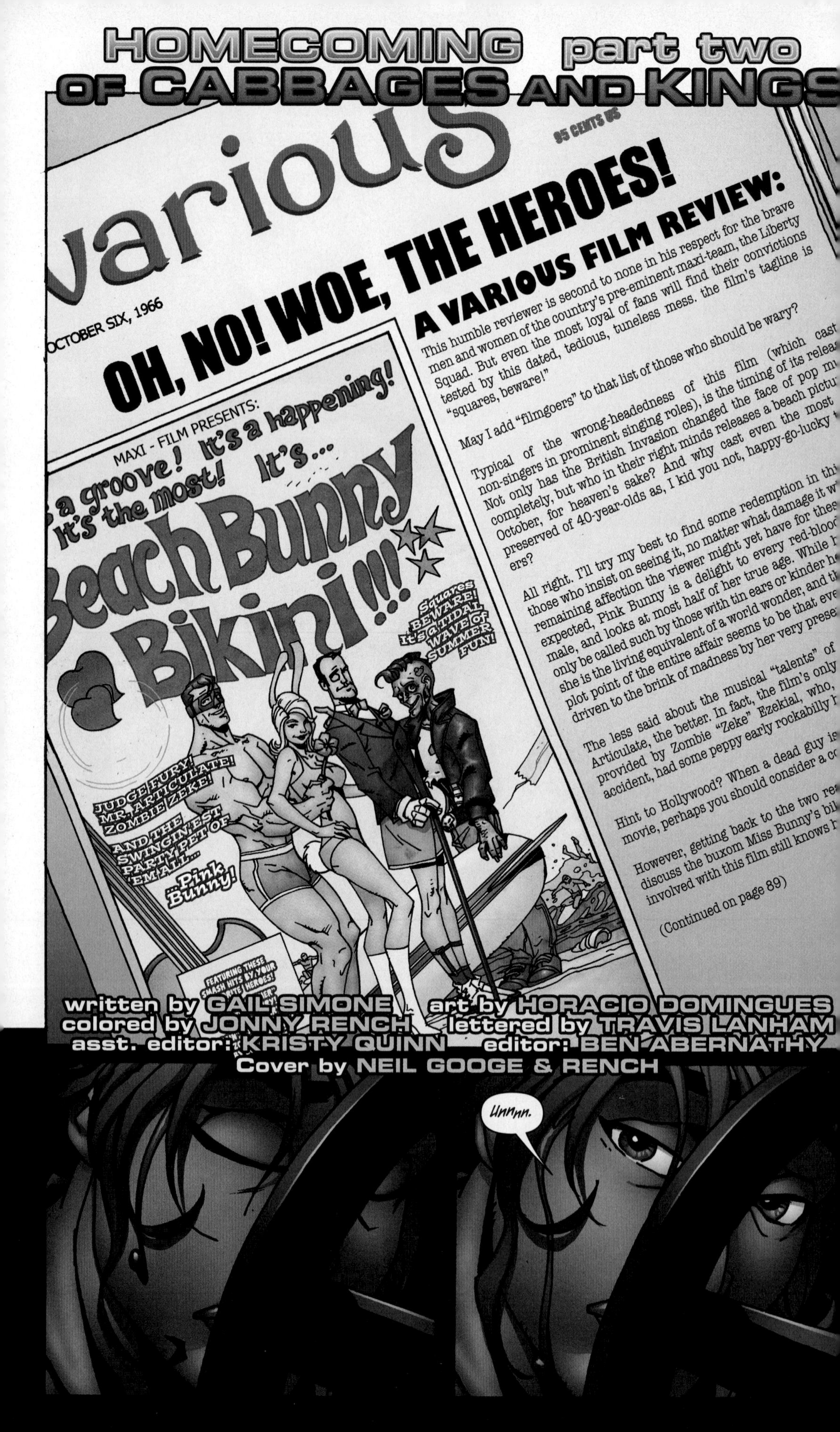
HOMECOMING part two
OF CABBAGES AND KINGS
Various
95 CENTS US
OCTOBER SIX, 1966
OH, NO! WOE, THE HEROES!
A VARIOUS FILM REVIEW:
This humble reviewer is second to none in his respect for the brave men and women of the country's pre-eminent maxi-team, the Liberty Squad. But even the most loyal of fans will find their convictions tested by this dated, tedious, tuneless mess. the film's tagline is "squares, beware!"
May I add "filmgoers" to that list of those who should be wary?
Typical of the wrong-headedness of this film (which cast non-singers in prominent singing roles), is the timing of its releas
Not only has the British Invasion changed the face of pop mu
completely, but who in their right minds releases a beach pictu
October, for heaven's sake? And why cast even the most
preserved of 40-year-olds as, I kid you not, happy-go-lucky
ers?
All right. I'll try my best to find some redemption in thi
those who insist on seeing it, no matter what damage it w
remaining affection the viewer might yet have for thes
expected, Pink Bunny is a delight to every red-blood
male, and looks at most half of her true age. While h
only be called such by those with tin ears or kinder h
she is the living equivalent of a world wonder, and th
plot point of the entire affair seems to be that eve
driven to the brink of madness by her very prese
The less said about the musical "talents" of
Articulate, the better. In fact, the film's only
provided by Zombie "Zeke" Ezekial, who,
accident, had some peppy early rockabilly h
Hint to Hollywood? When a dead guy is
movie, perhaps you should consider a co
However, getting back to the two re
discuss the buxom Miss Bunny's bi
involved with this film still knows h
(Continued on page 89)
MAXI - FILM PRESENTS:
It's a groove! It's a happening! It's the most! It's...
Beach Bunny Bikini!!!
Squares BEWARE! It's a TIDAL WAVE of SUMMER FUN!
JUDGE FURY! MR. ARTICULATE! ZOMBIE ZEKE!
AND THE SWINGIN'EST PARTY PET OF 'EM ALL... ...Pink Bunny!
FEATURING THESE SMASH HITS BY YOUR FAVORITE HEROES!
written by GAIL SIMONE art by HORACIO DOMINGUES
colored by JONNY RENCH lettered by TRAVIS LANHAM
asst. editor: KRISTY QUINN editor: BEN ABERNATHY
Cover by NEIL GOOGE & RENCH
Unnnn.

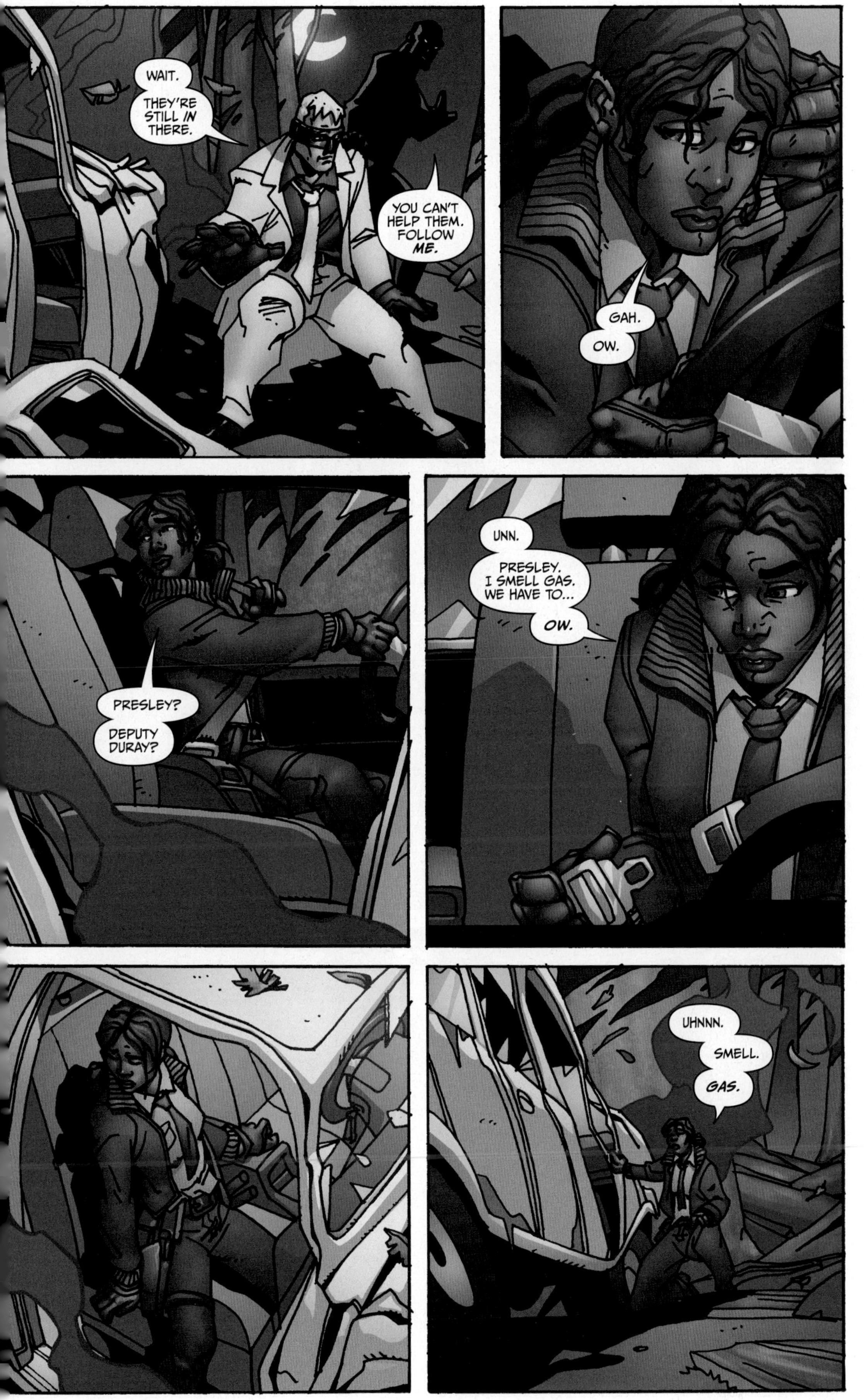
WAIT.
THEY'RE STILL *IN* THERE.
YOU CAN'T HELP THEM. FOLLOW *ME*.
GAH.
OW.
PRESLEY?
DEPUTY DURAY?
UNN.
PRESLEY. I SMELL GAS. WE HAVE TO...
OW.
UHNNN.
SMELL.
GAS.

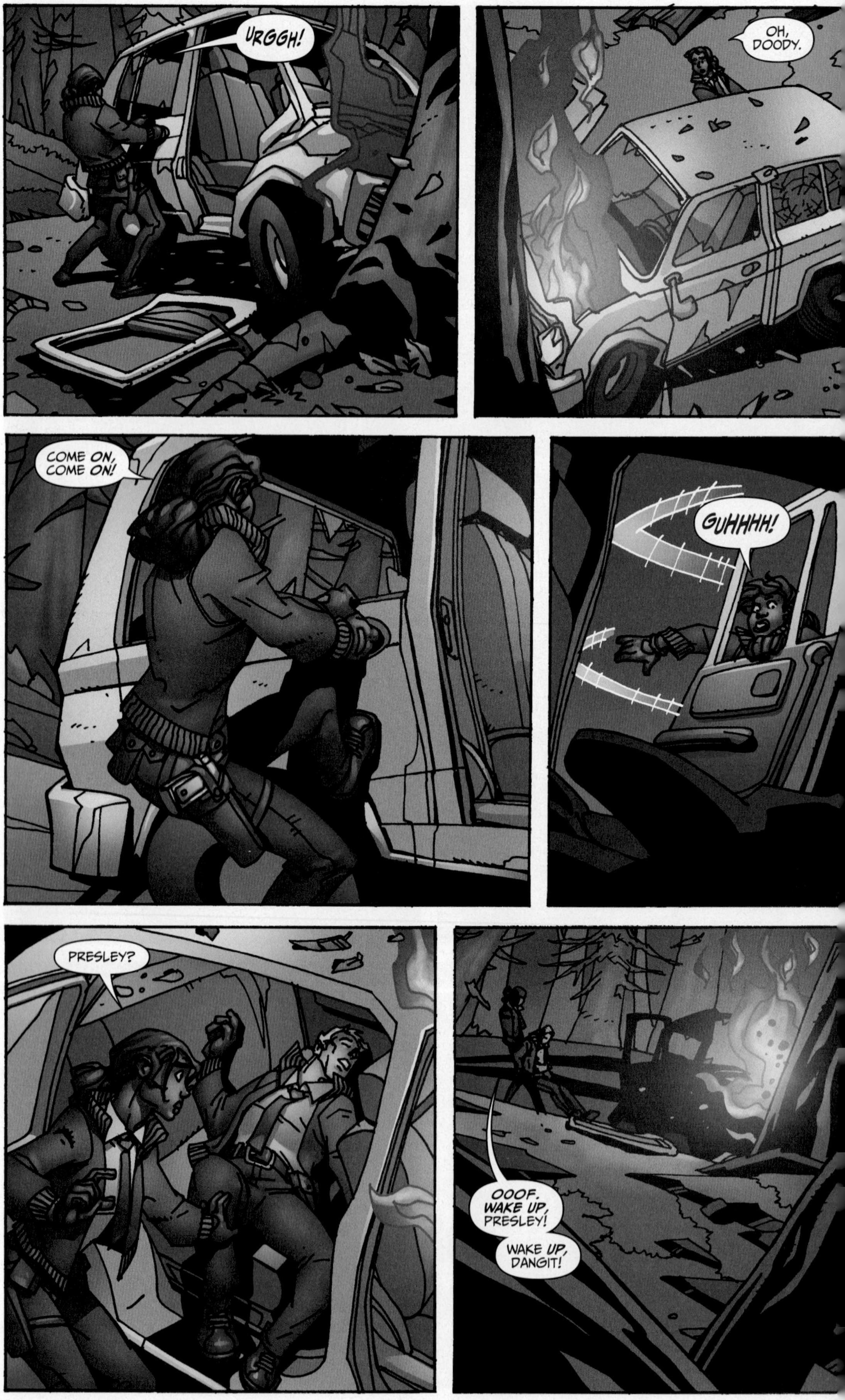
URGGH!
OH, DOODY.
COME ON, COME ON!
GUHHHH!
PRESLEY?
OOOF. WAKE UP, PRESLEY!
WAKE UP, DANGIT!

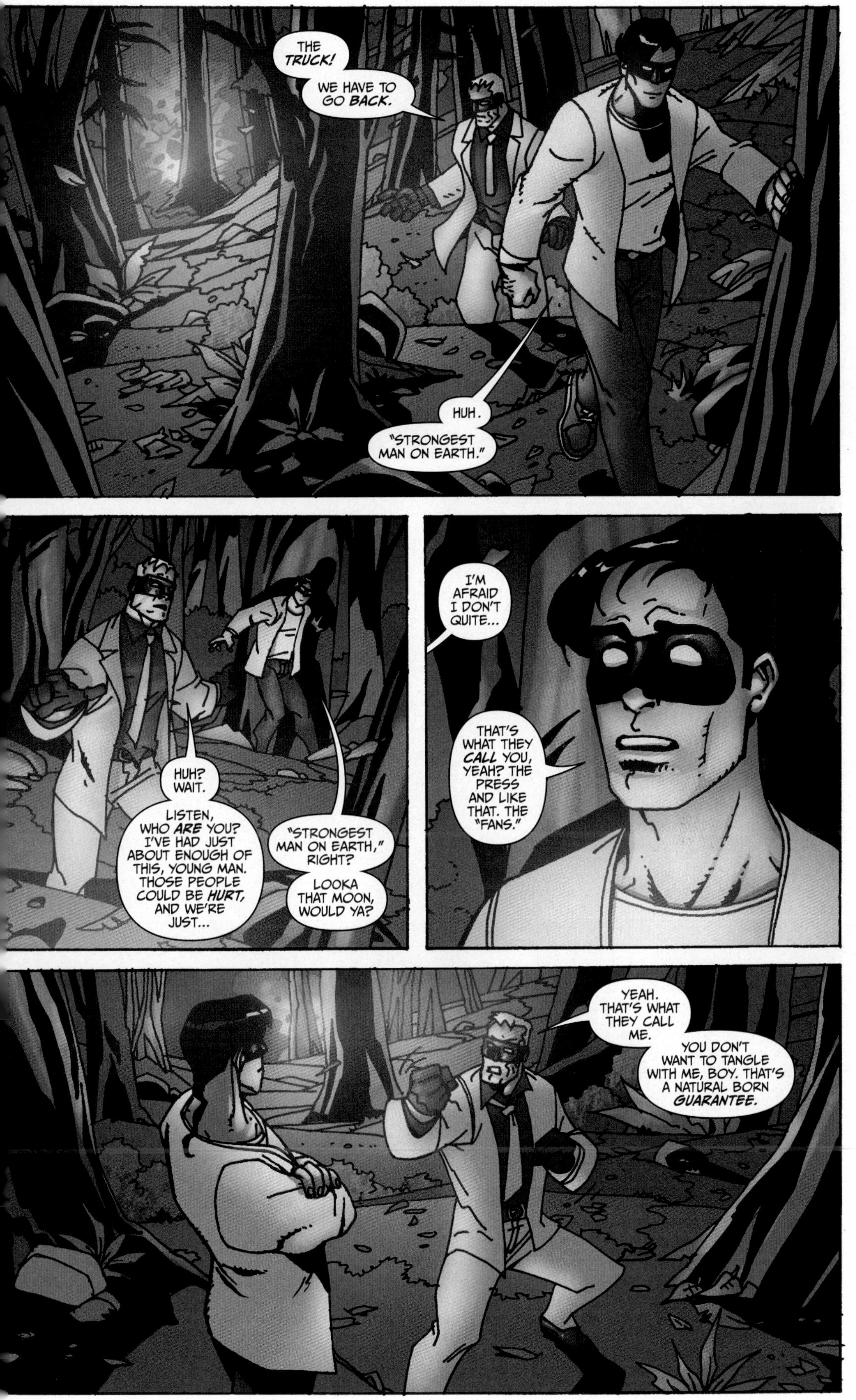
THE TRUCK!
WE HAVE TO GO BACK.
HUH. "STRONGEST MAN ON EARTH."
HUH? WAIT.
LISTEN, WHO ARE YOU? I'VE HAD JUST ABOUT ENOUGH OF THIS, YOUNG MAN. THOSE PEOPLE COULD BE HURT, AND WE'RE JUST...
"STRONGEST MAN ON EARTH," RIGHT?
LOOKA THAT MOON, WOULD YA?
I'M AFRAID I DON'T QUITE...
THAT'S WHAT THEY CALL YOU, YEAH? THE PRESS AND LIKE THAT. THE "FANS."
YEAH. THAT'S WHAT THEY CALL ME.
YOU DON'T WANT TO TANGLE WITH ME, BOY. THAT'S A NATURAL BORN GUARANTEE.

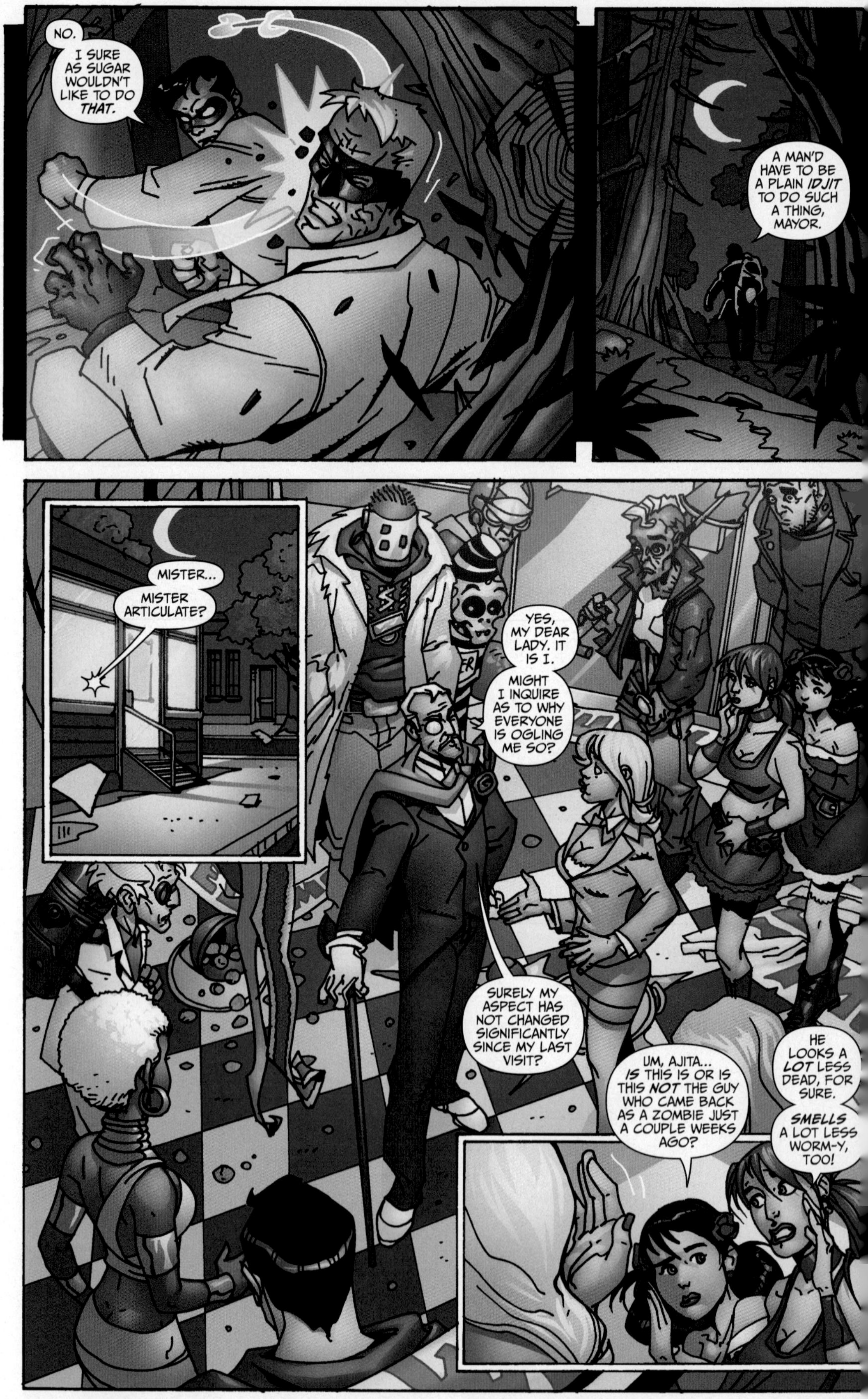
NO.
I SURE AS SUGAR WOULDN'T LIKE TO DO *THAT.*
A MAN'D HAVE TO BE A PLAIN *IDJIT* TO DO SUCH A THING, MAYOR.
MISTER...
MISTER ARTICULATE?
YES, MY DEAR LADY. IT IS I.
MIGHT I INQUIRE AS TO WHY EVERYONE IS OGLING ME SO?
SURELY MY ASPECT HAS NOT CHANGED SIGNIFICANTLY SINCE MY LAST VISIT?
UM, AJITA... *IS* THIS IS OR IS THIS *NOT* THE GUY WHO CAME BACK AS A ZOMBIE JUST A COUPLE WEEKS AGO?
HE LOOKS A *LOT* LESS DEAD, FOR SURE.
SMELLS A LOT LESS WORM-Y, TOO!

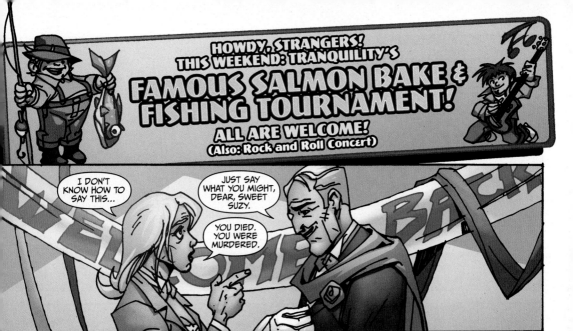

HOWDY, STRANGERS! THIS WEEKEND: TRANQUILITY'S **FAMOUS SALMON BAKE & FISHING TOURNAMENT!** ALL ARE WELCOME! (Also: Rock and Roll Concert)

I DON'T KNOW HOW TO SAY THIS...

JUST SAY WHAT YOU MIGHT, DEAR, SWEET SUZY.

YOU DIED. YOU WERE MURDERED.

MY COLONEL **CRAGG**, IN FACT.

THE DEUCE YOU SAY.

SEEMS LIKE I'D **REMEMBER** SUCH AN OCCASION!

ZEKE, I HATE TA ASK AN' DON'T TAKE THIS THE WRONG WAY, BUT WHAT WITH YOU BEIN' UNDEAD **YERSELF**, AN ALL...

YOU GOT ANY WAY A KNOWIN' IF MR. A'S A ZOMBIE HIMSELF AGAIN?

HUH.

I THINK SO, MR. SLAPJACK!

SLLAANNG

OWWW! WHAT IN **HADES'** NAME?

UM. SORRY.

ZOMBIE TEST.

YOU PASSED.

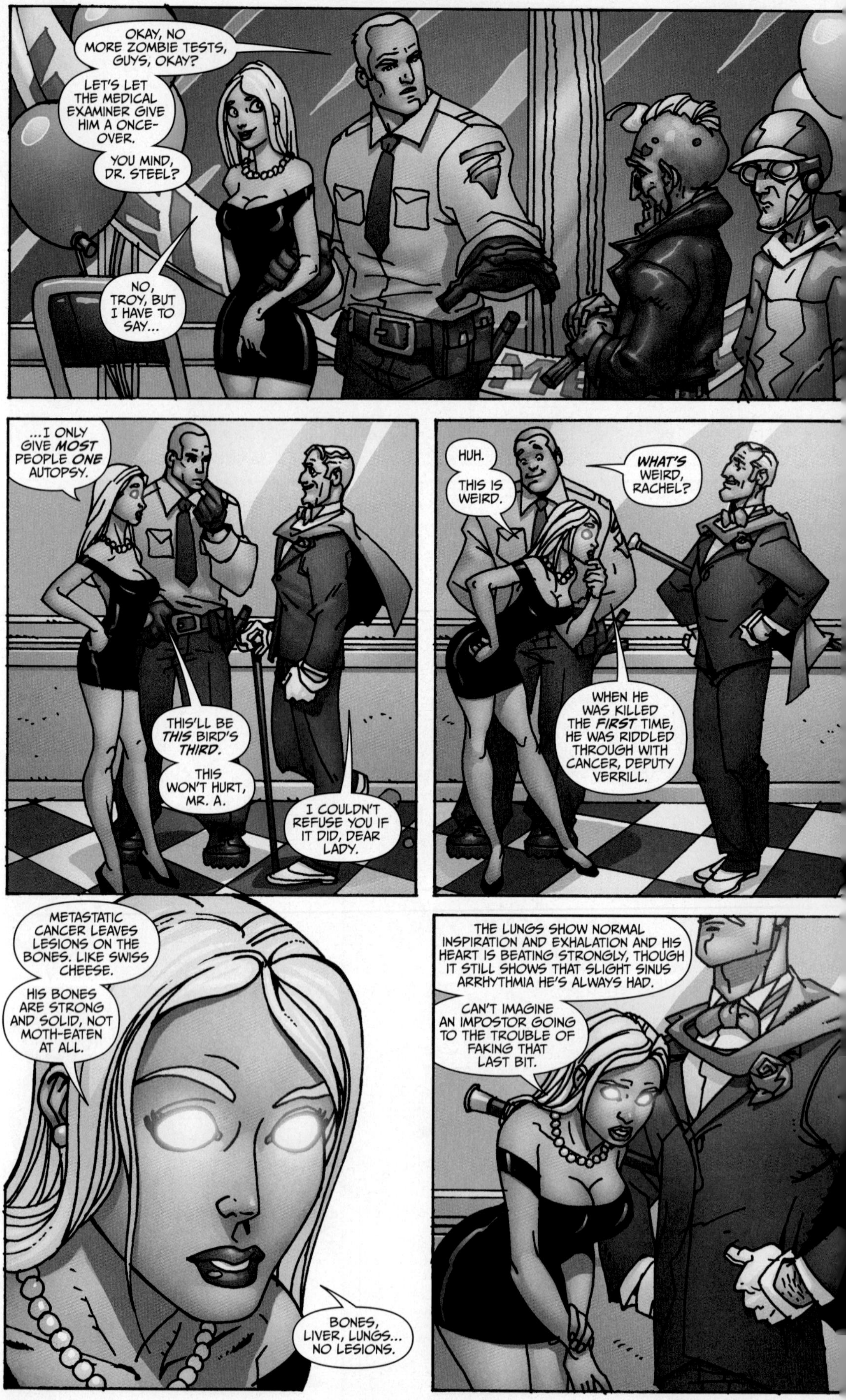
OKAY, NO MORE ZOMBIE TESTS, GUYS, OKAY?
LET'S LET THE MEDICAL EXAMINER GIVE HIM A ONCE-OVER.
YOU MIND, DR. STEEL?
NO, TROY, BUT I HAVE TO SAY...
...I ONLY GIVE MOST PEOPLE ONE AUTOPSY.
THIS'LL BE THIS BIRD'S THIRD.
THIS WON'T HURT, MR. A.
I COULDN'T REFUSE YOU IF IT DID, DEAR LADY.
HUH.
THIS IS WEIRD.
WHAT'S WEIRD, RACHEL?
WHEN HE WAS KILLED THE FIRST TIME, HE WAS RIDDLED THROUGH WITH CANCER, DEPUTY VERRILL.
METASTATIC CANCER LEAVES LESIONS ON THE BONES. LIKE SWISS CHEESE.
HIS BONES ARE STRONG AND SOLID, NOT MOTH-EATEN AT ALL.
BONES, LIVER, LUNGS... NO LESIONS.
THE LUNGS SHOW NORMAL INSPIRATION AND EXHALATION AND HIS HEART IS BEATING STRONGLY, THOUGH IT STILL SHOWS THAT SLIGHT SINUS ARRHYTHMIA HE'S ALWAYS HAD.
CAN'T IMAGINE AN IMPOSTOR GOING TO THE TROUBLE OF FAKING THAT LAST BIT.

THERE ARE PERISTALTIC WAVES IN THE INTESTINES, DENOTING A FUNCTIONING GASTROINTESTINAL TRACT. I CAN SEE THE FORMATION OF RED CORPUSCLES IN THE BONE MARROW.

THAT'S THE CAPPER, TROY. THIS MAN IS A GOING CONCERN, IF YOU GET MY DRIFT.

HE'S ALIVE, AND HE'S THE REAL *THING*.

WELL, IT'S ALWAYS NICE O HAVE ONE'S AFFAIRS IN ORDER IN MATTERS OF LIFE AND DEATH, I FIND.

YOU AIN'T OUT OF THE CLOUDS YET, MR. A.

I SAW YOUR CORPSE. GONNA TAKE A LOT OF CONVINCING FOR ME TO START INVITING YOU TO PARTIES AGAIN.

HENRY? YOU LOOK LIKE YOU HAVE SOMETHING TO *SAY*.

HMMM?

OH. NO. NOTHING SET IN STEEL, MAXI-MAN.

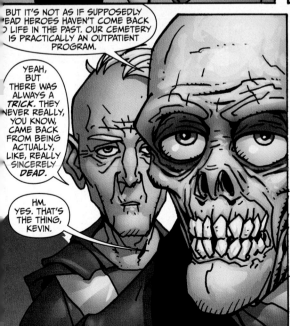

BUT IT'S NOT AS IF SUPPOSEDLY EAD HEROES HAVEN'T COME BACK O LIFE IN THE PAST. OUR CEMETERY IS PRACTICALLY AN OUTPATIENT PROGRAM.

YEAH, BUT THERE WAS ALWAYS A *TRICK*. THEY NEVER REALLY, YOU KNOW, CAME BACK FROM BEING ACTUALLY, LIKE, REALLY SINCERELY *DEAD*.

HM. YES. THAT'S THE THING, KEVIN.

THERE WAS ALWAYS A *TRICK*.

OKAY. DON'T *NO* ONE MAKE A BIG *THING* OF THIS.

IT DOESN'T *MEAN* NOTHING, ARE WE CLEAR ON *THAT*?

IT'S HIM. LET'S HAVE NO MORE FUSS ABOUT IT.

WHO WANTS MEATLOAF?

MY DEAR GOD IN HEAVEN.

UH, DISPATCH?

LISA, WE GOT AN E.T.A. ON THE SHERIFF'S RETURN? WE HAVE KIND OF...A SITUATION HERE, AND I COULD USE TOMMY'S...

TRUTH BE TOLD, TROY, I CAN'T RAISE HER OR PRESLEY ON THEIR RADIOS OR CELL PHONES. I'M GETTING A LITTLE NERVOUS.

THAT'S WEIRD.

SHALL I CALL THE STATE POLICE?

NAH, NO. SHE'S BRINGING BACK THE MAYOR. LET'S HANDLE THIS OURSELVES FOR NOW, OKAY?

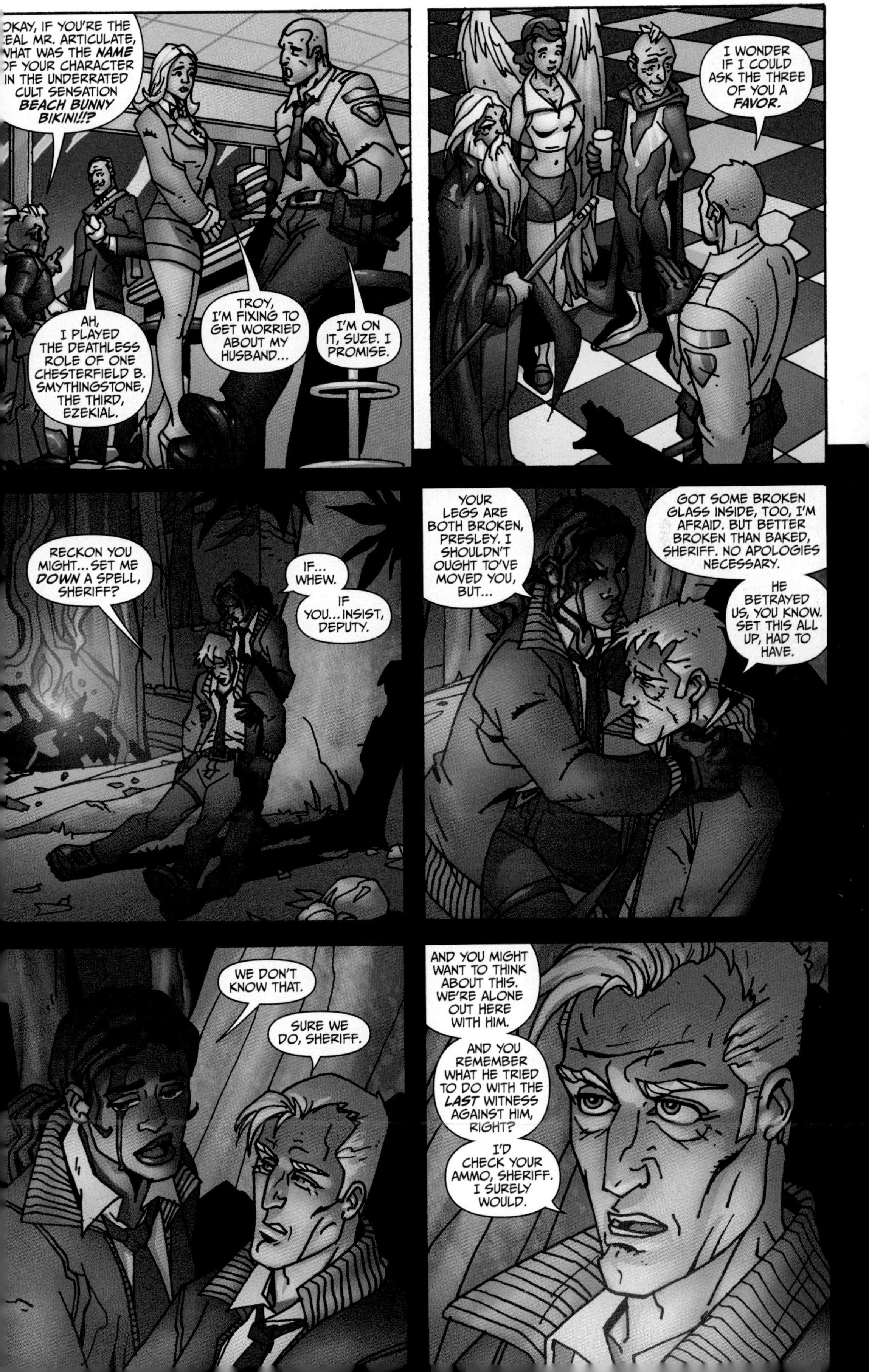
OKAY, IF YOU'RE THE EAL MR. ARTICULATE, WHAT WAS THE NAME OF YOUR CHARACTER IN THE UNDERRATED CULT SENSATION BEACH BUNNY BIKINI!!?
AH, I PLAYED THE DEATHLESS ROLE OF ONE CHESTERFIELD B. SMYTHINGSTONE, THE THIRD, EZEKIAL.
TROY, I'M FIXING TO GET WORRIED ABOUT MY HUSBAND...
I'M ON IT, SUZE. I PROMISE.
I WONDER IF I COULD ASK THE THREE OF YOU A FAVOR.
RECKON YOU MIGHT...SET ME DOWN A SPELL, SHERIFF?
IF... WHEW.
IF YOU...INSIST, DEPUTY.
YOUR LEGS ARE BOTH BROKEN, PRESLEY. I SHOULDN'T OUGHT TO'VE MOVED YOU, BUT...
GOT SOME BROKEN GLASS INSIDE, TOO, I'M AFRAID. BUT BETTER BROKEN THAN BAKED, SHERIFF. NO APOLOGIES NECESSARY.
HE BETRAYED US, YOU KNOW. SET THIS ALL UP, HAD TO HAVE.
WE DON'T KNOW THAT.
SURE WE DO, SHERIFF.
AND YOU MIGHT WANT TO THINK ABOUT THIS. WE'RE ALONE OUT HERE WITH HIM.
AND YOU REMEMBER WHAT HE TRIED TO DO WITH THE LAST WITNESS AGAINST HIM, RIGHT?
I'D CHECK YOUR AMMO, SHERIFF. I SURELY WOULD.

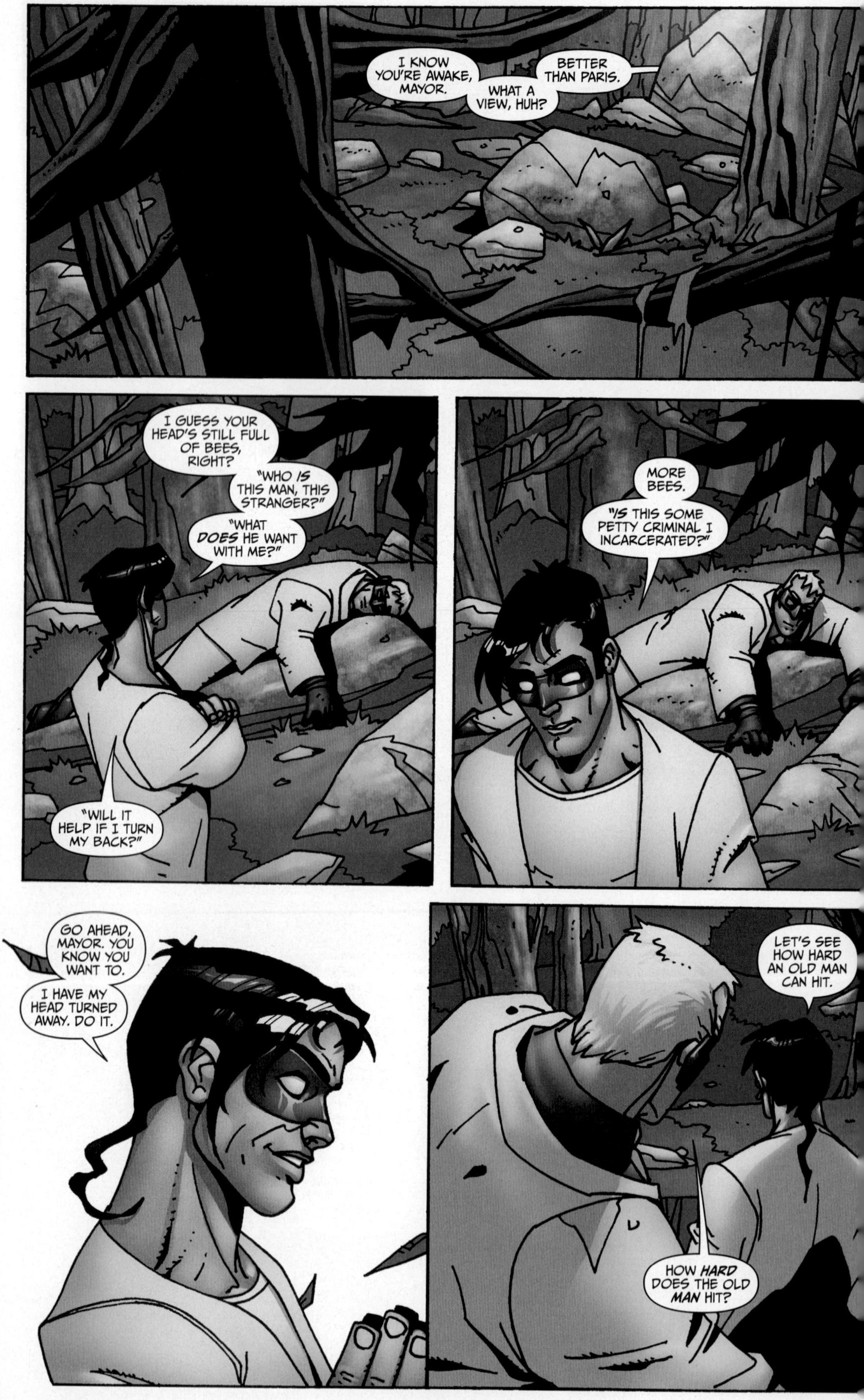
I KNOW YOU'RE AWAKE, MAYOR.
WHAT A VIEW, HUH?
BETTER THAN PARIS.
I GUESS YOUR HEAD'S STILL FULL OF BEES, RIGHT?
"WHO *IS* THIS MAN, THIS STRANGER?"
"WHAT *DOES* HE WANT WITH ME?"
"WILL IT HELP IF I TURN MY BACK?"
MORE BEES.
"*IS* THIS SOME PETTY CRIMINAL I INCARCERATED?"
GO AHEAD, MAYOR. YOU KNOW YOU WANT TO.
I HAVE MY HEAD TURNED AWAY. DO IT.
LET'S SEE HOW HARD AN OLD MAN CAN HIT.
HOW *HARD* DOES THE OLD *MAN* HIT?

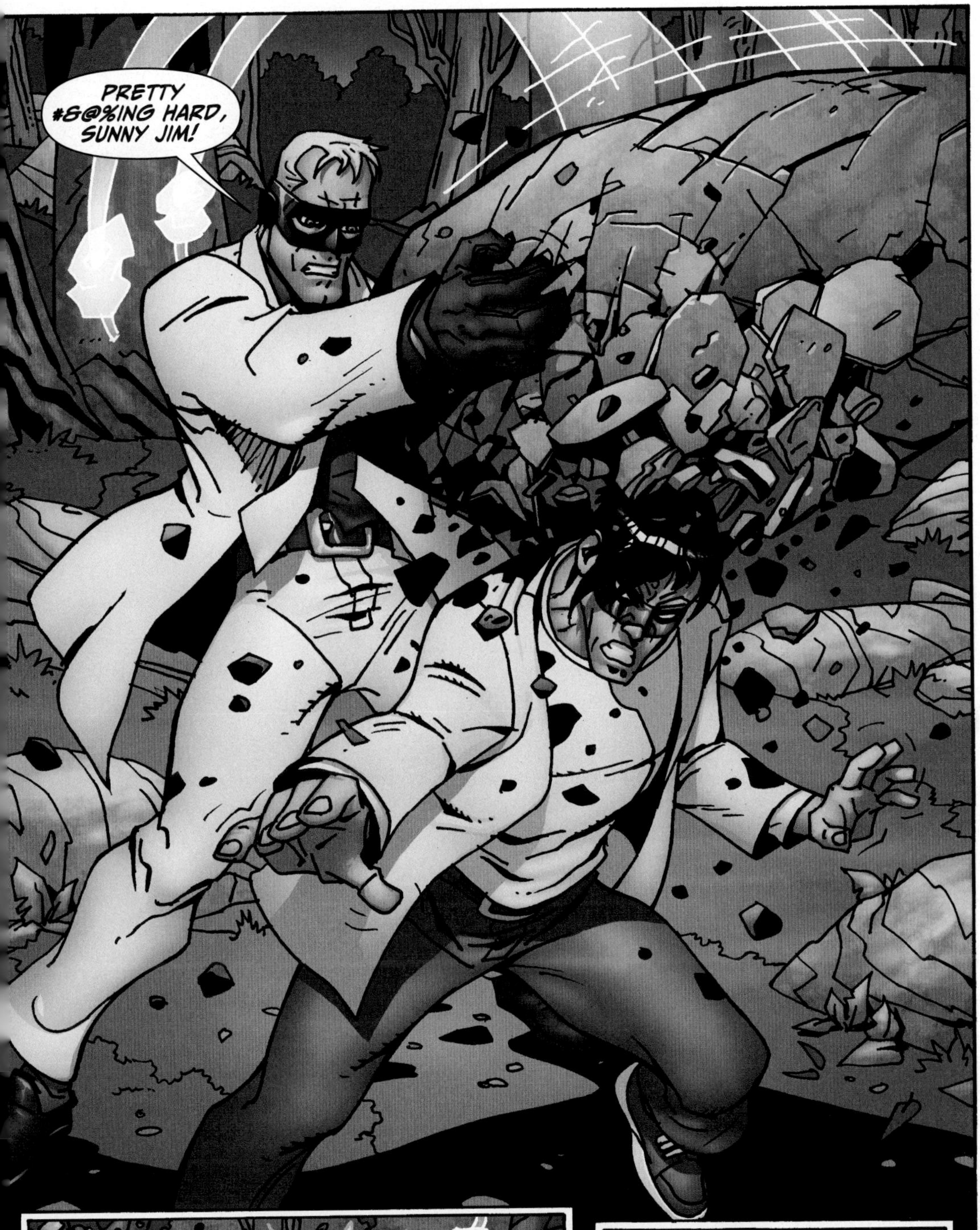
PRETTY #&@%ING HARD, SUNNY JIM!

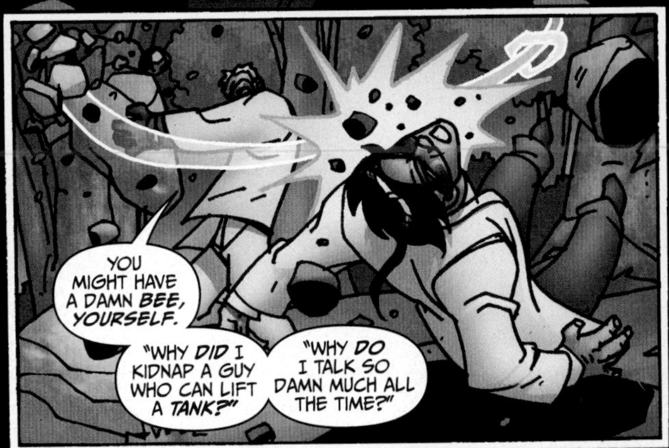
YOU MIGHT HAVE A DAMN BEE, YOURSELF.
"WHY DID I KIDNAP A GUY WHO CAN LIFT A TANK?"
"WHY DO I TALK SO DAMN MUCH ALL THE TIME?"

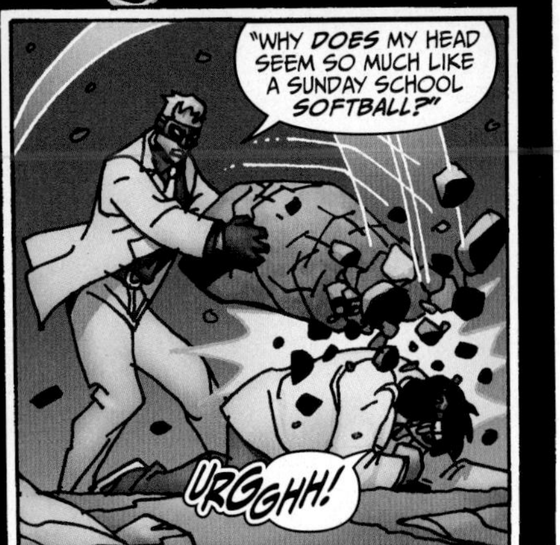
"WHY DOES MY HEAD SEEM SO MUCH LIKE A SUNDAY SCHOOL SOFTBALL?"
URGGHH!

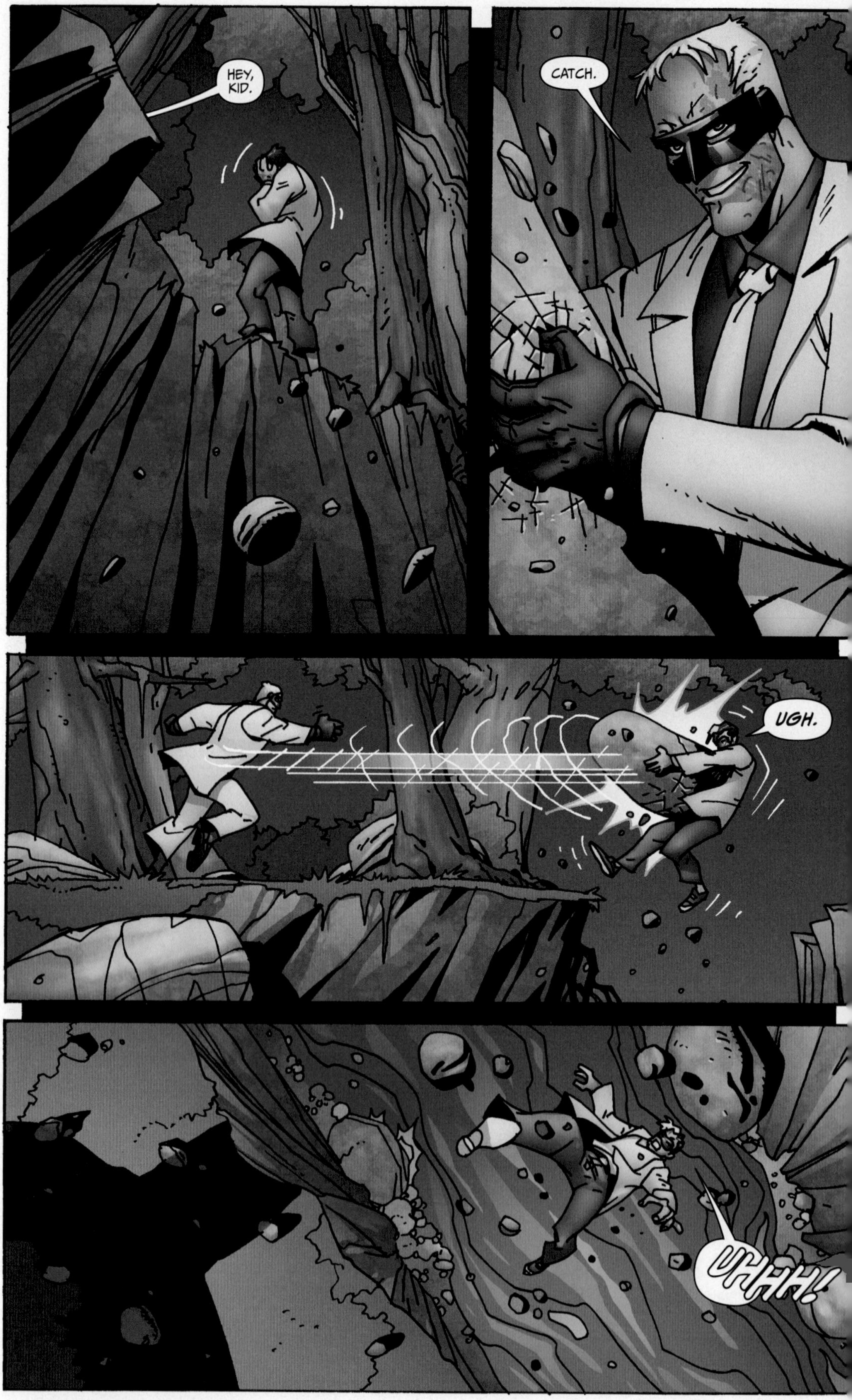
HEY, KID.
CATCH.
UGH.
UHHH!

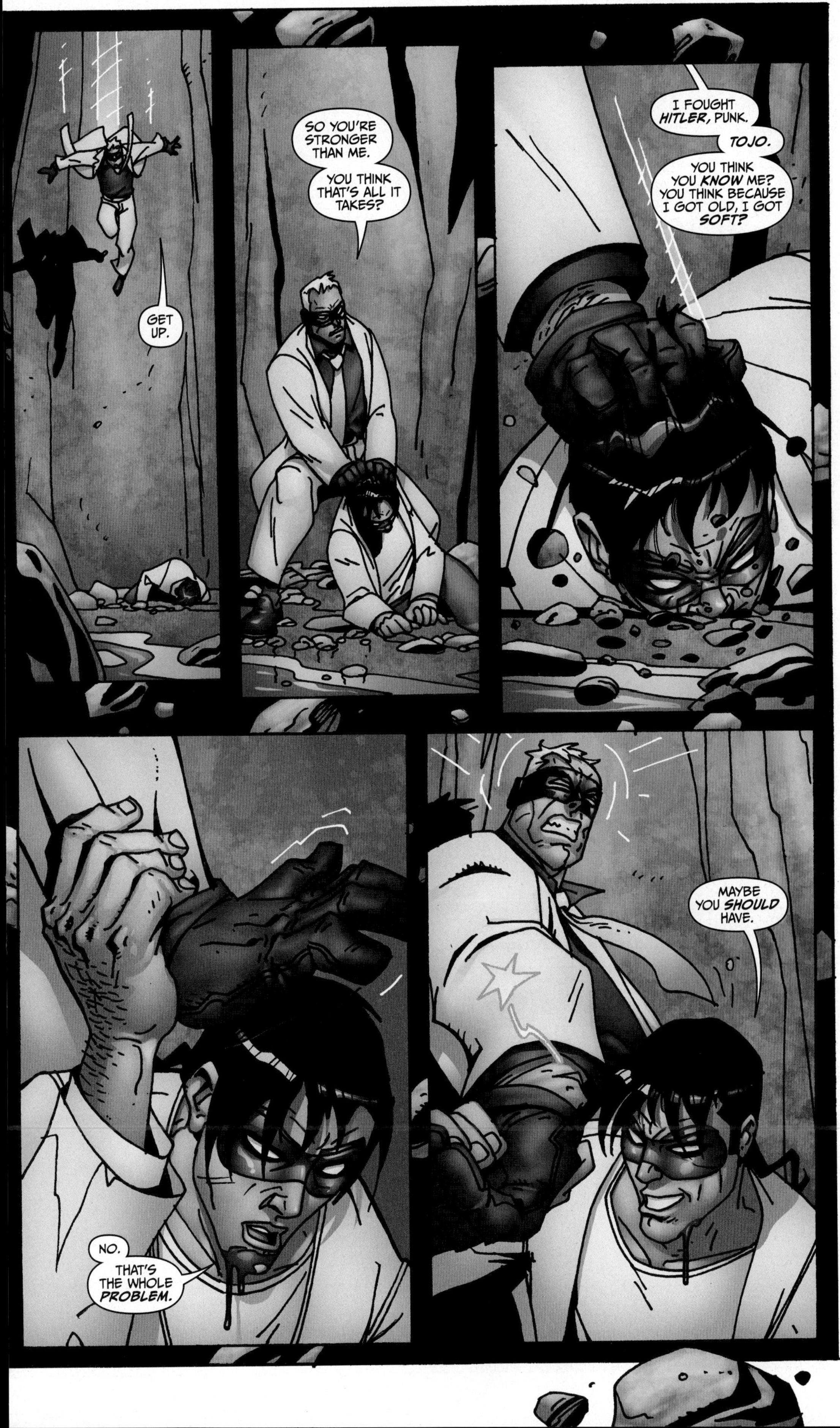
GET UP.
SO YOU'RE STRONGER THAN ME.
YOU THINK THAT'S ALL IT TAKES?
I FOUGHT HITLER, PUNK.
TOJO.
YOU THINK YOU KNOW ME? YOU THINK BECAUSE I GOT OLD, I GOT SOFT?
NO.
THAT'S THE WHOLE PROBLEM.
MAYBE YOU SHOULD HAVE.

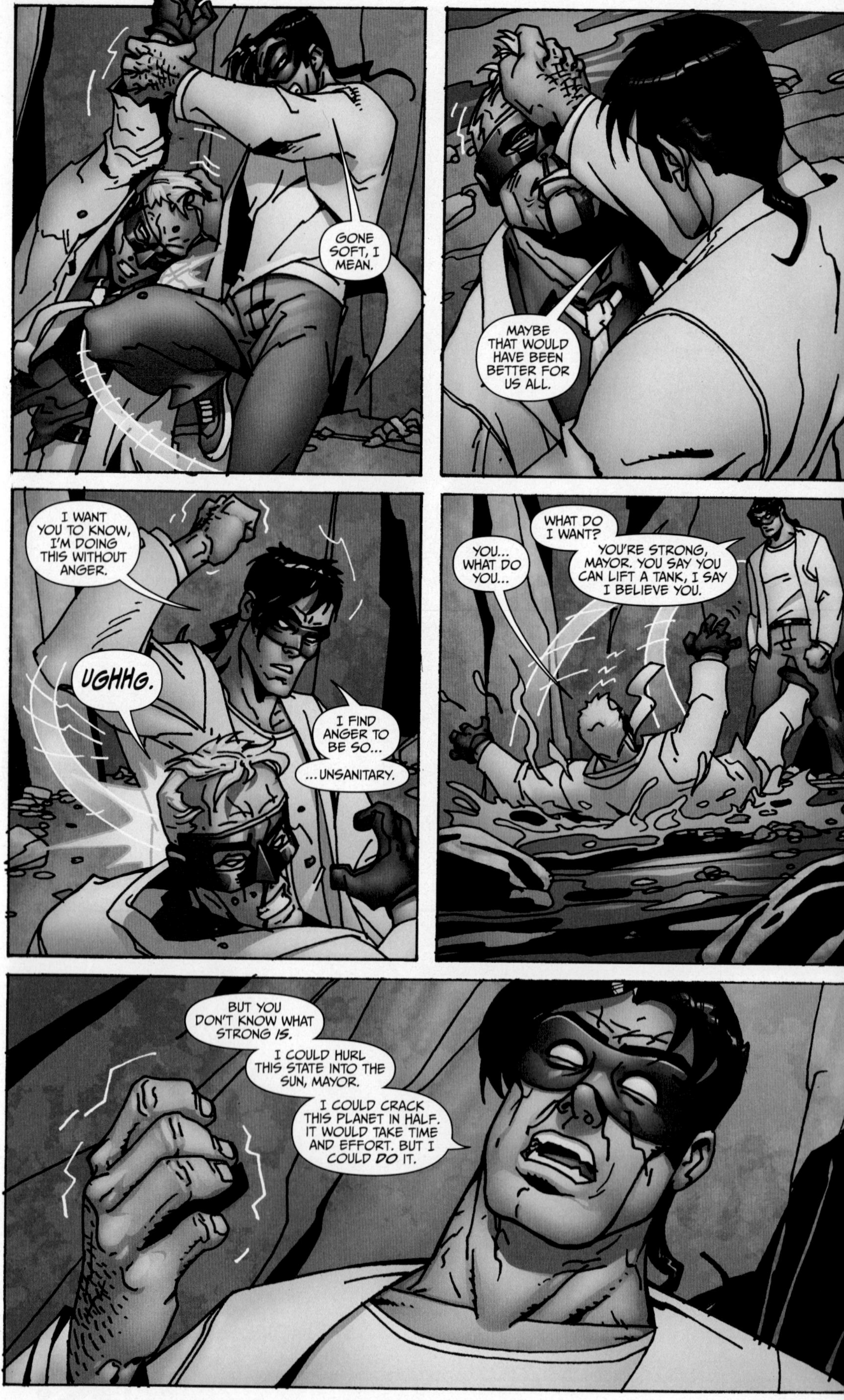
GONE SOFT, I MEAN.
MAYBE THAT WOULD HAVE BEEN BETTER FOR US ALL.
I WANT YOU TO KNOW, I'M DOING THIS WITHOUT ANGER.
UGHHG.
I FIND ANGER TO BE SO...
...UNSANITARY.
YOU... WHAT DO YOU...
WHAT DO I WANT?
YOU'RE STRONG, MAYOR. YOU SAY YOU CAN LIFT A TANK, I SAY I BELIEVE YOU.
BUT YOU DON'T KNOW WHAT STRONG *IS*.
I COULD HURL THIS STATE INTO THE SUN, MAYOR.
I COULD CRACK THIS PLANET IN HALF. IT WOULD TAKE TIME AND EFFORT. BUT I COULD *DO* IT.

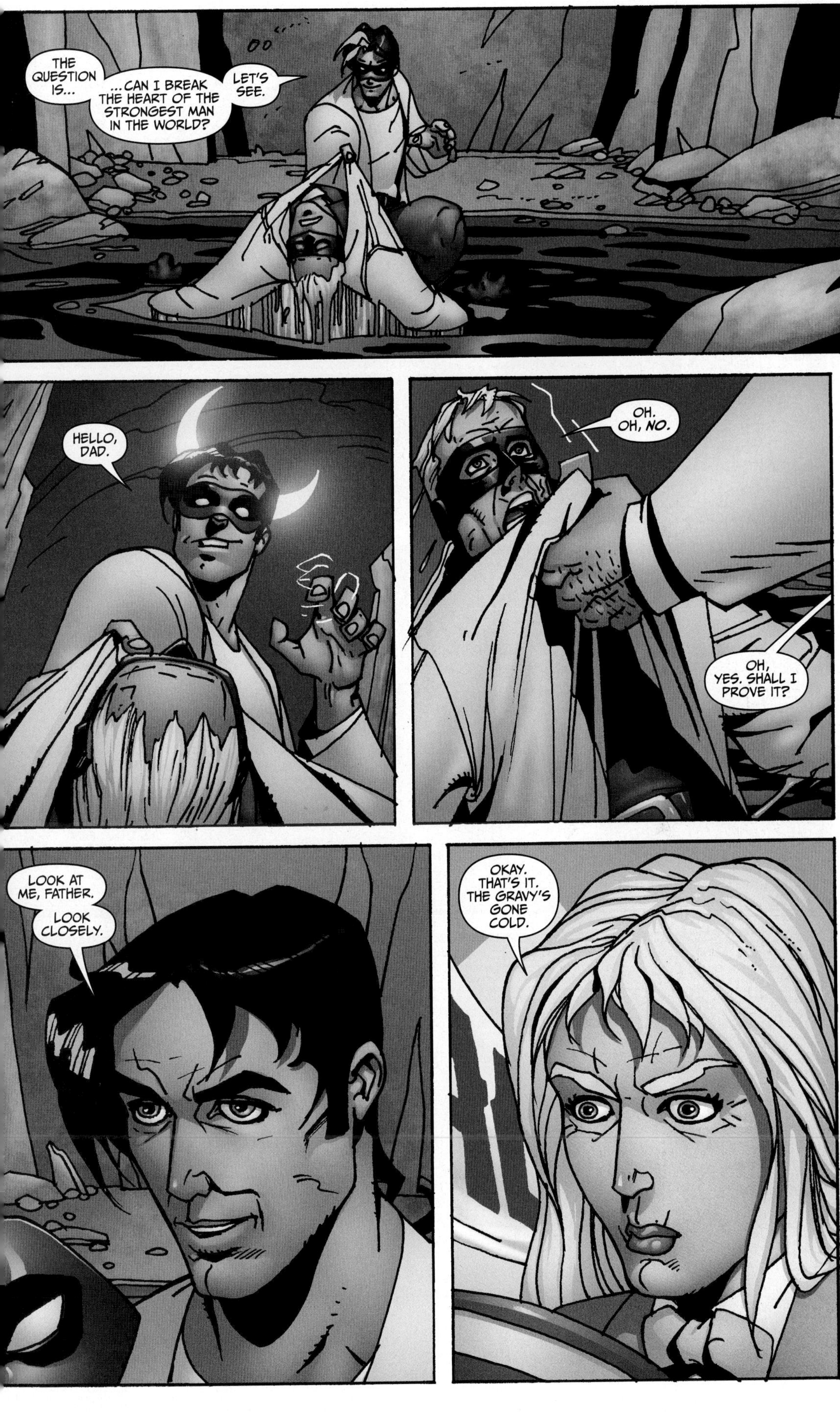
THE QUESTION IS...
...CAN I BREAK THE HEART OF THE STRONGEST MAN IN THE WORLD?
LET'S SEE.
HELLO, DAD.
OH. OH, NO.
OH, YES. SHALL I PROVE IT?
LOOK AT ME, FATHER.
LOOK CLOSELY.
OKAY. THAT'S IT. THE GRAVY'S GONE COLD.

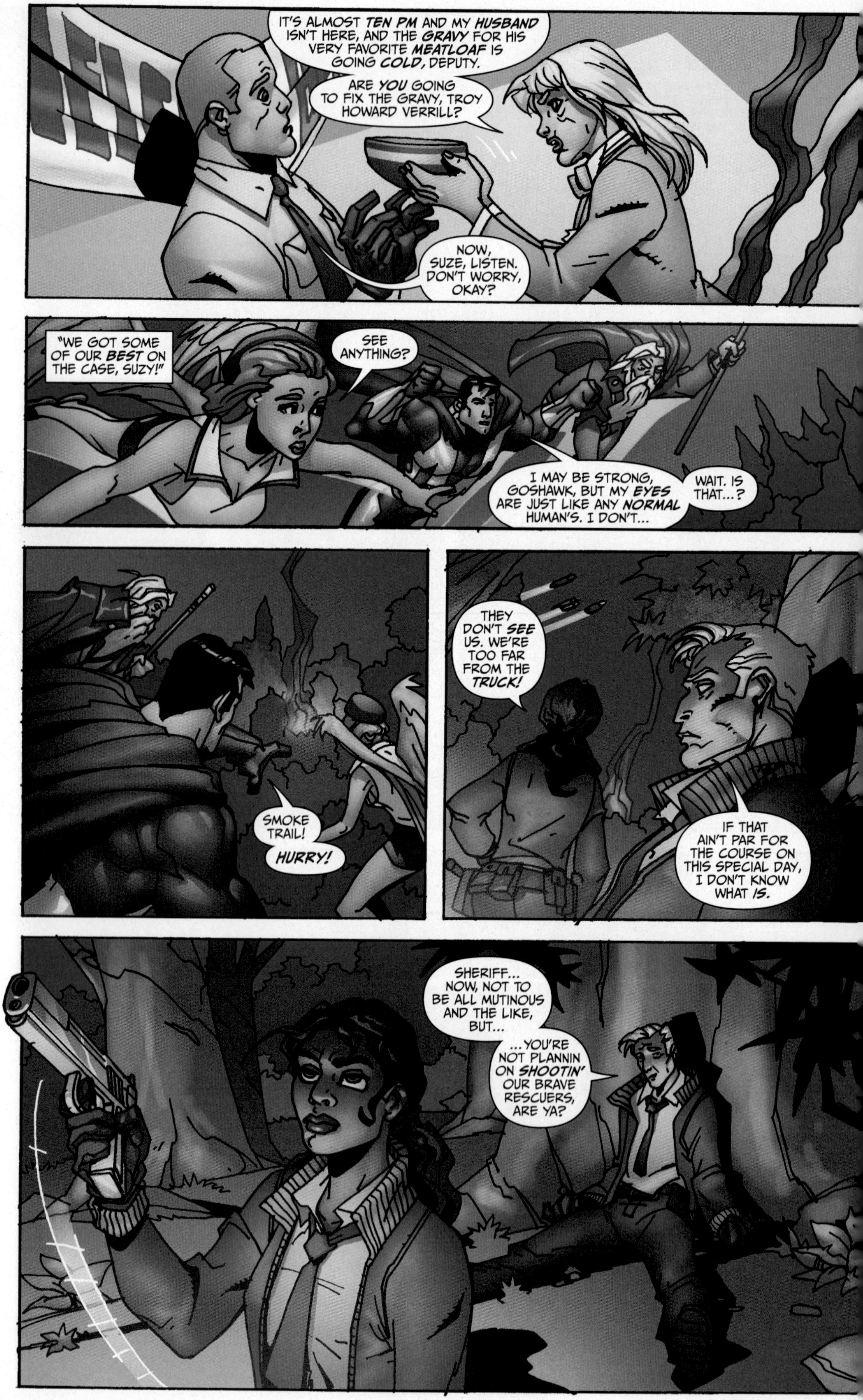
IT'S ALMOST **TEN PM** AND MY **HUSBAND** ISN'T HERE, AND THE **GRAVY** FOR HIS VERY FAVORITE **MEATLOAF** IS GOING **COLD**, DEPUTY.
ARE **YOU** GOING TO FIX THE GRAVY, TROY HOWARD VERRILL?
NOW, SUZE, LISTEN. DON'T WORRY, OKAY?
"WE GOT SOME OF OUR **BEST** ON THE CASE, SUZY!"
SEE ANYTHING?
I MAY BE STRONG, GOSHAWK, BUT MY **EYES** ARE JUST LIKE ANY **NORMAL** HUMAN'S. I DON'T...
WAIT. IS THAT...?
SMOKE TRAIL! **HURRY!**
THEY DON'T **SEE** US. WE'RE TOO FAR FROM THE **TRUCK!**
IF THAT AIN'T PAR FOR THE COURSE ON THIS SPECIAL DAY, I DON'T KNOW WHAT **IS.**
SHERIFF... NOW, NOT TO BE ALL MUTINOUS AND THE LIKE, BUT...
...YOU'RE NOT PLANNIN ON **SHOOTIN'** OUR BRAVE RESCUERS, ARE YA?

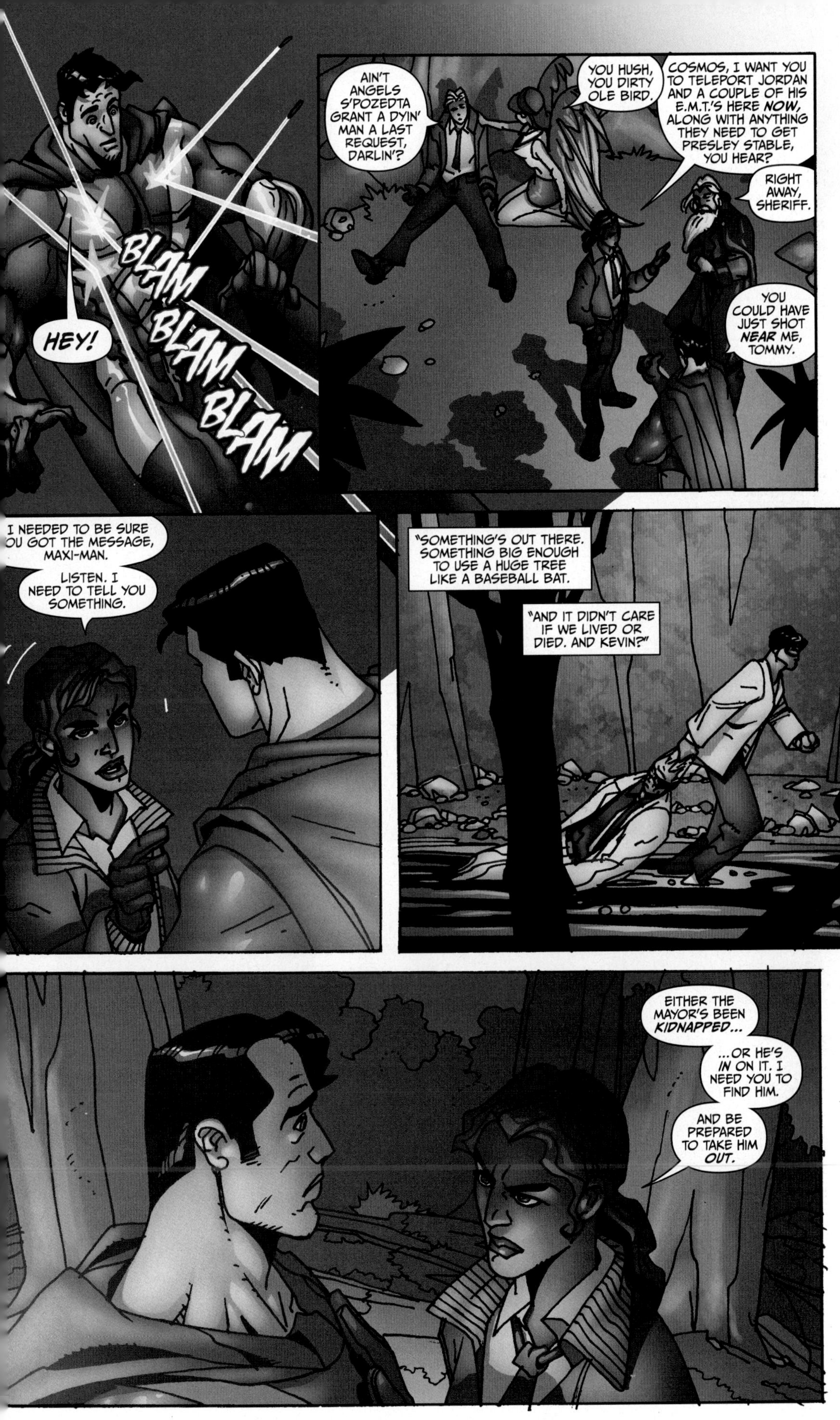
BLAM
BLAM
BLAM
BLAM
HEY!
AIN'T ANGELS S'POZEDTA GRANT A DYIN' MAN A LAST REQUEST, DARLIN'?
YOU HUSH, YOU DIRTY OLE BIRD.
COSMOS, I WANT YOU TO TELEPORT JORDAN AND A COUPLE OF HIS E.M.T.'S HERE NOW, ALONG WITH ANYTHING THEY NEED TO GET PRESLEY STABLE, YOU HEAR?
RIGHT AWAY, SHERIFF.
YOU COULD HAVE JUST SHOT NEAR ME, TOMMY.
I NEEDED TO BE SURE OU GOT THE MESSAGE, MAXI-MAN.
LISTEN. I NEED TO TELL YOU SOMETHING.
"SOMETHING'S OUT THERE. SOMETHING BIG ENOUGH TO USE A HUGE TREE LIKE A BASEBALL BAT.
"AND IT DIDN'T CARE IF WE LIVED OR DIED. AND KEVIN?"
EITHER THE MAYOR'S BEEN KIDNAPPED...
...OR HE'S IN ON IT. I NEED YOU TO FIND HIM.
AND BE PREPARED TO TAKE HIM OUT.

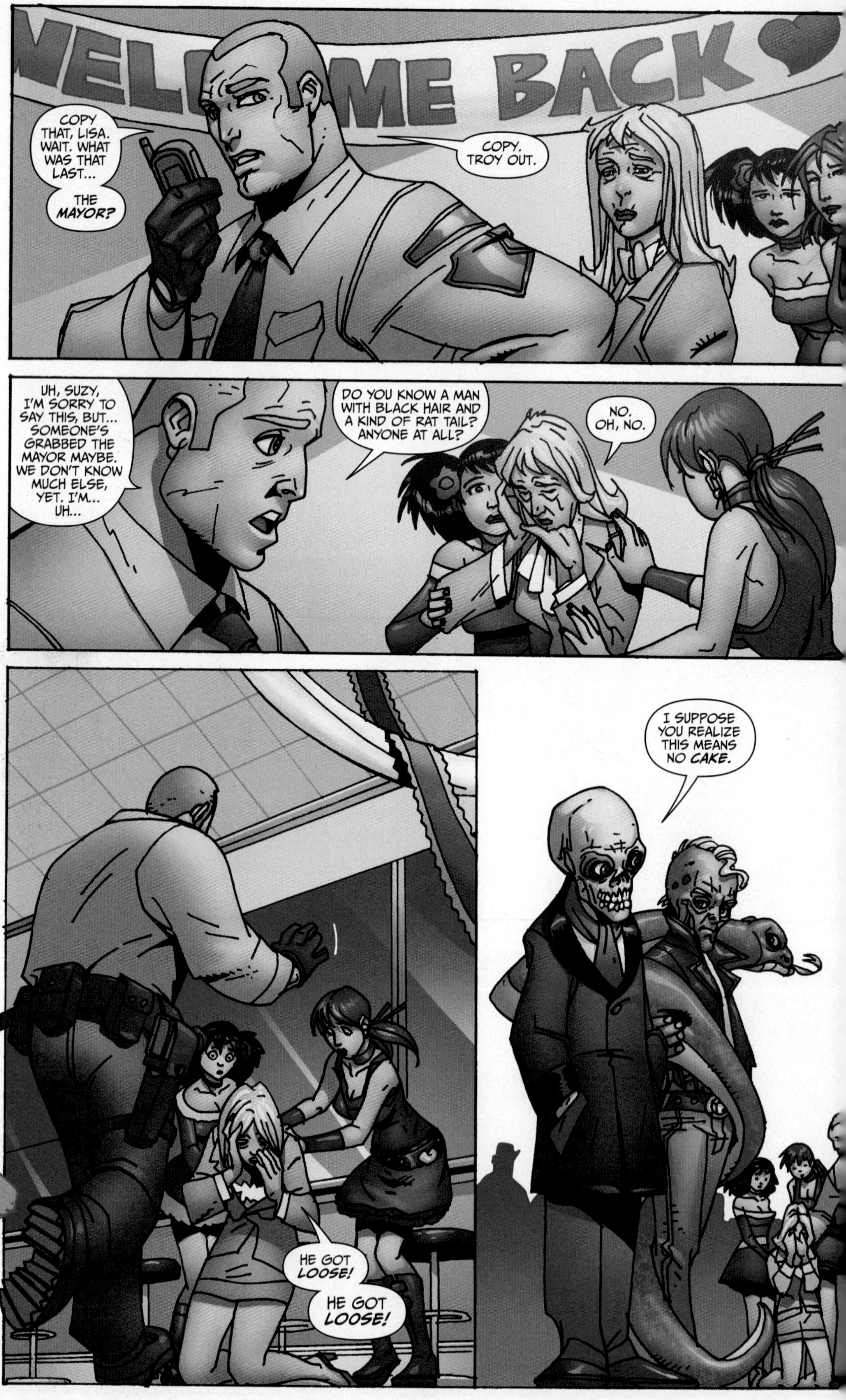
WELC ME BACK
COPY THAT, LISA. WAIT. WHAT WAS THAT LAST...
THE MAYOR?
COPY. TROY OUT.
UH, SUZY, I'M SORRY TO SAY THIS, BUT... SOMEONE'S GRABBED THE MAYOR MAYBE. WE DON'T KNOW MUCH ELSE, YET. I'M... UH...
DO YOU KNOW A MAN WITH BLACK HAIR AND A KIND OF RAT TAIL? ANYONE AT ALL?
NO. OH, NO.
HE GOT LOOSE!
HE GOT LOOSE!
I SUPPOSE YOU REALIZE THIS MEANS NO CAKE.

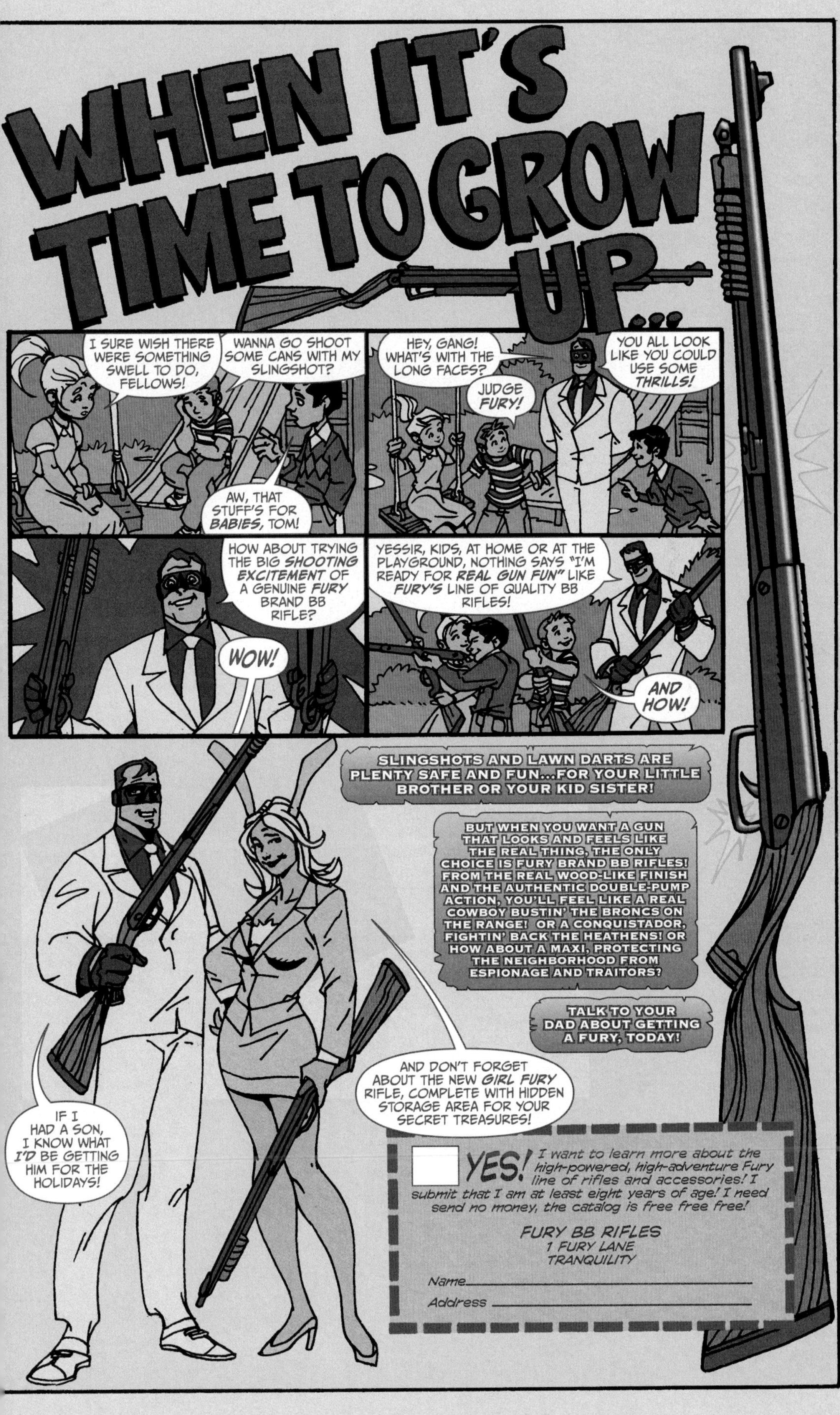
WHEN IT'S TIME TO GROW UP...
I SURE WISH THERE WERE SOMETHING SWELL TO DO, FELLOWS!
WANNA GO SHOOT SOME CANS WITH MY SLINGSHOT?
AW, THAT STUFF'S FOR BABIES, TOM!
HEY, GANG! WHAT'S WITH THE LONG FACES?
JUDGE FURY!
YOU ALL LOOK LIKE YOU COULD USE SOME THRILLS!
HOW ABOUT TRYING THE BIG SHOOTING EXCITEMENT OF A GENUINE FURY BRAND BB RIFLE?
WOW!
YESSIR, KIDS, AT HOME OR AT THE PLAYGROUND, NOTHING SAYS "I'M READY FOR REAL GUN FUN" LIKE FURY'S LINE OF QUALITY BB RIFLES!
AND HOW!
SLINGSHOTS AND LAWN DARTS ARE PLENTY SAFE AND FUN...FOR YOUR LITTLE BROTHER OR YOUR KID SISTER!
BUT WHEN YOU WANT A GUN THAT LOOKS AND FEELS LIKE THE REAL THING, THE ONLY CHOICE IS FURY BRAND BB RIFLES! FROM THE REAL WOOD-LIKE FINISH AND THE AUTHENTIC DOUBLE-PUMP ACTION, YOU'LL FEEL LIKE A REAL COWBOY BUSTIN' THE BRONCS ON THE RANGE! OR A CONQUISTADOR, FIGHTIN' BACK THE HEATHENS! OR HOW ABOUT A MAXI, PROTECTING THE NEIGHBORHOOD FROM ESPIONAGE AND TRAITORS?
TALK TO YOUR DAD ABOUT GETTING A FURY, TODAY!
IF I HAD A SON, I KNOW WHAT I'D BE GETTING HIM FOR THE HOLIDAYS!
AND DON'T FORGET ABOUT THE NEW GIRL FURY RIFLE, COMPLETE WITH HIDDEN STORAGE AREA FOR YOUR SECRET TREASURES!
YES! I want to learn more about the high-powered, high-adventure Fury line of rifles and accessories! I submit that I am at least eight years of age! I need send no money, the catalog is free free free!
FURY BB RIFLES
1 FURY LANE
TRANQUILITY
Name
Address

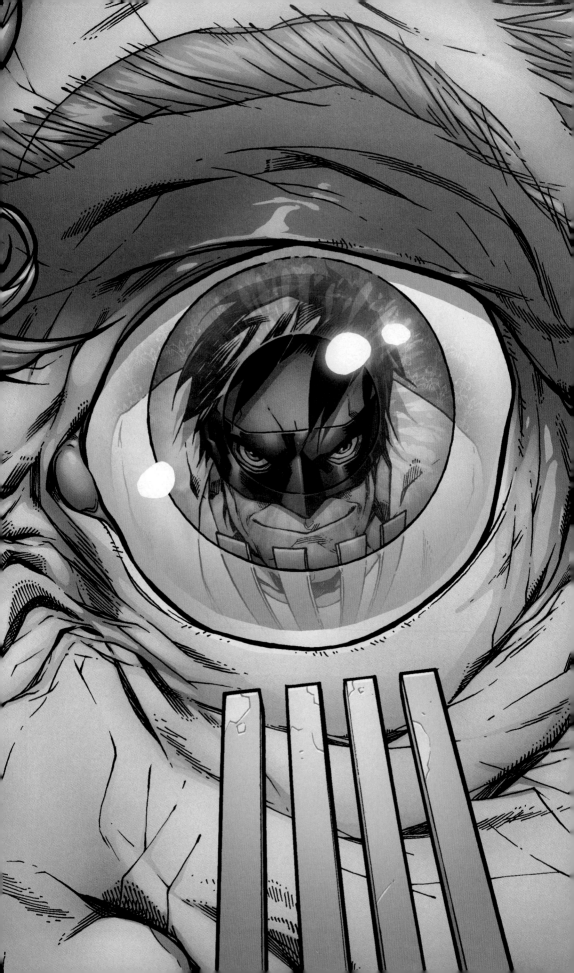

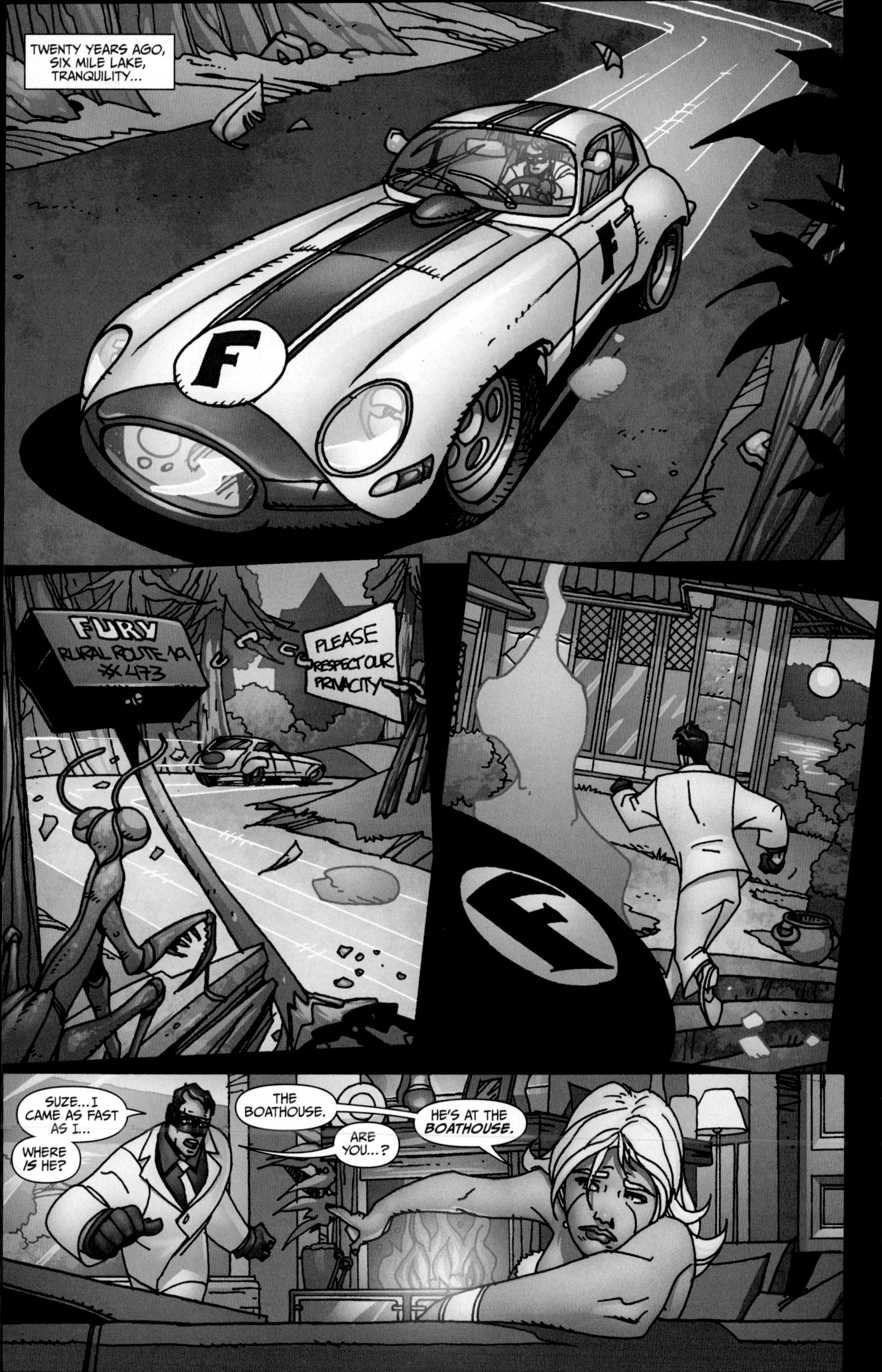
TWENTY YEARS AGO, SIX MILE LAKE, TRANQUILITY...
F
FURY
RURAL ROUTE 19
#473
PLEASE RESPECT OUR PRIVACITY
SUZE... I CAME AS FAST AS I...
WHERE *IS* HE?
THE BOATHOUSE.
ARE YOU...?
HE'S AT THE *BOATHOUSE.*

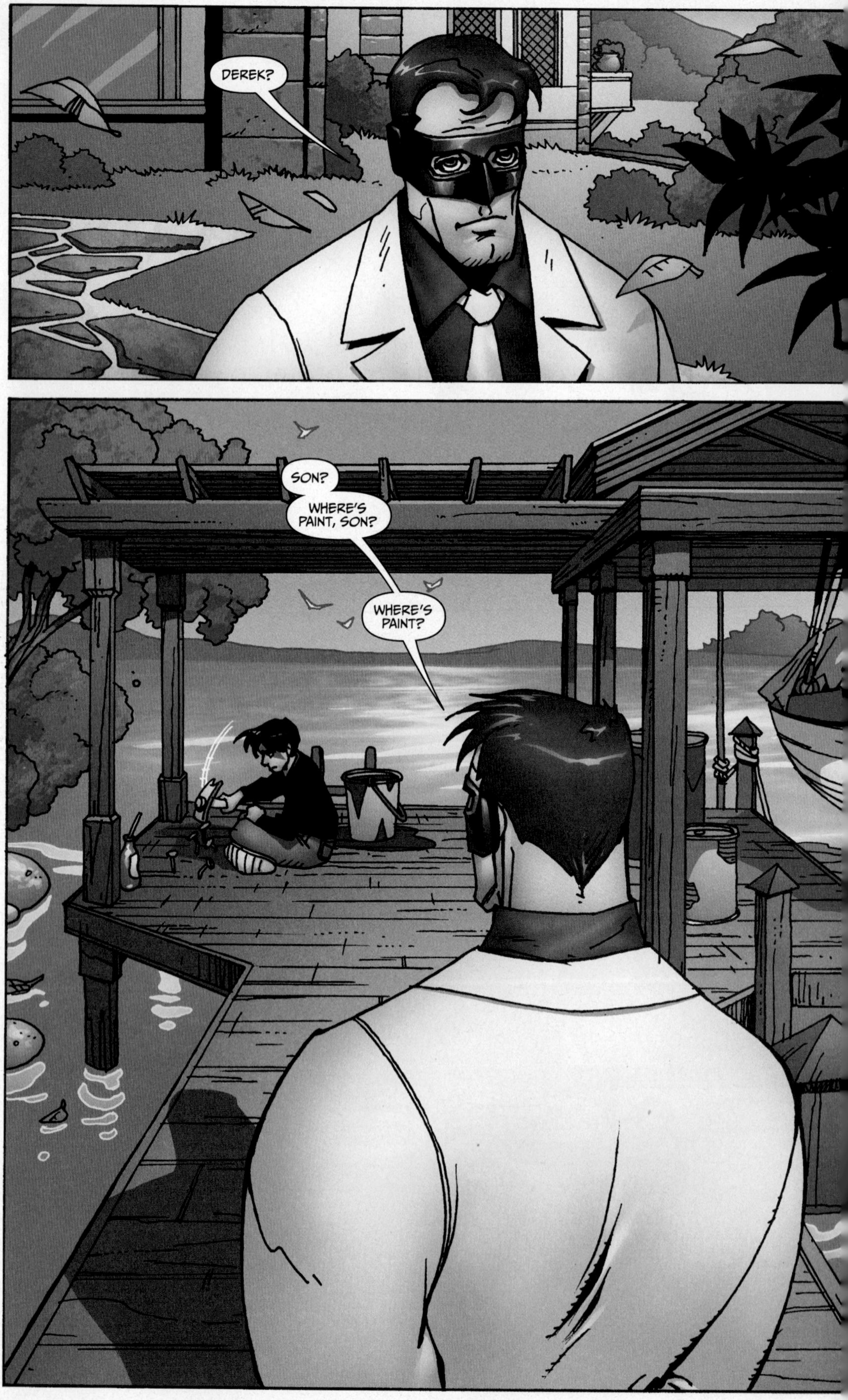
DEREK?
SON?
WHERE'S PAINT, SON?
WHERE'S PAINT?

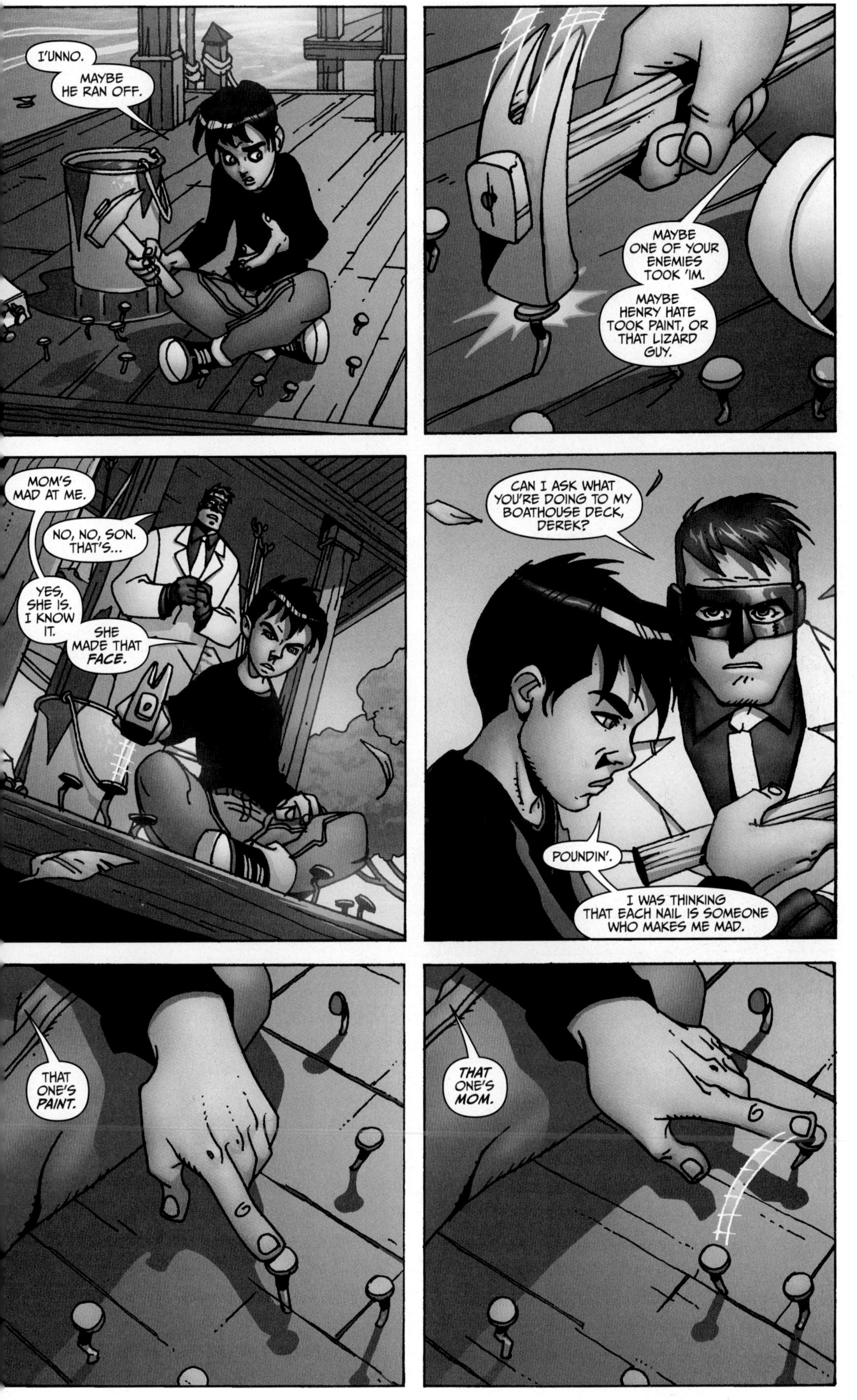
I'UNNO.
MAYBE HE RAN OFF.
MAYBE ONE OF YOUR ENEMIES TOOK 'IM.
MAYBE HENRY HATE TOOK PAINT, OR THAT LIZARD GUY.
MOM'S MAD AT ME.
NO, NO, SON. THAT'S...
YES, SHE IS. I KNOW IT.
SHE MADE THAT *FACE.*
CAN I ASK WHAT YOU'RE DOING TO MY BOATHOUSE DECK, DEREK?
POUNDIN'.
I WAS THINKING THAT EACH NAIL IS SOMEONE WHO MAKES ME MAD.
THAT ONE'S *PAINT.*
THAT ONE'S *MOM.*

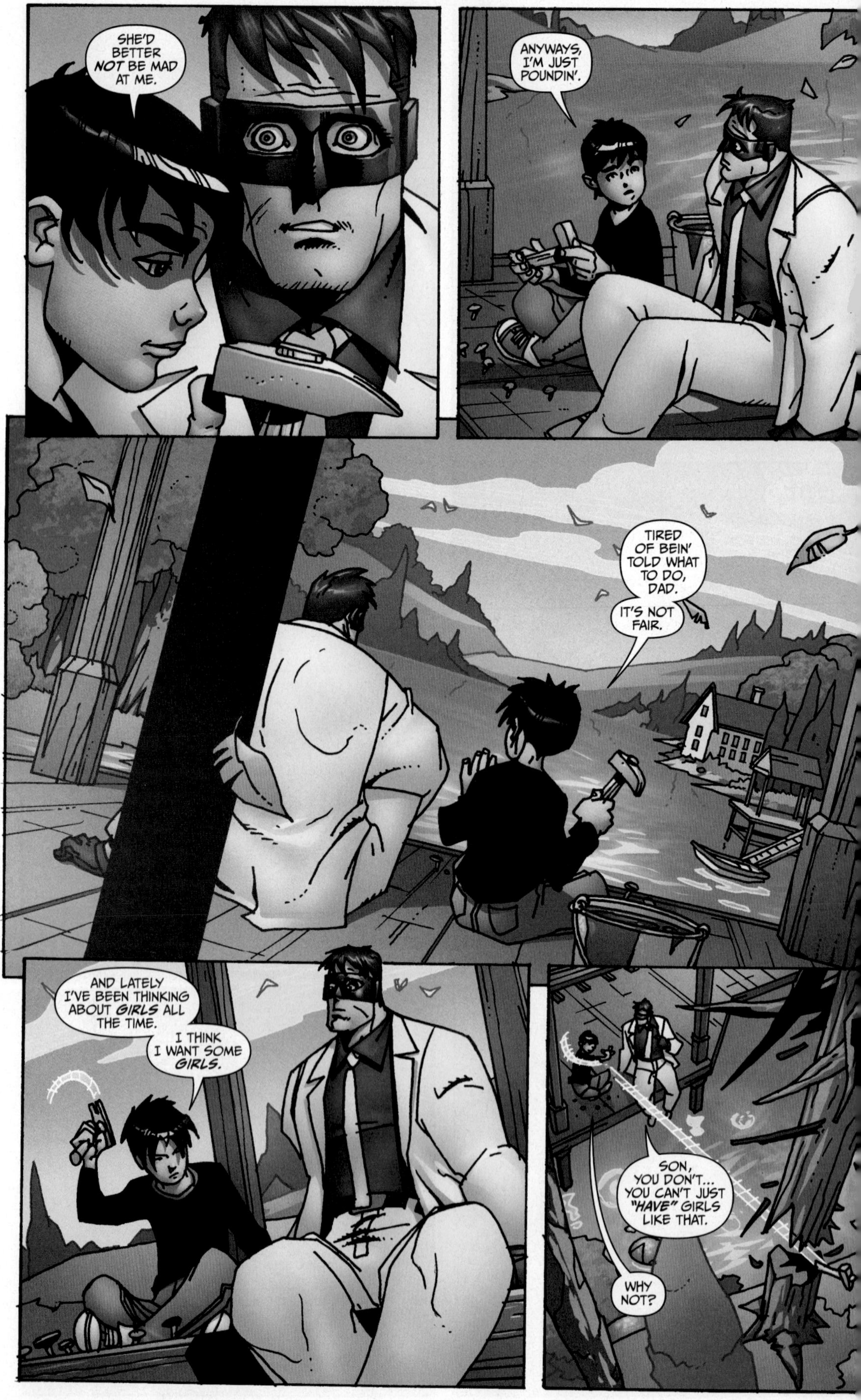
SHE'D BETTER NOT BE MAD AT ME.
ANYWAYS, I'M JUST POUNDIN'.
TIRED OF BEIN' TOLD WHAT TO DO, DAD.
IT'S NOT FAIR.
AND LATELY I'VE BEEN THINKING ABOUT GIRLS ALL THE TIME.
I THINK I WANT SOME GIRLS.
SON, YOU DON'T... YOU CAN'T JUST "HAVE" GIRLS LIKE THAT.
WHY NOT?

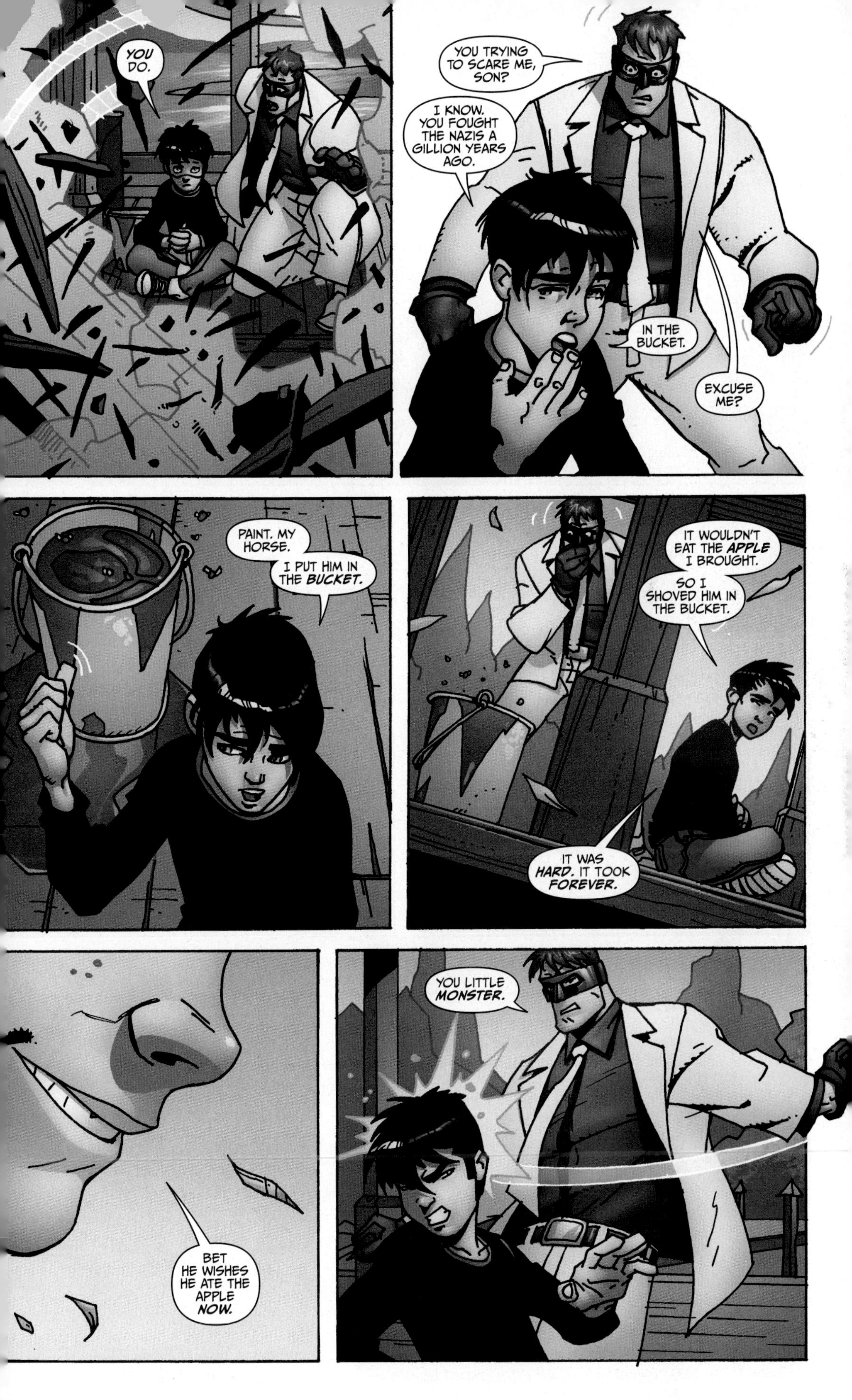

YOU DO.
YOU TRYING TO SCARE ME, SON?
I KNOW. YOU FOUGHT THE NAZIS A GILLION YEARS AGO.
IN THE BUCKET.
EXCUSE ME?
PAINT. MY HORSE.
I PUT HIM IN THE BUCKET.
IT WOULDN'T EAT THE APPLE I BROUGHT.
SO I SHOVED HIM IN THE BUCKET.
IT WAS HARD. IT TOOK FOREVER.
BET HE WISHES HE ATE THE APPLE NOW.
YOU LITTLE MONSTER.

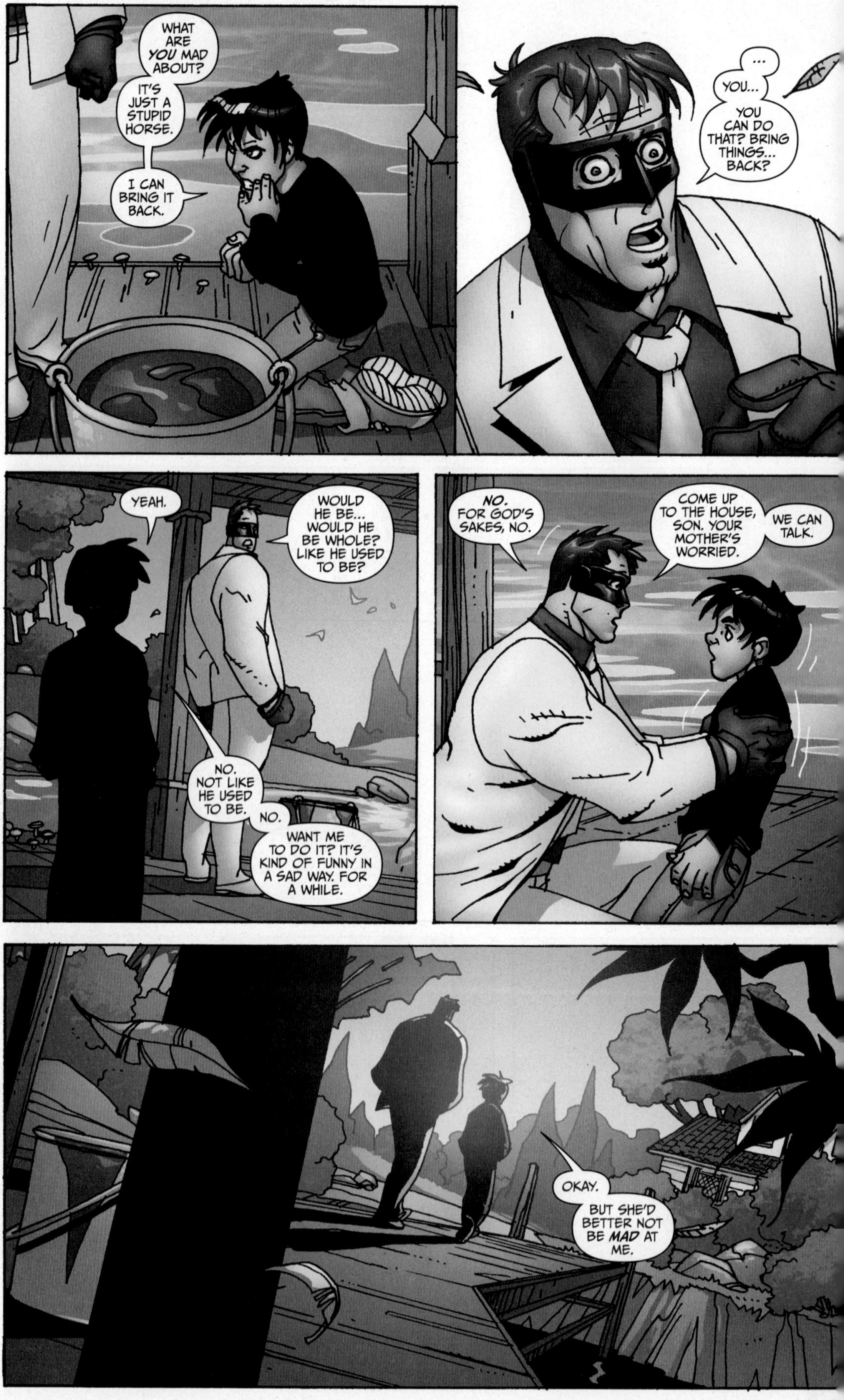
WHAT ARE *YOU* MAD ABOUT?
IT'S JUST A STUPID HORSE.
I CAN BRING IT BACK.
...
YOU...
YOU CAN DO THAT? BRING THINGS... BACK?
YEAH.
WOULD HE BE... WOULD HE BE WHOLE? LIKE HE USED TO BE?
NO. NOT LIKE HE USED TO BE.
NO.
WANT ME TO DO IT? IT'S KIND OF FUNNY IN A SAD WAY. FOR A WHILE.
NO. FOR GOD'S SAKES, NO.
COME UP TO THE HOUSE, SON. YOUR MOTHER'S WORRIED.
WE CAN TALK.
OKAY.
BUT SHE'D BETTER NOT BE *MAD* AT ME.

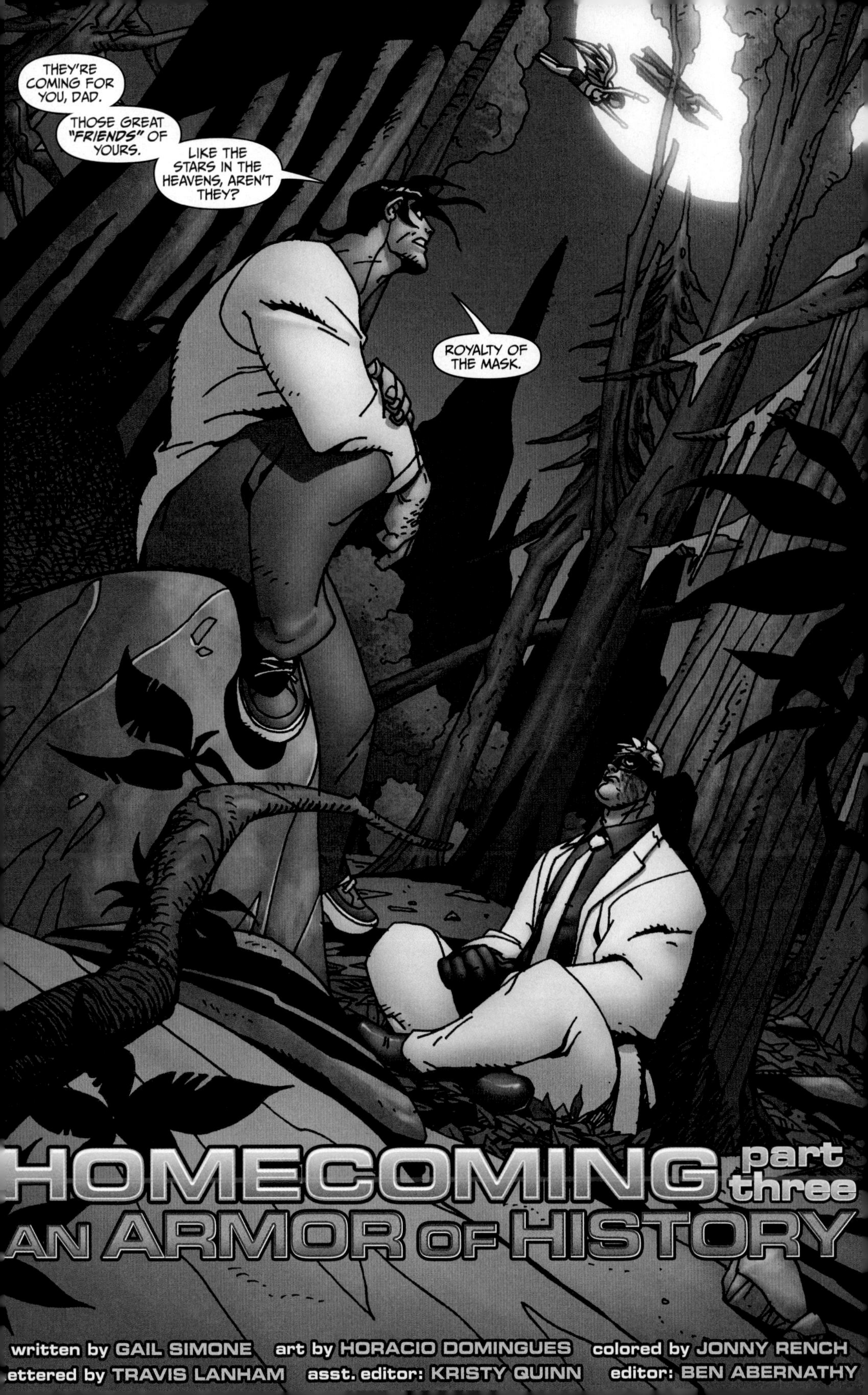
THEY'RE COMING FOR YOU, DAD.
THOSE GREAT "FRIENDS" OF YOURS.
LIKE THE STARS IN THE HEAVENS, AREN'T THEY?
ROYALTY OF THE MASK.
HOMECOMING part three
AN ARMOR OF HISTORY
written by GAIL SIMONE art by HORACIO DOMINGUES colored by JONNY RENCH
ettered by TRAVIS LANHAM asst. editor: KRISTY QUINN editor: BEN ABERNATHY

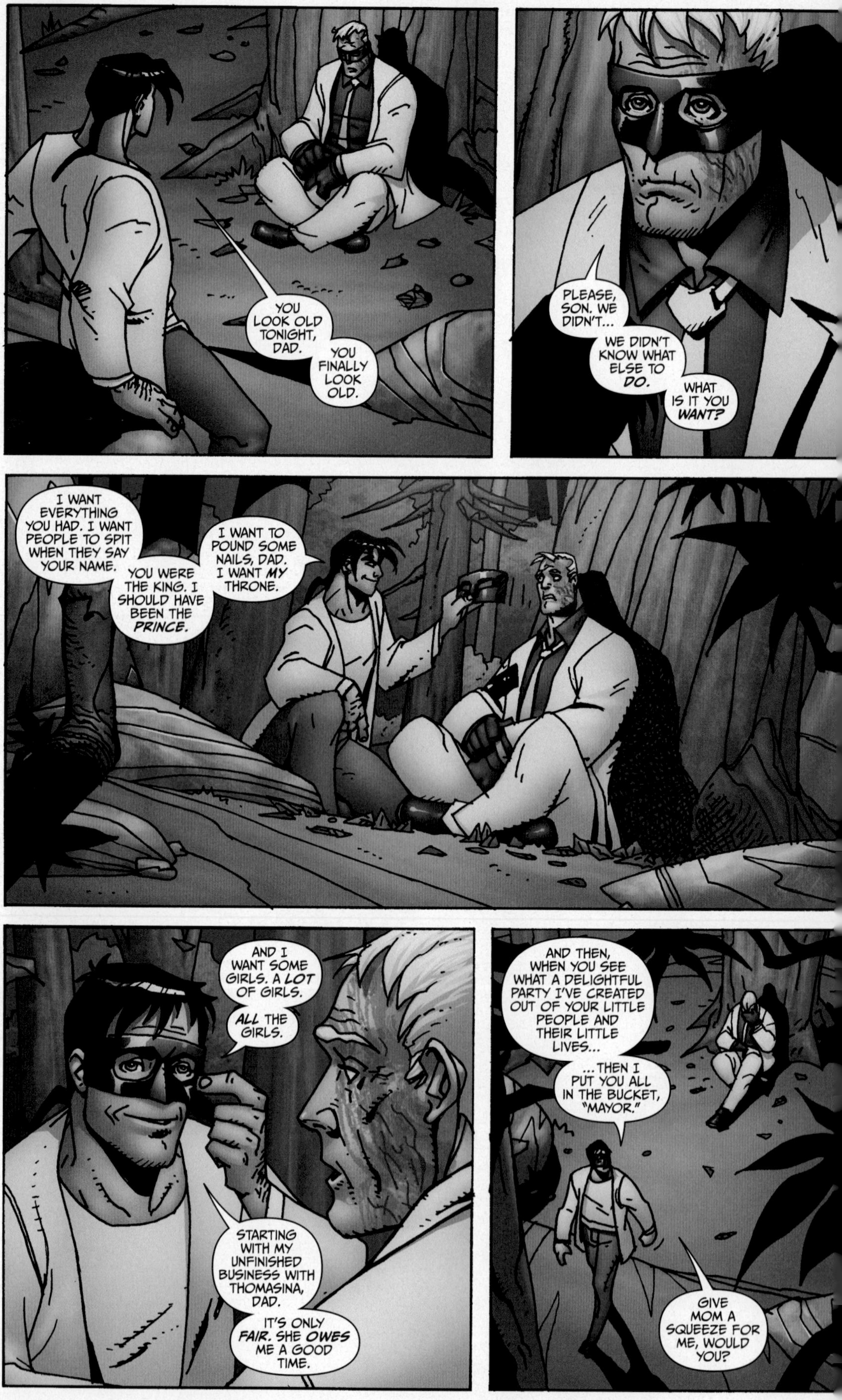
YOU LOOK OLD TONIGHT, DAD.
YOU FINALLY LOOK OLD.
PLEASE, SON. WE DIDN'T...
WE DIDN'T KNOW WHAT ELSE TO DO.
WHAT IS IT YOU WANT?
I WANT EVERYTHING YOU HAD. I WANT PEOPLE TO SPIT WHEN THEY SAY YOUR NAME.
YOU WERE THE KING. I SHOULD HAVE BEEN THE PRINCE.
I WANT TO POUND SOME NAILS, DAD. I WANT MY THRONE.
AND I WANT SOME GIRLS. A LOT OF GIRLS.
ALL THE GIRLS.
STARTING WITH MY UNFINISHED BUSINESS WITH THOMASINA, DAD.
IT'S ONLY FAIR. SHE OWES ME A GOOD TIME.
AND THEN, WHEN YOU SEE WHAT A DELIGHTFUL PARTY I'VE CREATED OUT OF YOUR LITTLE PEOPLE AND THEIR LITTLE LIVES...
...THEN I PUT YOU ALL IN THE BUCKET, "MAYOR."
GIVE MOM A SQUEEZE FOR ME, WOULD YOU?

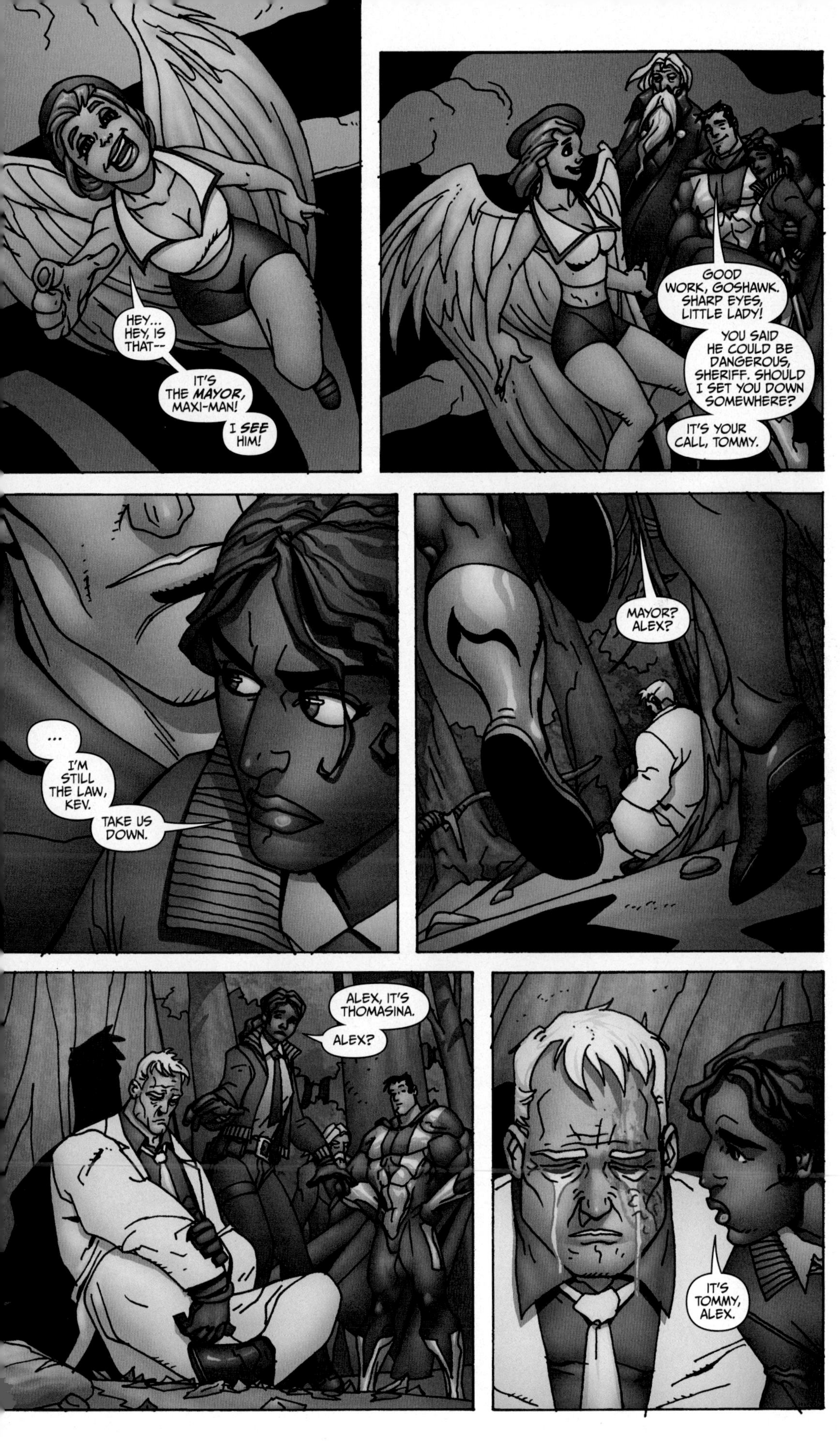
HEY... HEY, IS THAT--
IT'S THE *MAYOR*, MAXI-MAN!
I *SEE* HIM!
GOOD WORK, GOSHAWK. SHARP EYES, LITTLE LADY!
YOU SAID HE COULD BE DANGEROUS, SHERIFF. SHOULD I SET YOU DOWN SOMEWHERE?
IT'S YOUR CALL, TOMMY.
...
I'M STILL THE LAW, KEV.
TAKE US DOWN.
MAYOR? ALEX?
ALEX, IT'S THOMASINA.
ALEX?
IT'S TOMMY, ALEX.

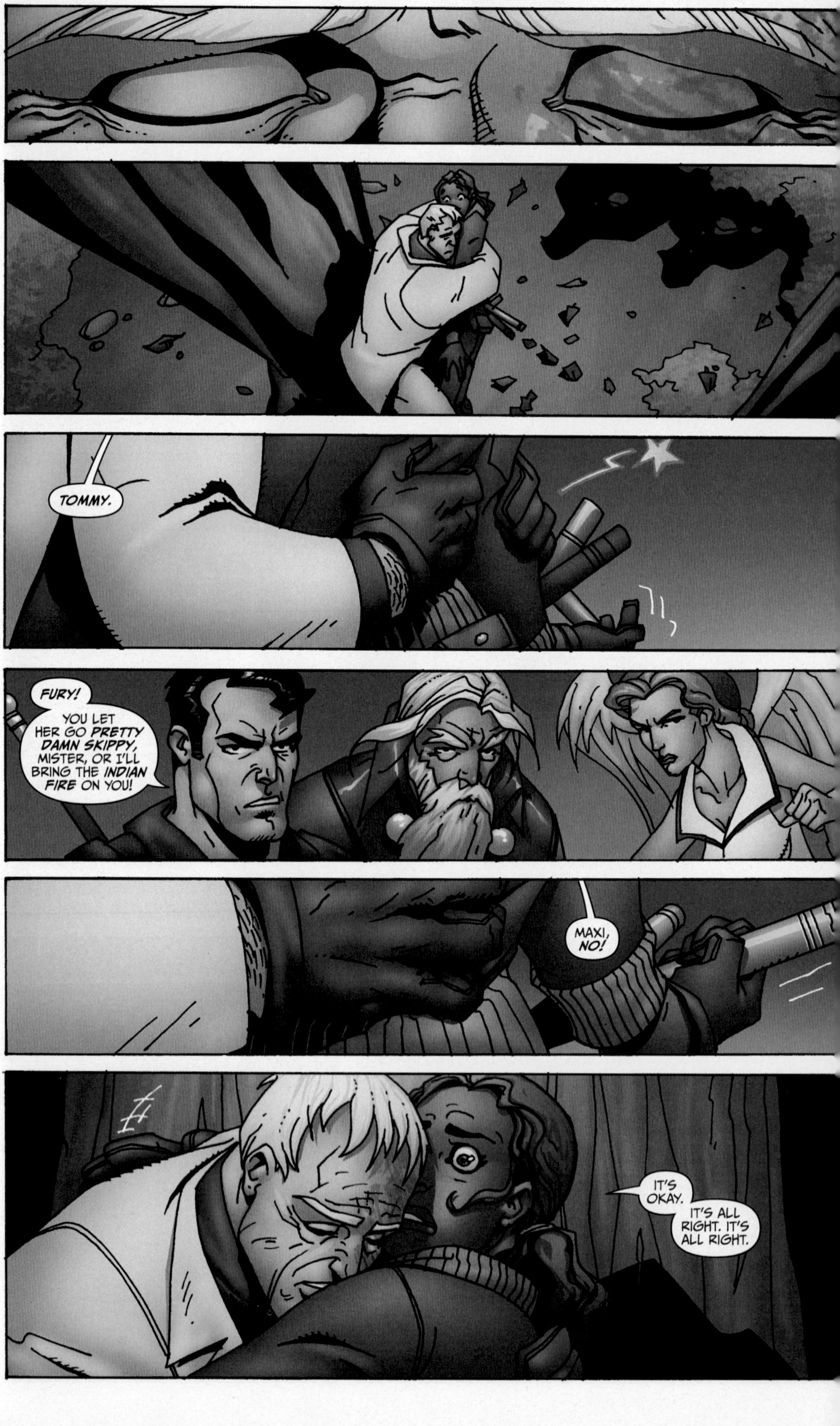

TOMMY.
FURY!
YOU LET HER GO PRETTY DAMN SKIPPY, MISTER, OR I'LL BRING THE INDIAN FIRE ON YOU!
MAXI, NO!
IT'S OKAY.
IT'S ALL RIGHT. IT'S ALL RIGHT.

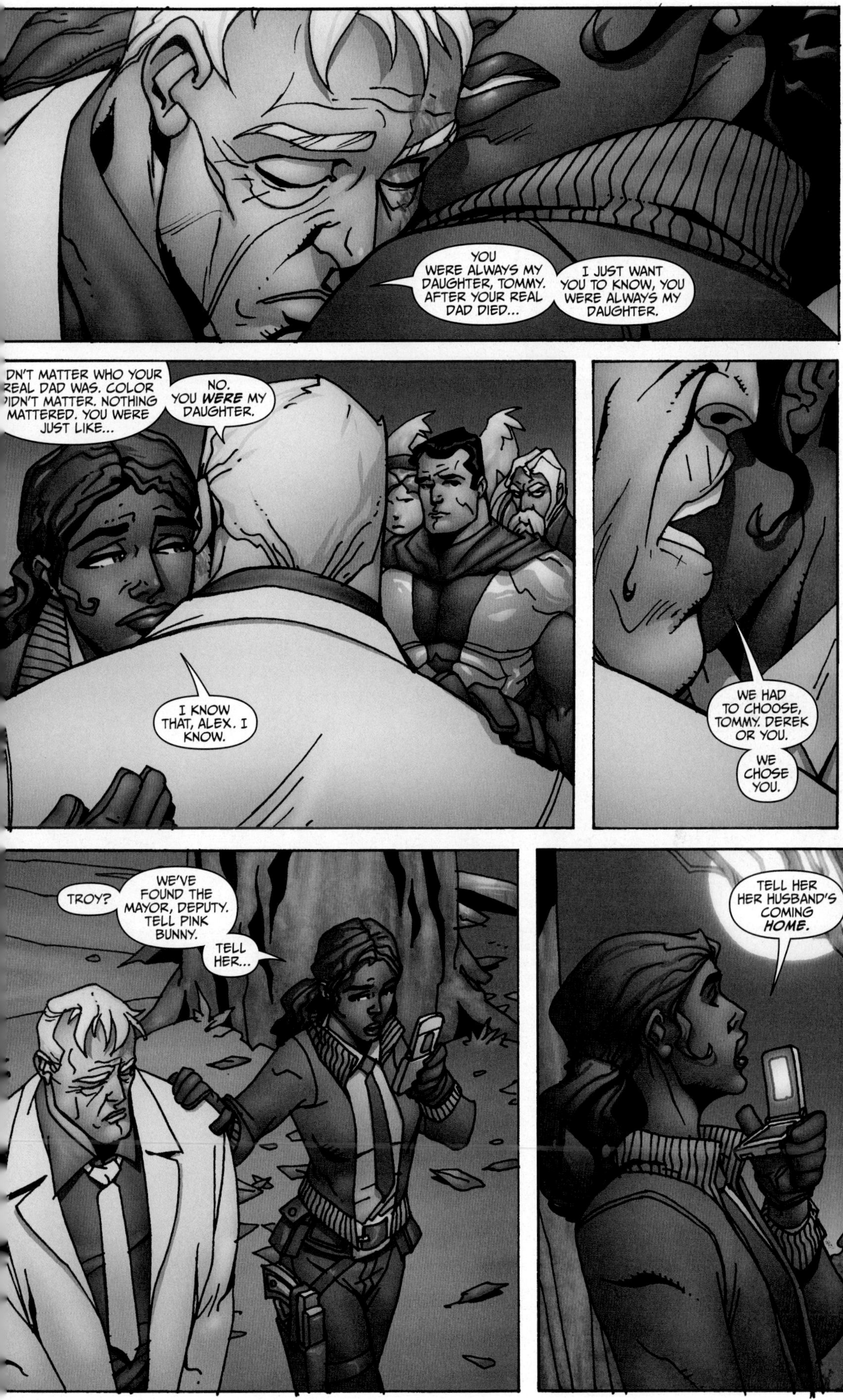
I JUST WANT YOU TO KNOW, YOU WERE ALWAYS MY DAUGHTER.
YOU WERE ALWAYS MY DAUGHTER, TOMMY. AFTER YOUR REAL DAD DIED...
DN'T MATTER WHO YOUR REAL DAD WAS. COLOR DIDN'T MATTER. NOTHING MATTERED. YOU WERE JUST LIKE...
NO. YOU ***WERE*** MY DAUGHTER.
I KNOW THAT, ALEX. I KNOW.
WE HAD TO CHOOSE, TOMMY. DEREK OR YOU.
WE CHOSE YOU.
TROY?
WE'VE FOUND THE MAYOR, DEPUTY. TELL PINK BUNNY.
TELL HER...
TELL HER HER HUSBAND'S COMING ***HOME.***

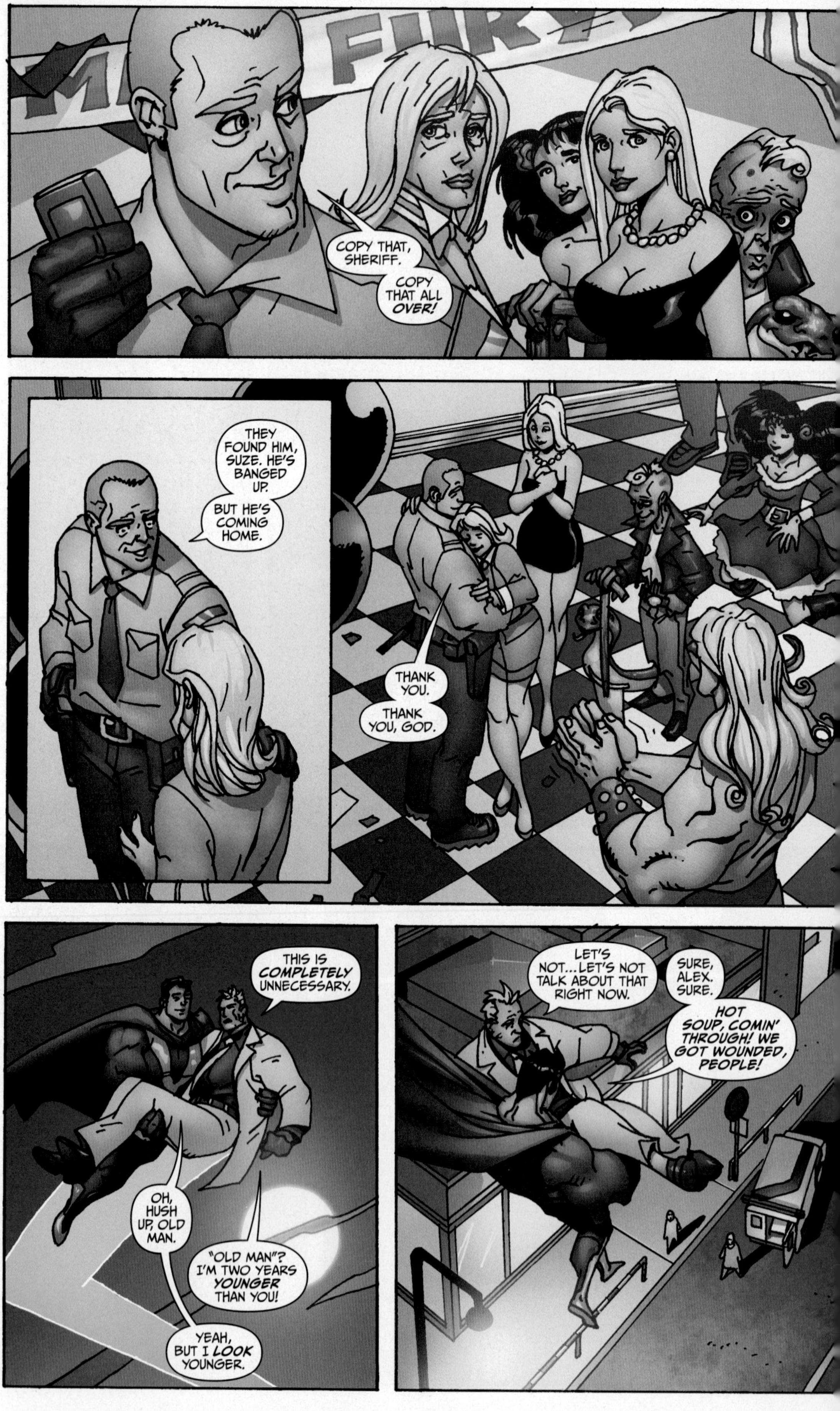

COPY THAT, SHERIFF.
COPY THAT ALL *OVER!*
THEY FOUND HIM, SUZE. HE'S BANGED UP.
BUT HE'S COMING HOME.
THANK YOU.
THANK YOU, GOD.
THIS IS *COMPLETELY* UNNECESSARY.
OH, HUSH UP, OLD MAN.
"OLD MAN"? I'M TWO YEARS *YOUNGER* THAN YOU!
YEAH, BUT I *LOOK* YOUNGER.
LET'S NOT...LET'S NOT TALK ABOUT THAT RIGHT NOW.
SURE, ALEX. SURE.
HOT SOUP, COMIN' THROUGH! WE GOT WOUNDED, PEOPLE!

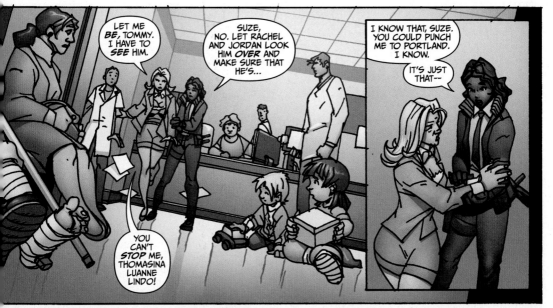

LET ME *BE*, TOMMY. I HAVE TO *SEE* HIM.

SUZE, NO. LET RACHEL AND JORDAN LOOK HIM *OVER* AND MAKE SURE THAT HE'S...

I KNOW THAT, SUZE. YOU COULD PUNCH ME TO PORTLAND. I KNOW.

IT'S JUST THAT--

YOU CAN'T *STOP* ME, THOMASINA LUANNE LINDO!

--WELL, YOU WOULDN'T WANT TO RESIST AN OFFICER OF THE LAW IN FRONT OF KIDS, WOULD YOU?

WHAT SORT OF MESSAGE DOES THAT SEND?

ALL RIGHT, TOMMY. I'LL BEHAVE. FOR A *WHILE*.

BUT THEY'D *BETTER* HAVE SOME RECENT DAMN *MAGAZINES* IN HERE!

THERE AIN'T NO ONE ELSE LEFT, MISTER HENRY HATE, SIR.

THAT IS TRUE.

BE A SHAME TO LET ALL THIS BOUNTY GO TO WASTE.

THIS *ALSO* IS TRUE.

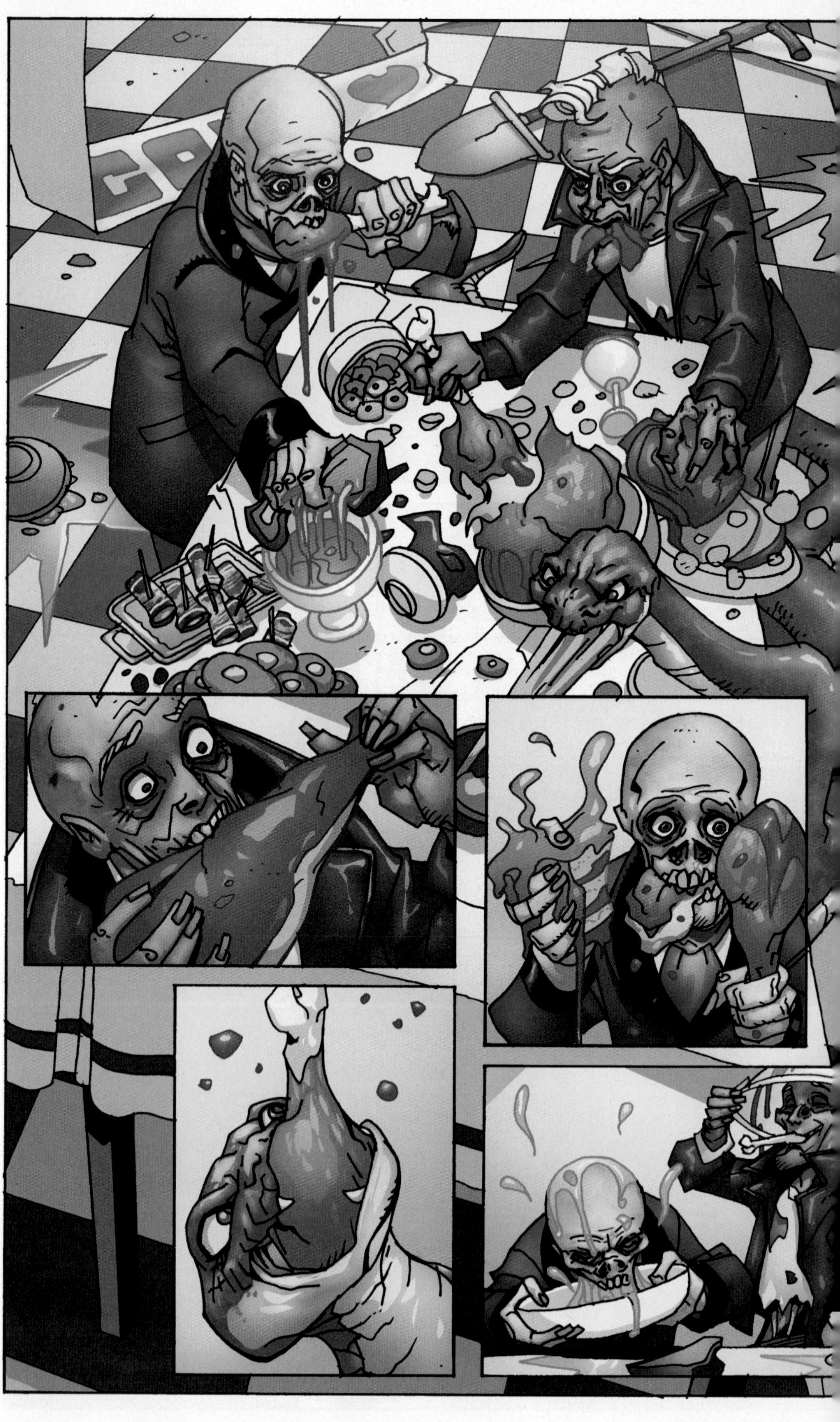

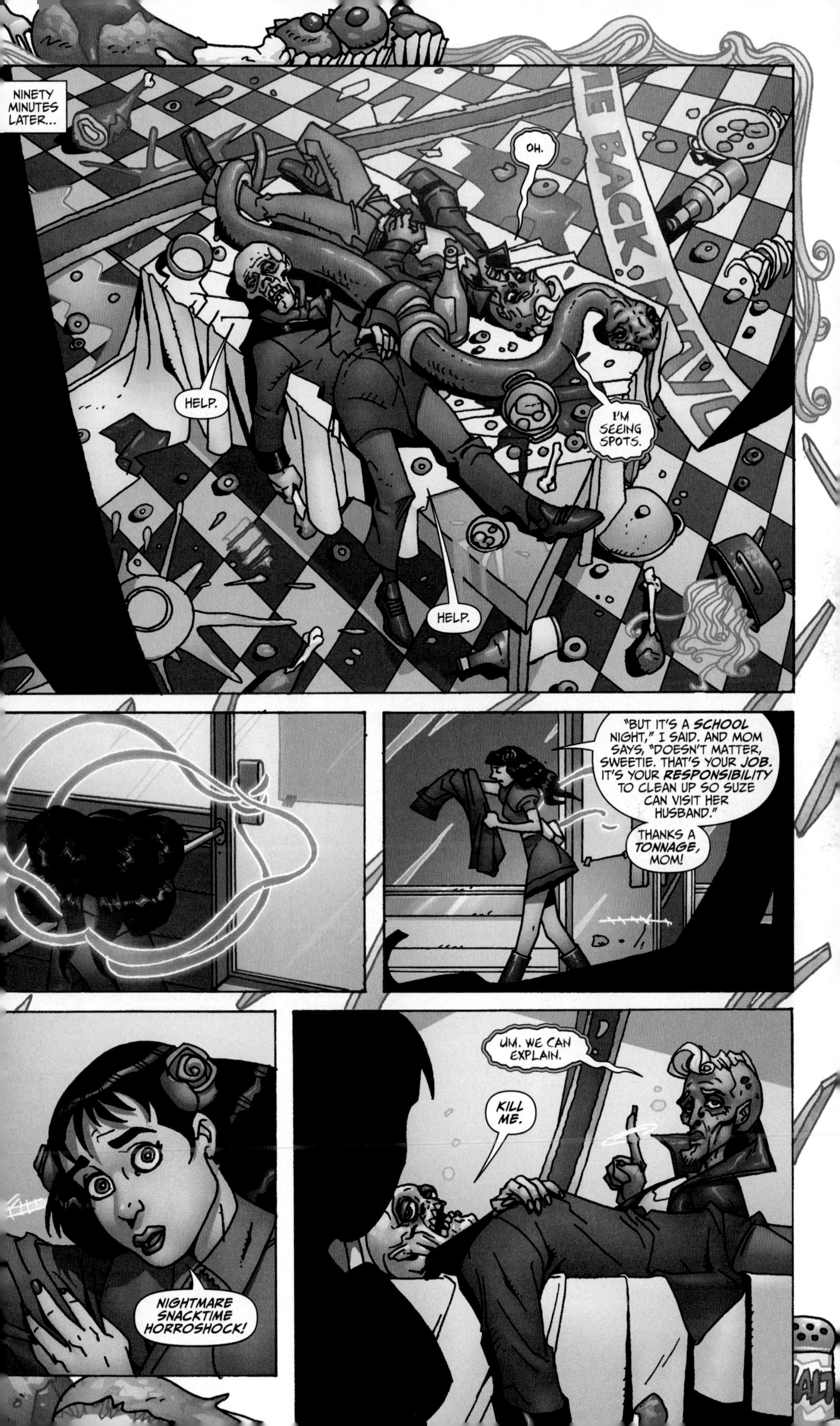
NINETY MINUTES LATER...
OH.
HELP.
I'M SEEING SPOTS.
HELP.
"BUT IT'S A SCHOOL NIGHT," I SAID. AND MOM SAYS, "DOESN'T MATTER, SWEETIE. THAT'S YOUR JOB. IT'S YOUR RESPONSIBILITY TO CLEAN UP SO SUZE CAN VISIT HER HUSBAND."
THANKS A TONNAGE, MOM!
NIGHTMARE SNACKTIME HORROSHOCK!
UM. WE CAN EXPLAIN.
KILL ME.

ADVERTISEMENT

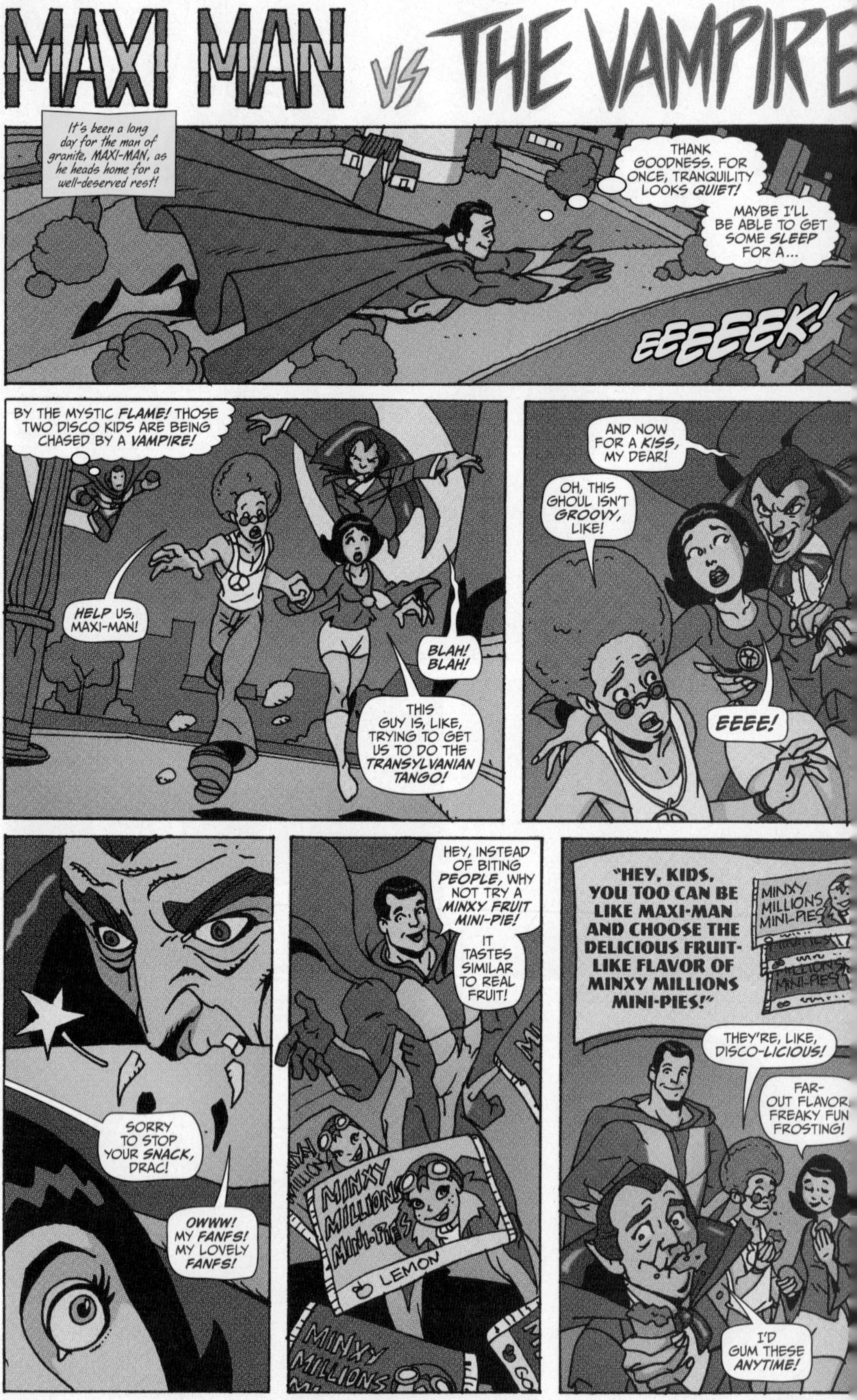

MAXI MAN VS THE VAMPIRE
It's been a long day for the man of granite, MAXI-MAN, as he heads home for a well-deserved rest!
THANK GOODNESS. FOR ONCE, TRANQUILITY LOOKS QUIET!
MAYBE I'LL BE ABLE TO GET SOME SLEEP FOR A...
EEEEEK!
BY THE MYSTIC FLAME! THOSE TWO DISCO KIDS ARE BEING CHASED BY A VAMPIRE!
HELP US, MAXI-MAN!
BLAH! BLAH!
THIS GUY IS, LIKE, TRYING TO GET US TO DO THE TRANSYLVANIAN TANGO!
AND NOW FOR A KISS, MY DEAR!
OH, THIS GHOUL ISN'T GROOVY, LIKE!
EEEE!
SORRY TO STOP YOUR SNACK, DRAC!
OWWW! MY FANFS! MY LOVELY FANFS!
HEY, INSTEAD OF BITING PEOPLE, WHY NOT TRY A MINXY FRUIT MINI-PIE!
IT TASTES SIMILAR TO REAL FRUIT!
MINXY MILLIONS MINI-PIES
LEMON
"HEY, KIDS, YOU TOO CAN BE LIKE MAXI-MAN AND CHOOSE THE DELICIOUS FRUIT-LIKE FLAVOR OF MINXY MILLIONS MINI-PIES!"
THEY'RE, LIKE, DISCO-LICIOUS!
FAR-OUT FLAVOR, FREAKY FUN FROSTING!
I'D GUM THESE ANYTIME!

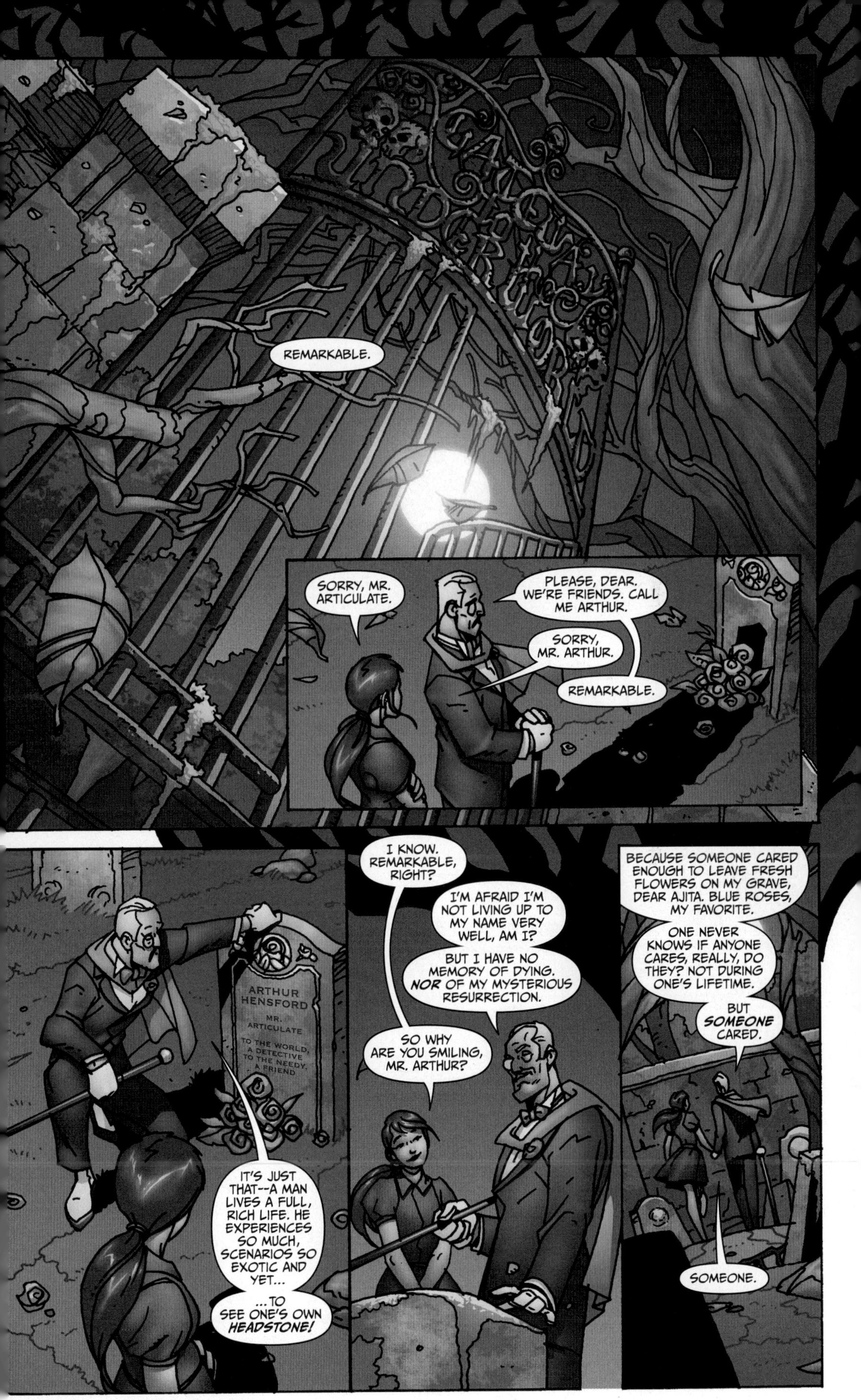
REMARKABLE.
SORRY, MR. ARTICULATE.
PLEASE, DEAR. WE'RE FRIENDS. CALL ME ARTHUR.
SORRY, MR. ARTHUR.
REMARKABLE.
ARTHUR HENSFORD
MR. ARTICULATE
TO THE WORLD, A DETECTIVE TO THE NEEDY, A FRIEND
IT'S JUST THAT--A MAN LIVES A FULL, RICH LIFE. HE EXPERIENCES SO MUCH, SCENARIOS SO EXOTIC AND YET...
...TO SEE ONE'S OWN **HEADSTONE!**
I KNOW. REMARKABLE, RIGHT?
I'M AFRAID I'M NOT LIVING UP TO MY NAME VERY WELL, AM I?
BUT I HAVE NO MEMORY OF DYING. ***NOR*** OF MY MYSTERIOUS RESURRECTION.
SO WHY ARE YOU SMILING, MR. ARTHUR?
BECAUSE SOMEONE CARED ENOUGH TO LEAVE FRESH FLOWERS ON MY GRAVE, DEAR AJITA. BLUE ROSES, MY FAVORITE.
ONE NEVER KNOWS IF ANYONE CARES, REALLY, DO THEY? NOT DURING ONE'S LIFETIME.
BUT ***SOMEONE*** CARED.
SOMEONE.

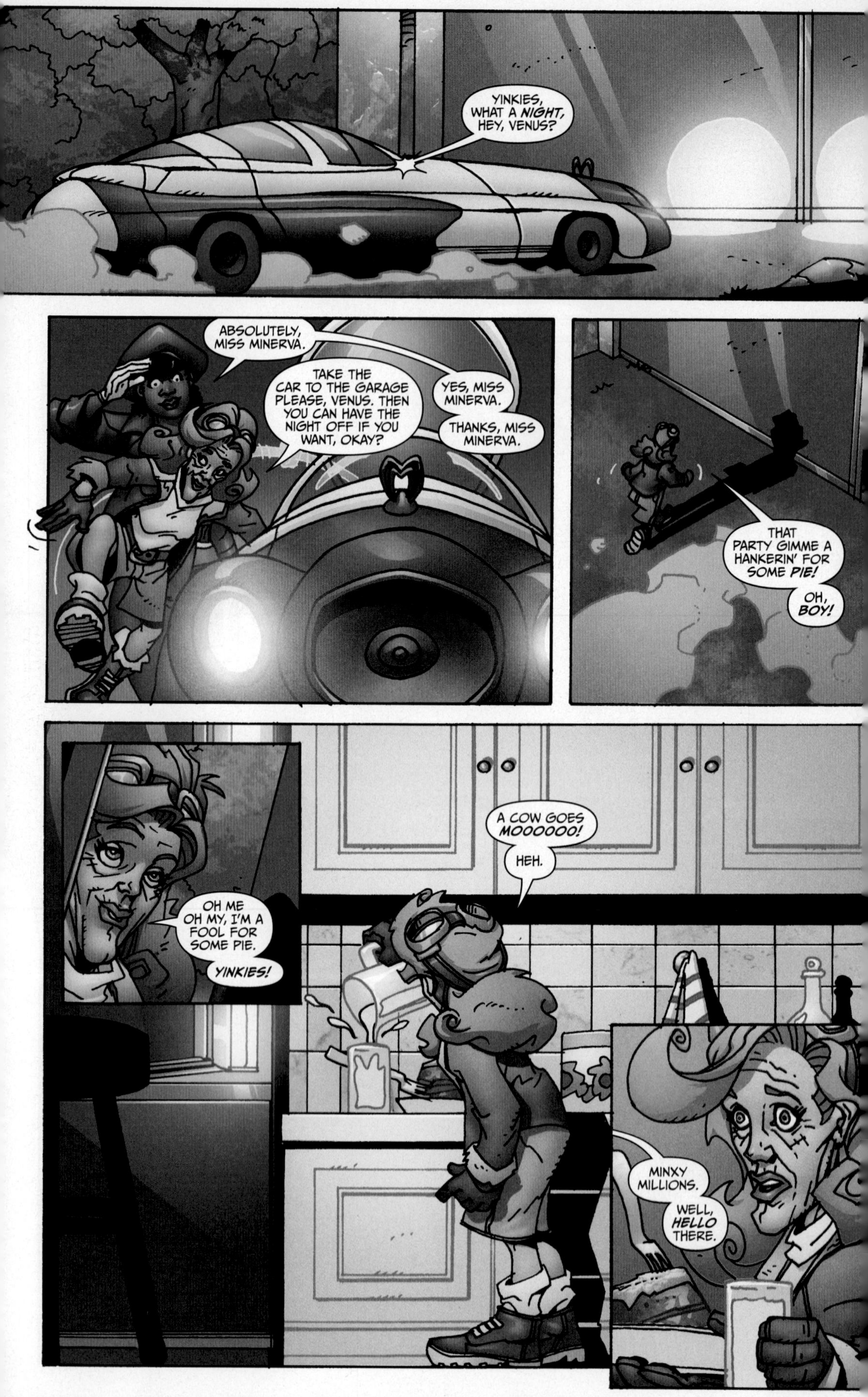
YINKIES, WHAT A NIGHT, HEY, VENUS?
ABSOLUTELY, MISS MINERVA.
TAKE THE CAR TO THE GARAGE PLEASE, VENUS. THEN YOU CAN HAVE THE NIGHT OFF IF YOU WANT, OKAY?
YES, MISS MINERVA.
THANKS, MISS MINERVA.
THAT PARTY GIMME A HANKERIN' FOR SOME PIE!
OH, BOY!
OH ME OH MY, I'M A FOOL FOR SOME PIE.
YINKIES!
A COW GOES MOOOOOO!
HEH.
MINXY MILLIONS.
WELL, HELLO THERE.

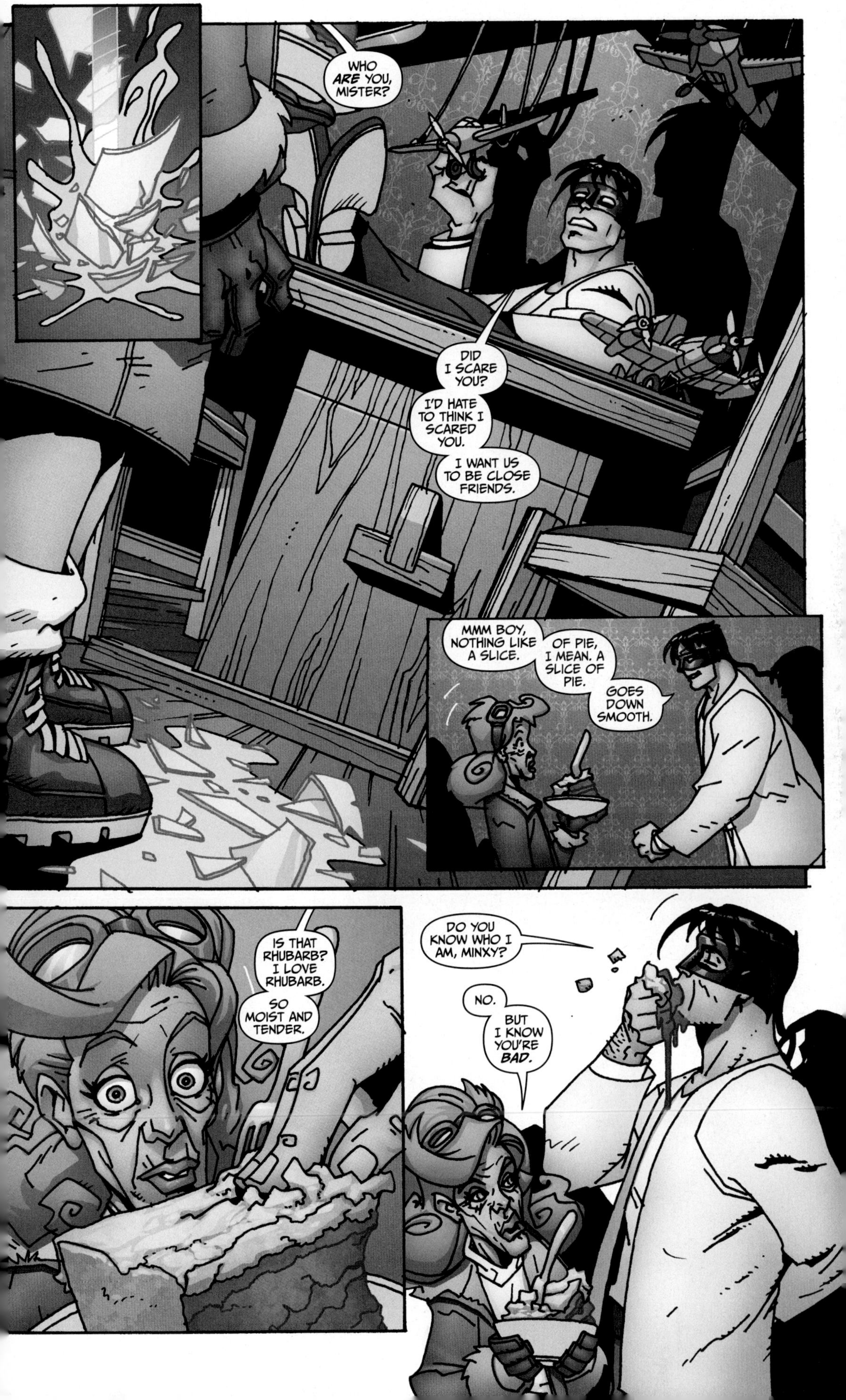
WHO ARE YOU, MISTER?
DID I SCARE YOU?
I'D HATE TO THINK I SCARED YOU.
I WANT US TO BE CLOSE FRIENDS.
MMM BOY, NOTHING LIKE A SLICE.
OF PIE, I MEAN. A SLICE OF PIE.
GOES DOWN SMOOTH.
IS THAT RHUBARB? I LOVE RHUBARB.
SO MOIST AND TENDER.
DO YOU KNOW WHO I AM, MINXY?
NO.
BUT I KNOW YOU'RE BAD.

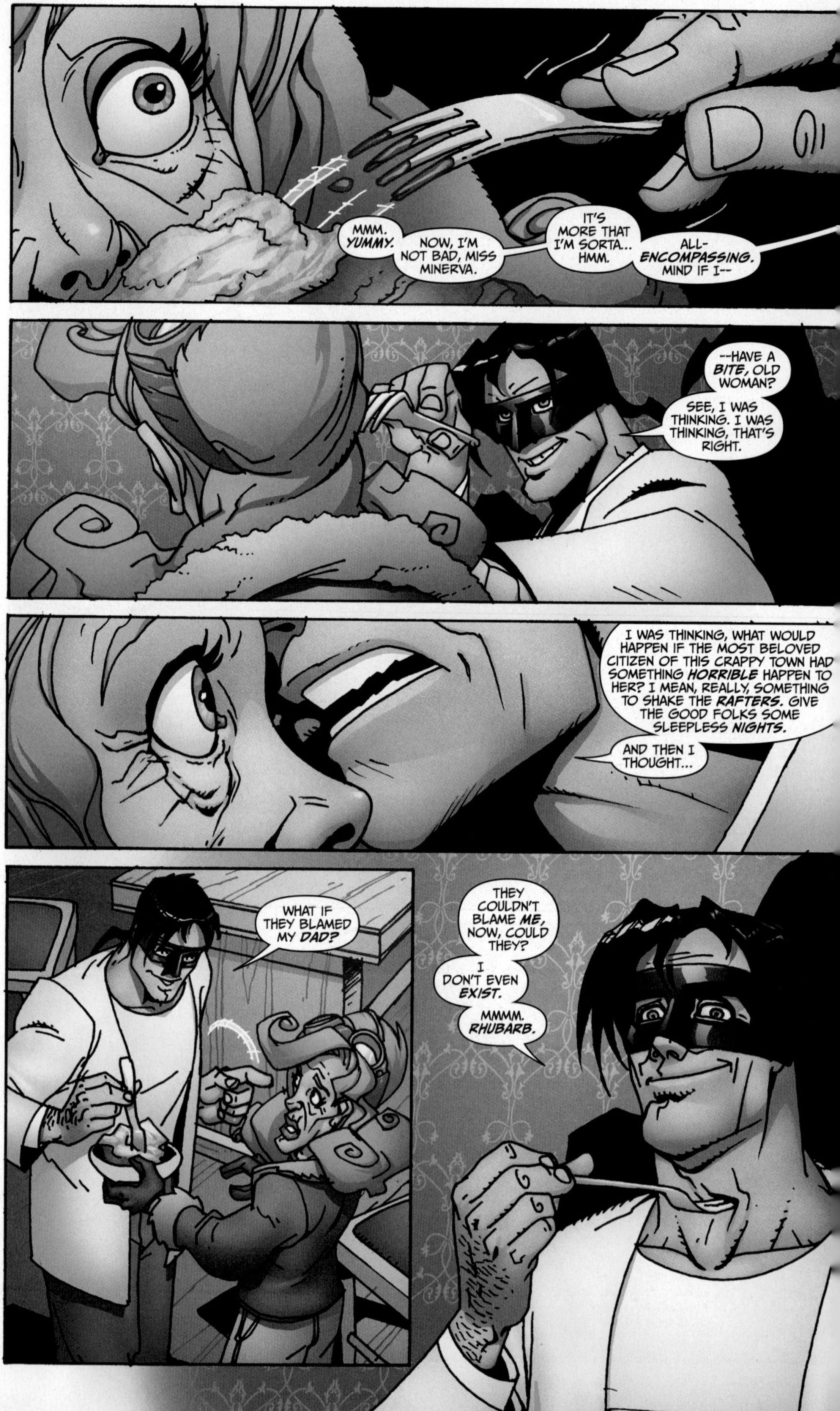
MMM. YUMMY.
NOW, I'M NOT BAD, MISS MINERVA.
IT'S MORE THAT I'M SORTA... HMM.
ALL-ENCOMPASSING. MIND IF I--
--HAVE A BITE, OLD WOMAN?
SEE, I WAS THINKING. I WAS THINKING, THAT'S RIGHT.
I WAS THINKING, WHAT WOULD HAPPEN IF THE MOST BELOVED CITIZEN OF THIS CRAPPY TOWN HAD SOMETHING HORRIBLE HAPPEN TO HER? I MEAN, REALLY, SOMETHING TO SHAKE THE RAFTERS. GIVE THE GOOD FOLKS SOME SLEEPLESS NIGHTS.
AND THEN I THOUGHT...
WHAT IF THEY BLAMED MY DAD?
THEY COULDN'T BLAME ME, NOW, COULD THEY?
I DON'T EVEN EXIST.
MMMM. RHUBARB.

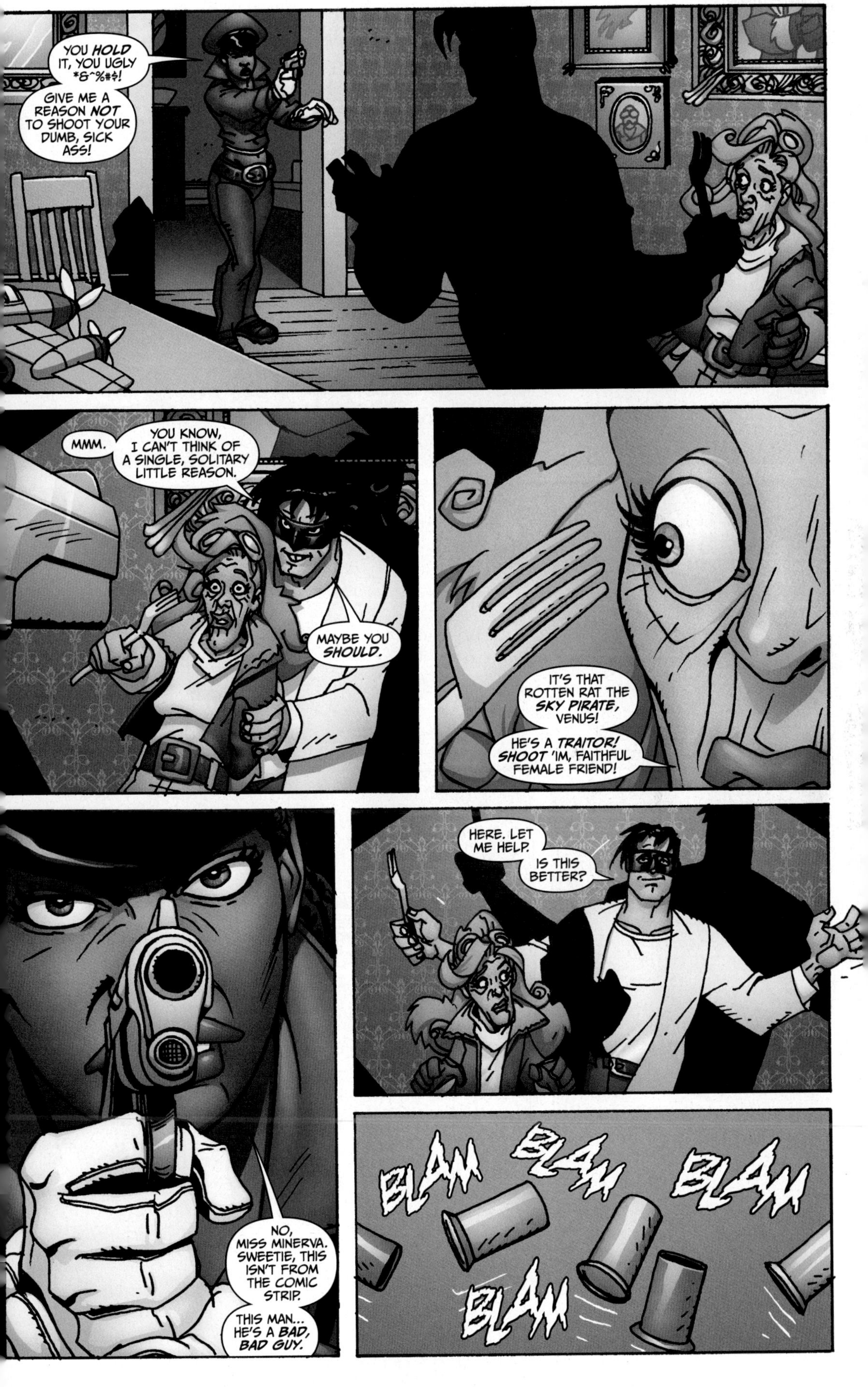
YOU HOLD IT, YOU UGLY *&^%#$!
GIVE ME A REASON NOT TO SHOOT YOUR DUMB, SICK ASS!
MMM.
YOU KNOW, I CAN'T THINK OF A SINGLE, SOLITARY LITTLE REASON.
MAYBE YOU SHOULD.
IT'S THAT ROTTEN RAT THE SKY PIRATE, VENUS!
HE'S A TRAITOR! SHOOT 'IM, FAITHFUL FEMALE FRIEND!
NO, MISS MINERVA. SWEETIE, THIS ISN'T FROM THE COMIC STRIP.
THIS MAN... HE'S A BAD, BAD GUY.
HERE. LET ME HELP.
IS THIS BETTER?
BLAM
BLAM
BLAM
BLAM

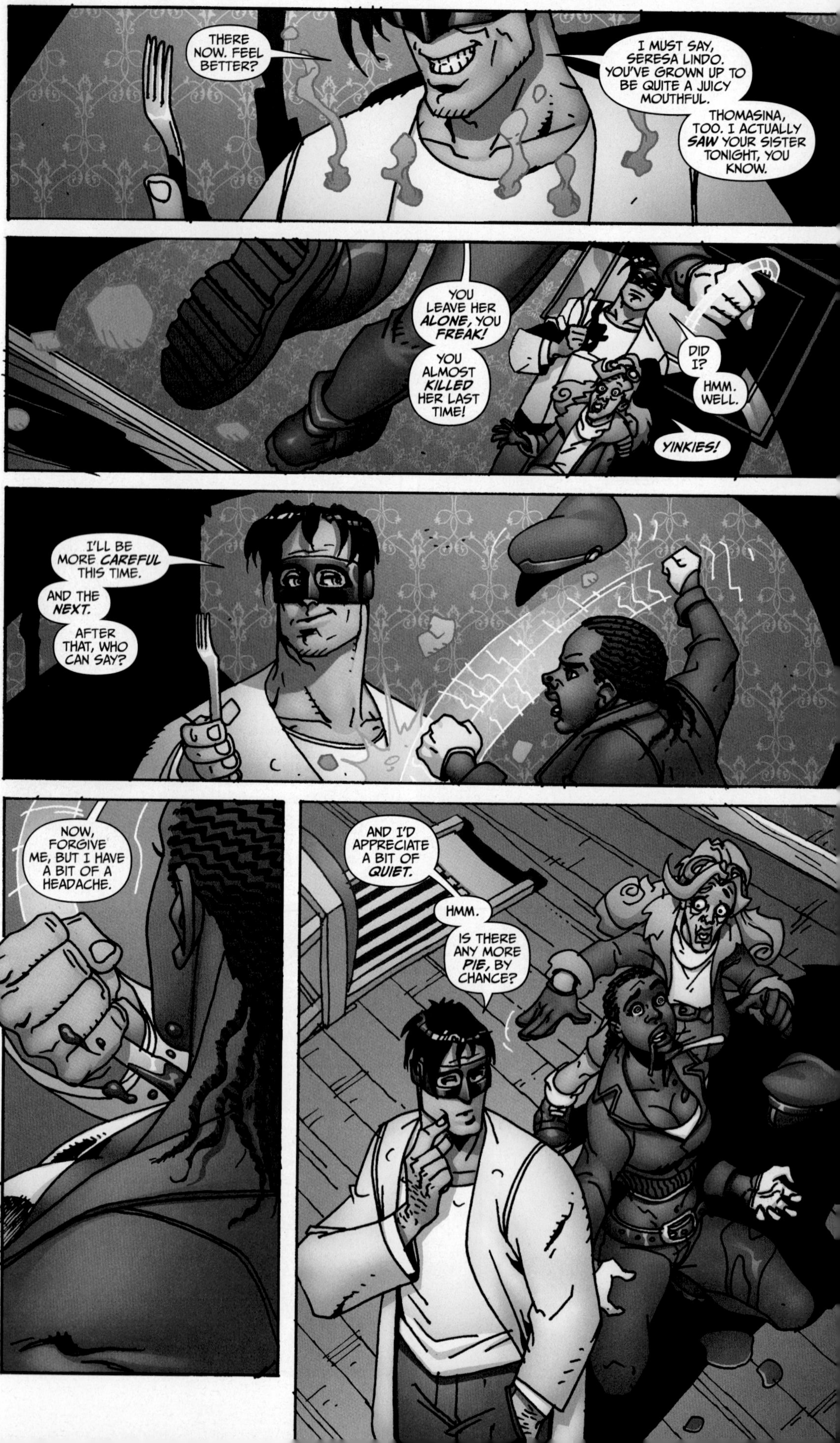
THERE NOW. FEEL BETTER?
I MUST SAY, SERESA LINDO. YOU'VE GROWN UP TO BE QUITE A JUICY MOUTHFUL.
THOMASINA, TOO. I ACTUALLY SAW YOUR SISTER TONIGHT, YOU KNOW.
YOU LEAVE HER ALONE, YOU FREAK!
YOU ALMOST KILLED HER LAST TIME!
DID I?
HMM. WELL.
YINKIES!
I'LL BE MORE CAREFUL THIS TIME.
AND THE NEXT.
AFTER THAT, WHO CAN SAY?
NOW, FORGIVE ME, BUT I HAVE A BIT OF A HEADACHE.
AND I'D APPRECIATE A BIT OF QUIET.
HMM.
IS THERE ANY MORE PIE, BY CHANCE?

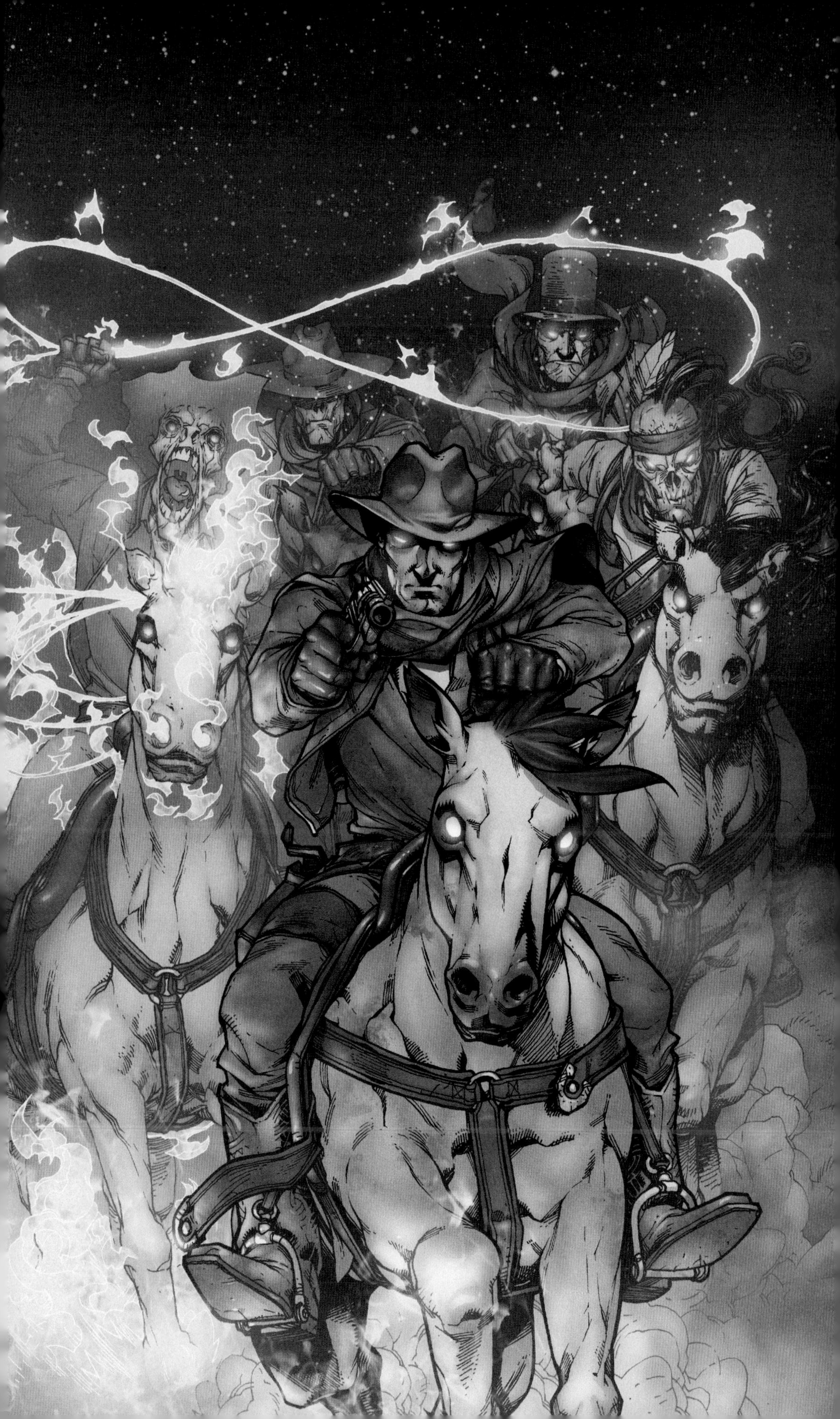

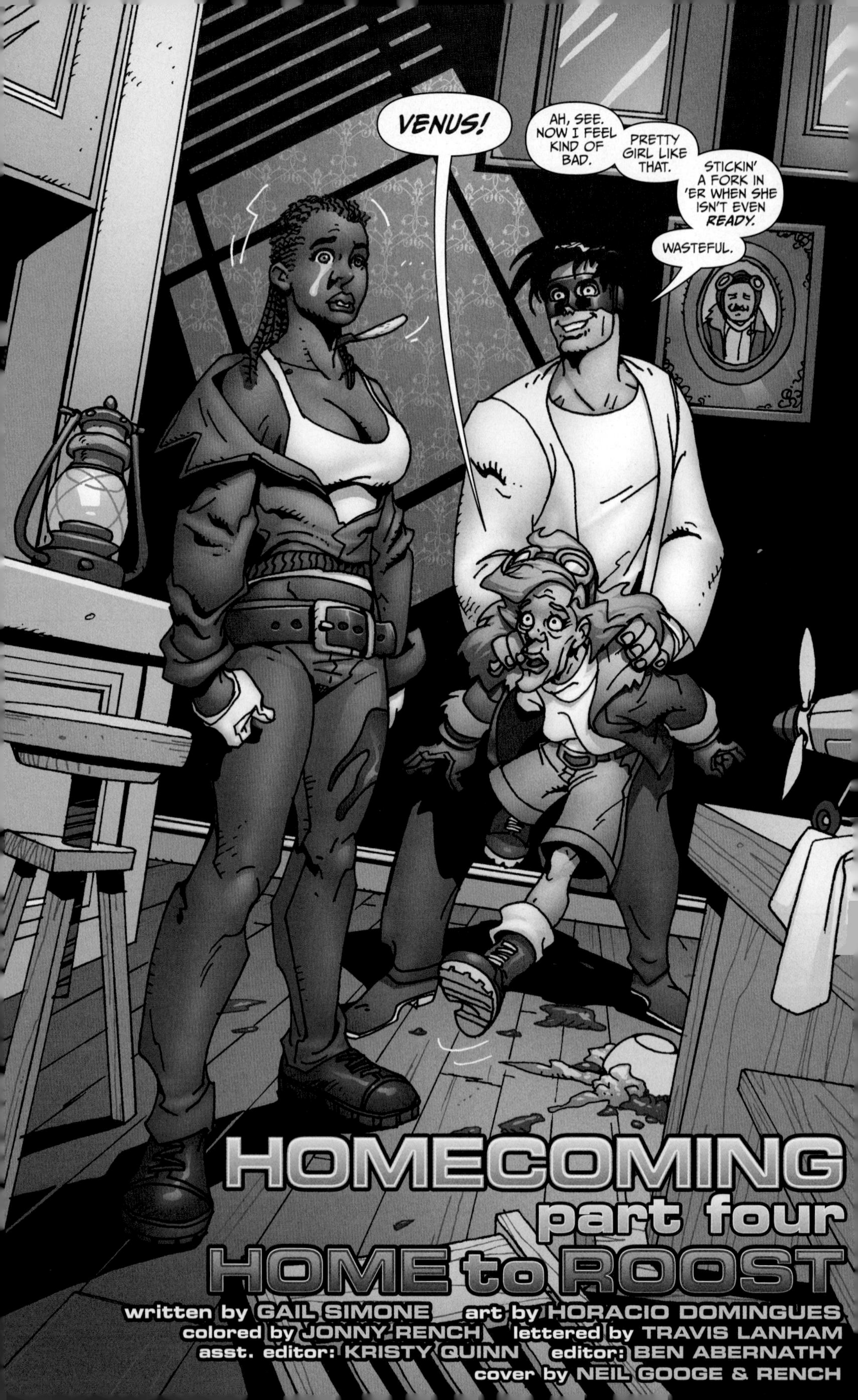
VENUS!
AH, SEE. NOW I FEEL KIND OF BAD.
PRETTY GIRL LIKE THAT.
STICKIN' A FORK IN 'ER WHEN SHE ISN'T EVEN READY.
WASTEFUL.
HOMECOMING
part four
HOME to ROOST
written by GAIL SIMONE art by HORACIO DOMINGUES
colored by JONNY RENCH lettered by TRAVIS LANHAM
asst. editor: KRISTY QUINN editor: BEN ABERNATHY
cover by NEIL GOOGE & RENCH

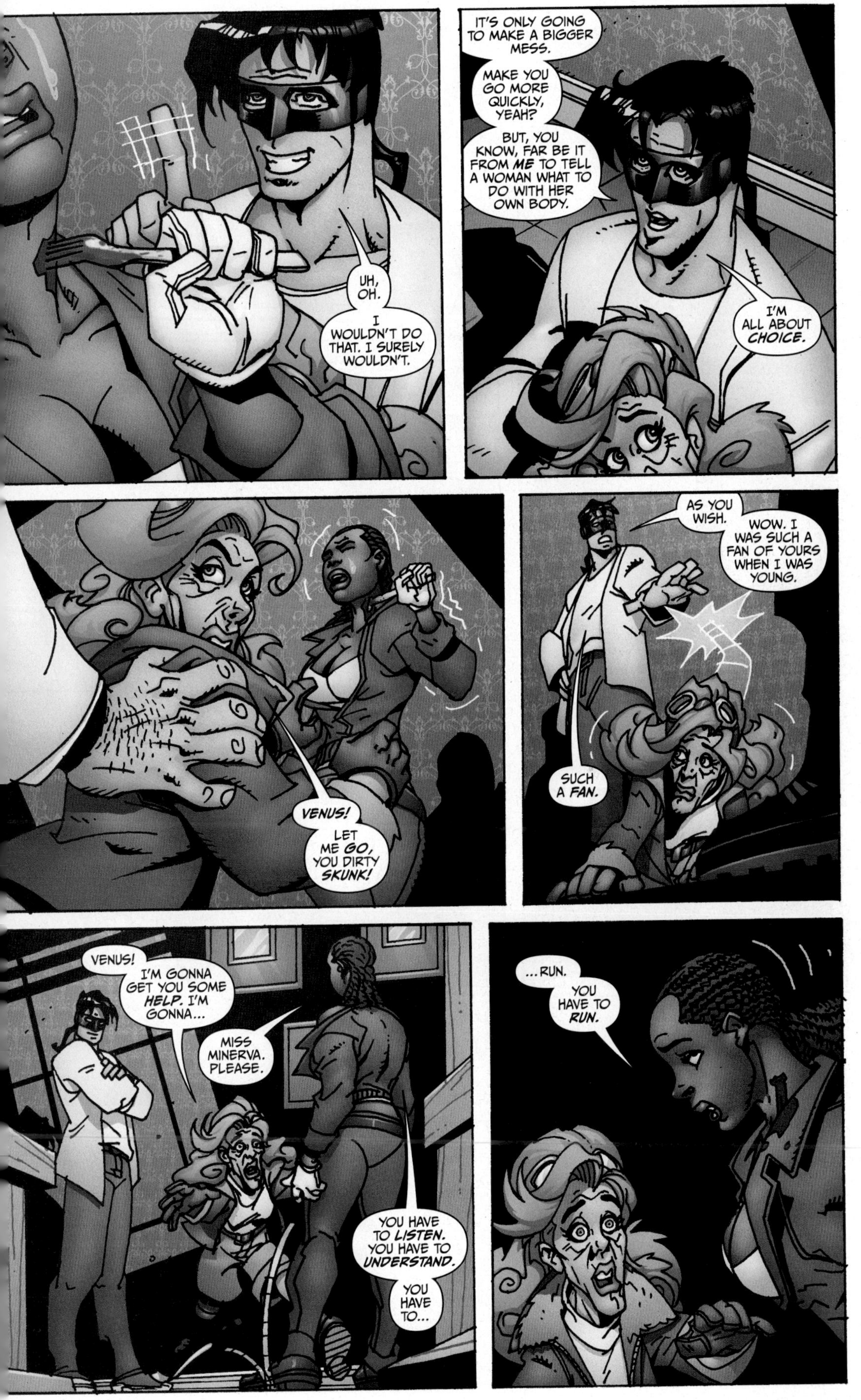
UH, OH.
I WOULDN'T DO THAT. I SURELY WOULDN'T.
IT'S ONLY GOING TO MAKE A BIGGER MESS.
MAKE YOU GO MORE QUICKLY, YEAH?
BUT, YOU KNOW, FAR BE IT FROM *ME* TO TELL A WOMAN WHAT TO DO WITH HER OWN BODY.
I'M ALL ABOUT *CHOICE.*
VENUS!
LET ME *GO,* YOU DIRTY *SKUNK!*
AS YOU WISH.
WOW. I WAS SUCH A FAN OF YOURS WHEN I WAS YOUNG.
SUCH A *FAN.*
VENUS!
I'M GONNA GET YOU SOME *HELP.* I'M GONNA...
MISS MINERVA. PLEASE.
YOU HAVE TO *LISTEN.* YOU HAVE TO *UNDERSTAND.*
YOU HAVE TO...
...RUN.
YOU HAVE TO *RUN.*

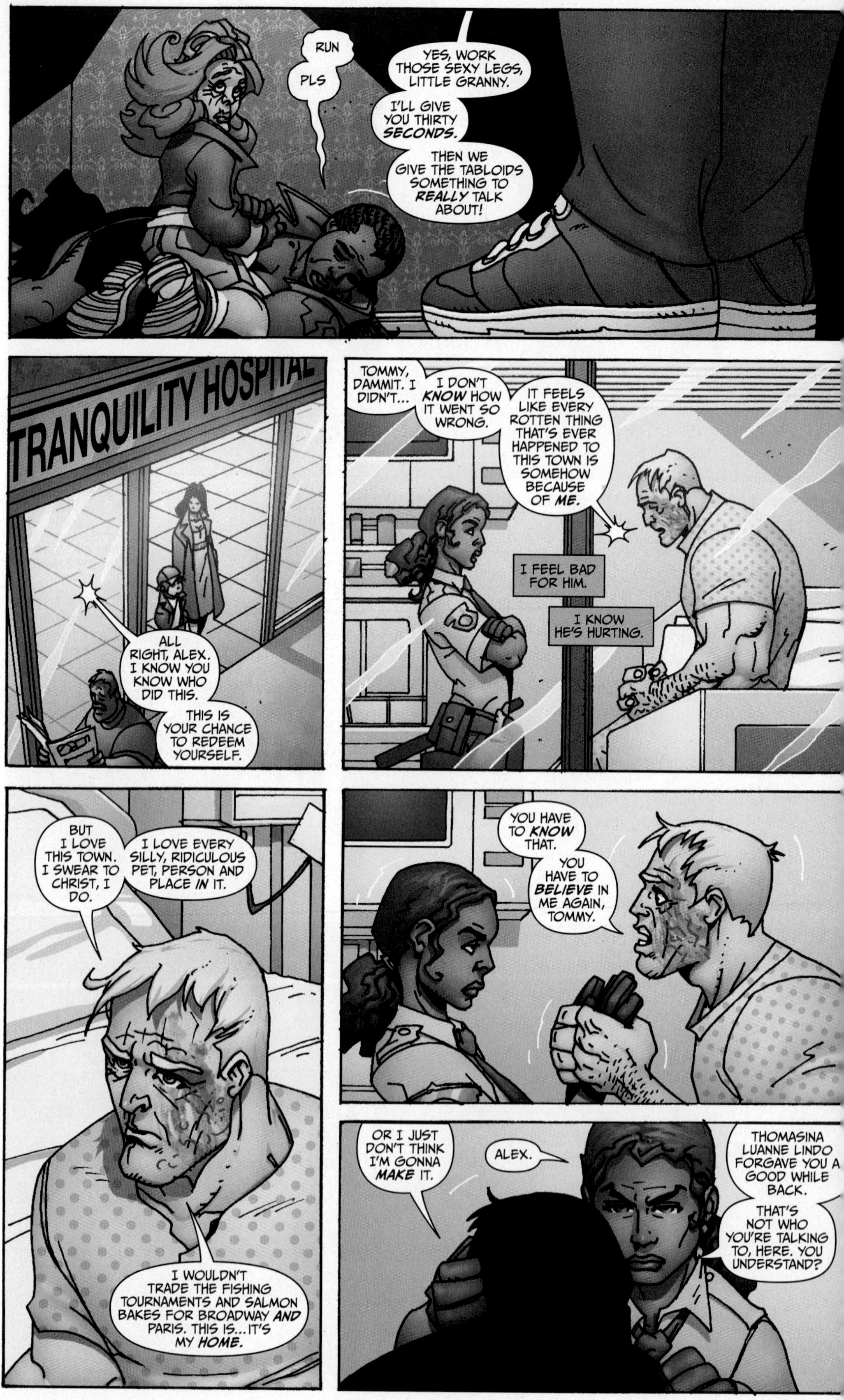
RUN
PLS
YES, WORK THOSE SEXY LEGS, LITTLE GRANNY.
I'LL GIVE YOU THIRTY *SECONDS.*
THEN WE GIVE THE TABLOIDS SOMETHING TO *REALLY* TALK ABOUT!
TRANQUILITY HOSPITAL
ALL RIGHT, ALEX. I KNOW YOU KNOW WHO DID THIS.
THIS IS YOUR CHANCE TO REDEEM YOURSELF.
TOMMY, DAMMIT. I DIDN'T...
I DON'T *KNOW* HOW IT WENT SO WRONG.
IT FEELS LIKE EVERY ROTTEN THING THAT'S EVER HAPPENED TO THIS TOWN IS SOMEHOW BECAUSE OF *ME.*
I FEEL BAD FOR HIM.
I KNOW HE'S HURTING.
BUT I LOVE THIS TOWN. I SWEAR TO CHRIST, I DO.
I LOVE EVERY SILLY, RIDICULOUS PET, PERSON AND PLACE *IN* IT.
I WOULDN'T TRADE THE FISHING TOURNAMENTS AND SALMON BAKES FOR BROADWAY *AND* PARIS. THIS IS... IT'S MY *HOME.*
YOU HAVE TO *KNOW* THAT.
YOU HAVE TO *BELIEVE* IN ME AGAIN, TOMMY.
OR I JUST DON'T THINK I'M GONNA *MAKE* IT.
ALEX.
THOMASINA LUANNE LINDO FORGAVE YOU A GOOD WHILE BACK.
THAT'S NOT WHO YOU'RE TALKING TO, HERE. YOU UNDERSTAND?

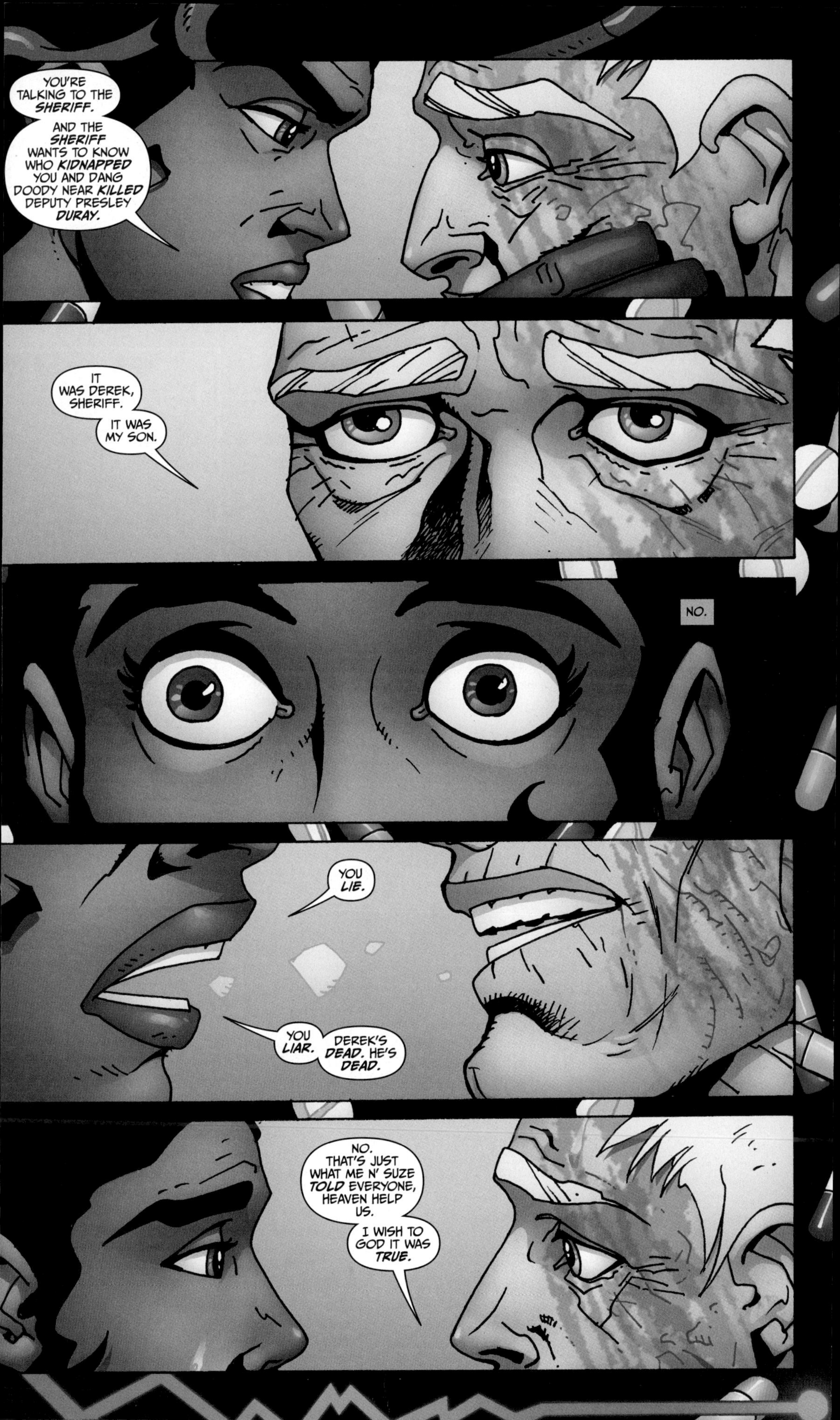
YOU'RE TALKING TO THE SHERIFF.
AND THE SHERIFF WANTS TO KNOW WHO KIDNAPPED YOU AND DANG DOODY NEAR KILLED DEPUTY PRESLEY DURAY.
IT WAS DEREK, SHERIFF.
IT WAS MY SON.
NO.
YOU LIE.
YOU LIAR.
DEREK'S DEAD. HE'S DEAD.
NO. THAT'S JUST WHAT ME N' SUZE TOLD EVERYONE, HEAVEN HELP US.
I WISH TO GOD IT WAS TRUE.

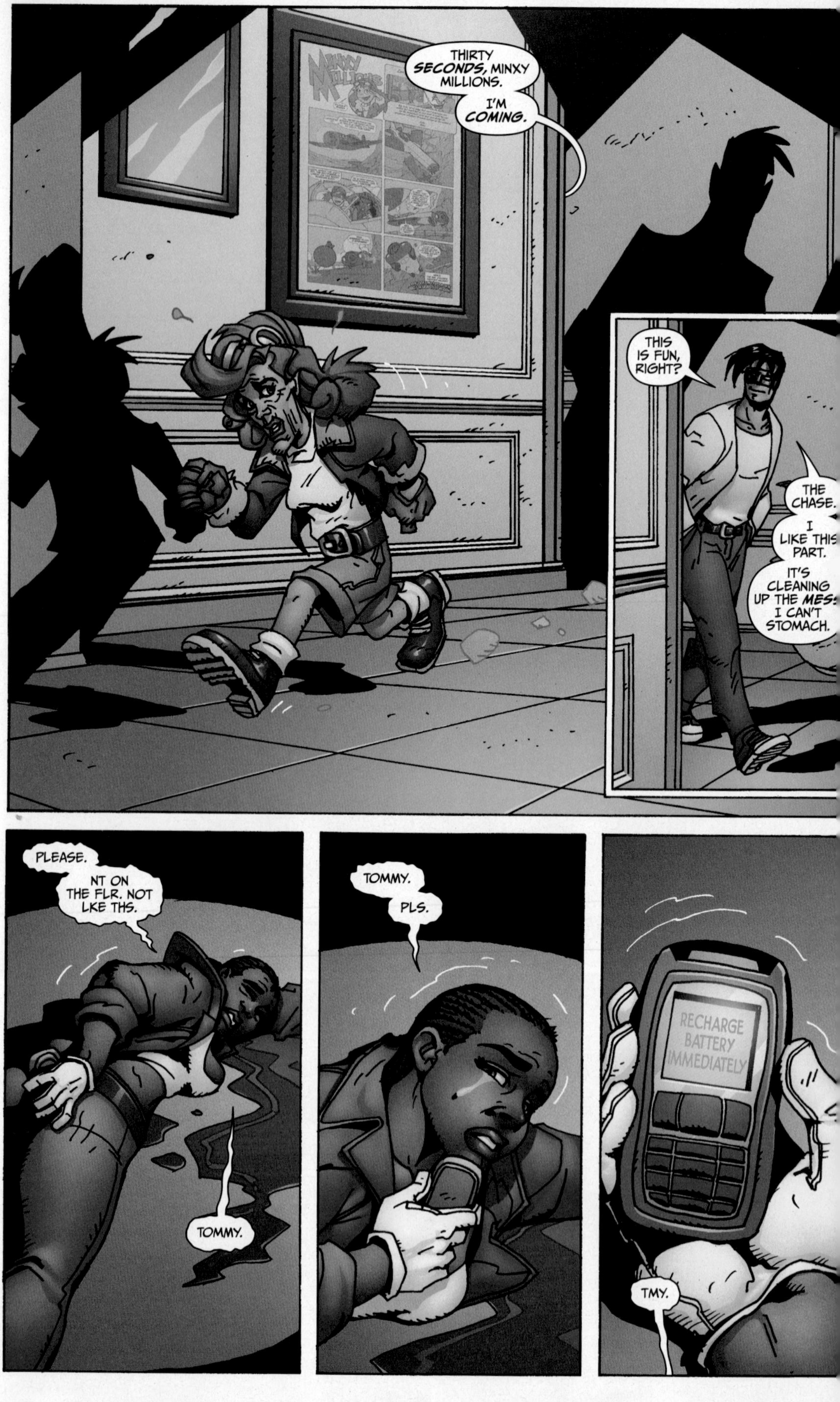
THIRTY SECONDS, MINXY MILLIONS.
I'M COMING.
THIS IS FUN, RIGHT?
THE CHASE.
I LIKE THIS PART.
IT'S CLEANING UP THE MESS I CAN'T STOMACH.
PLEASE.
NT ON THE FLR. NOT LKE THS.
TOMMY.
TOMMY.
PLS.
RECHARGE BATTERY IMMEDIATELY
TMY.

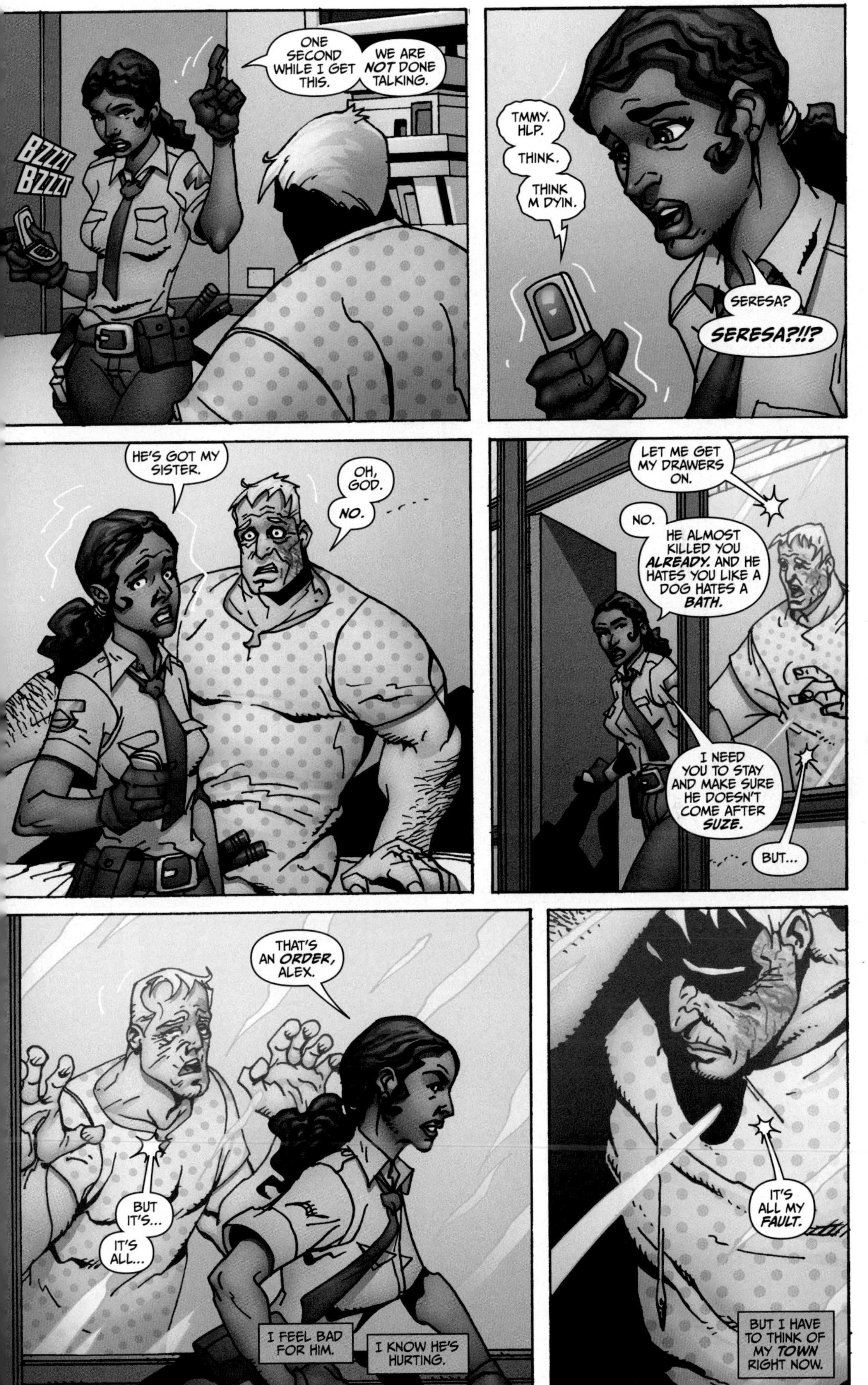
BZZZT
BZZZT
ONE SECOND WHILE I GET THIS.
WE ARE NOT DONE TALKING.
TMMY. HLP.
THINK.
THINK M DYIN.
SERESA?
SERESA?!!?
HE'S GOT MY SISTER.
OH, GOD.
NO.
LET ME GET MY DRAWERS ON.
NO.
HE ALMOST KILLED YOU ALREADY. AND HE HATES YOU LIKE A DOG HATES A BATH.
I NEED YOU TO STAY AND MAKE SURE HE DOESN'T COME AFTER SUZE.
BUT...
THAT'S AN ORDER, ALEX.
BUT IT'S...
IT'S ALL...
I FEEL BAD FOR HIM.
I KNOW HE'S HURTING.
IT'S ALL MY FAULT.
BUT I HAVE TO THINK OF MY TOWN RIGHT NOW.

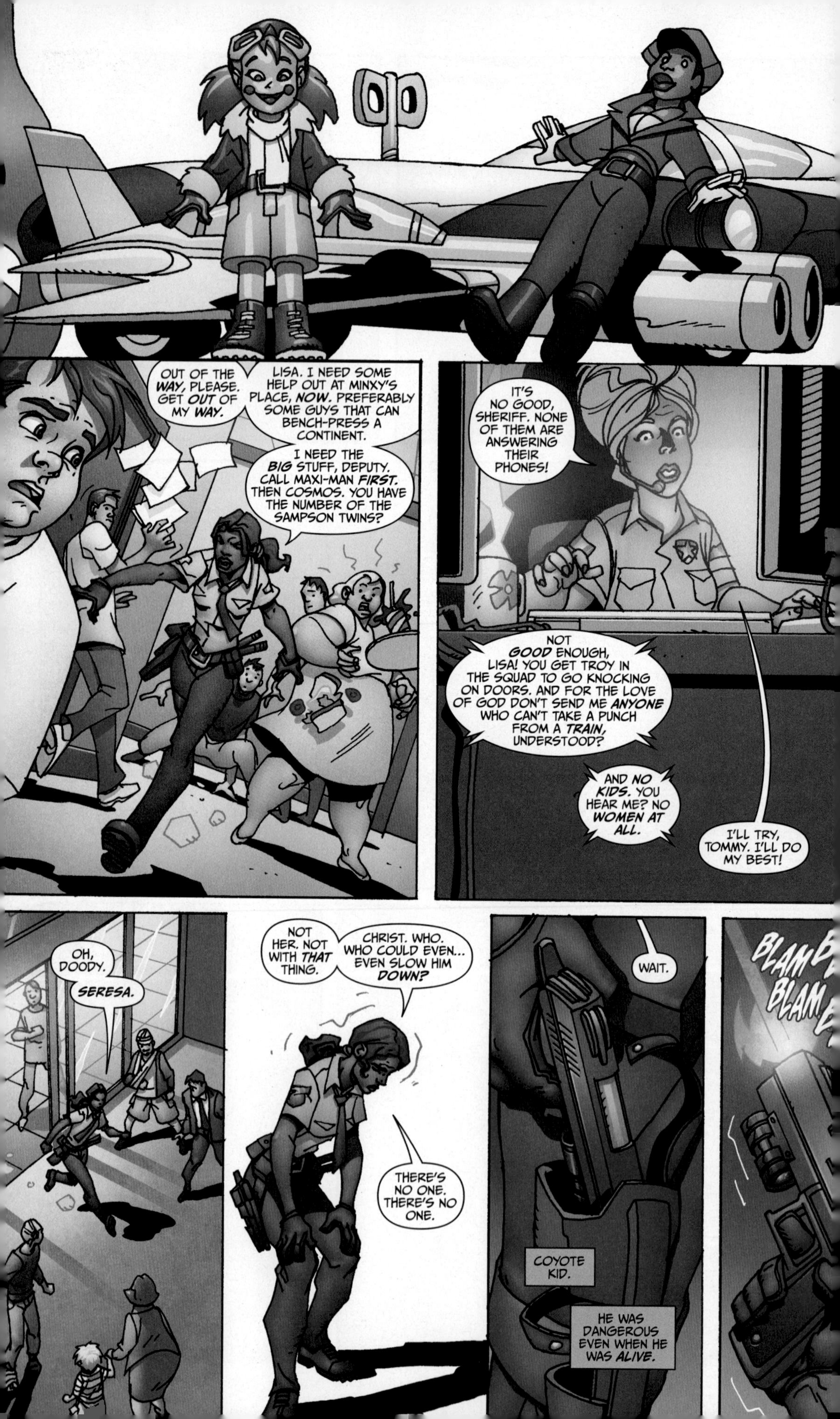
OUT OF THE WAY, PLEASE. GET OUT OF MY WAY.
LISA. I NEED SOME HELP OUT AT MINXY'S PLACE, NOW. PREFERABLY SOME GUYS THAT CAN BENCH-PRESS A CONTINENT.
I NEED THE BIG STUFF, DEPUTY. CALL MAXI-MAN FIRST. THEN COSMOS. YOU HAVE THE NUMBER OF THE SAMPSON TWINS?
IT'S NO GOOD, SHERIFF. NONE OF THEM ARE ANSWERING THEIR PHONES!
NOT GOOD ENOUGH, LISA! YOU GET TROY IN THE SQUAD TO GO KNOCKING ON DOORS. AND FOR THE LOVE OF GOD DON'T SEND ME ANYONE WHO CAN'T TAKE A PUNCH FROM A TRAIN, UNDERSTOOD?
AND NO KIDS. YOU HEAR ME? NO WOMEN AT ALL.
I'LL TRY, TOMMY. I'LL DO MY BEST!
OH, DOODY.
SERESA.
NOT HER. NOT WITH THAT THING.
CHRIST. WHO. WHO COULD EVEN... EVEN SLOW HIM DOWN?
THERE'S NO ONE. THERE'S NO ONE.
WAIT.
COYOTE KID.
HE WAS DANGEROUS EVEN WHEN HE WAS ALIVE.
BLAM
BLAM

OUR FATHER, WHO ART IN HEAVEN.

PLEASE GOD. PLEASE.

I RECKON THAT'S YORE WAY A *CALLIN'* ME, SHERIFF.

YES. YES.

WELP. YA *GOT* ME.

WHAT'S ALL THE *COMMOTION?*

ALL RIGHT. [YO]U'RE *DEAD,* RIGHT?

THAT I AM, MA'AM.

AND NOTHING, *NOTHING* ANYONE DOES TO YOU IS GONNA MAKE YOU, WHAT, ANY *MORE* DEAD, I GUESS, RIGHT?

I RECKON YOU AIN'T TRYING TO CHEER ME *UP* NONE WITH THIS LINE O' QUESTIONIN'.

KID. HE... A *RAPIST* HAS MY SISTER.

...

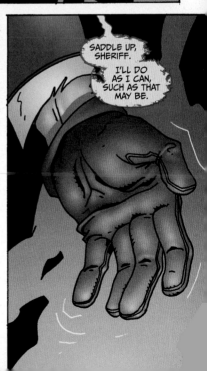

SADDLE UP, SHERIFF.

I'LL DO AS I CAN, SUCH AS THAT MAY BE.

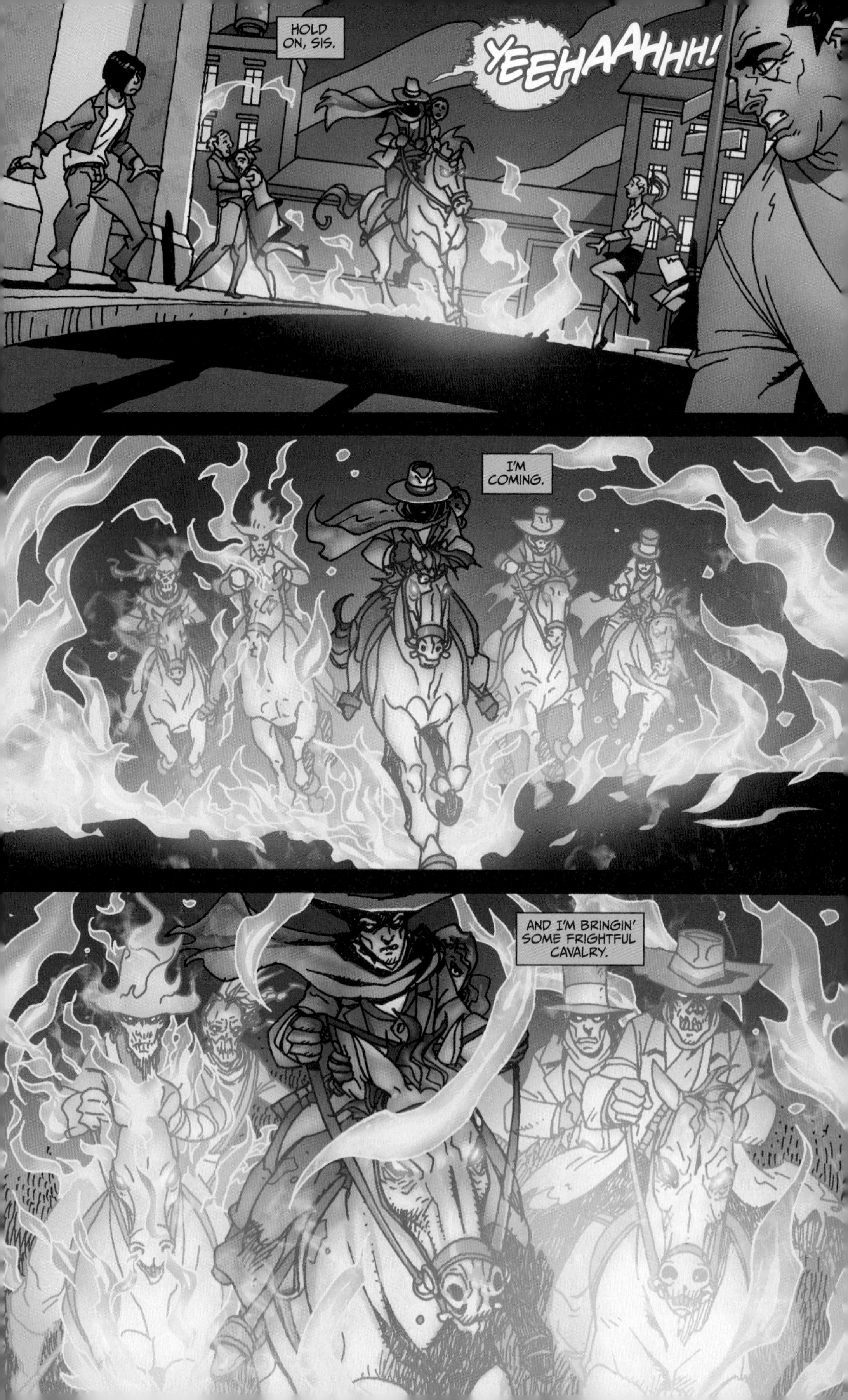
HOLD ON, SIS.
YEEHAAHHH!
I'M COMING.
AND I'M BRINGIN' SOME FRIGHTFUL CAVALRY.

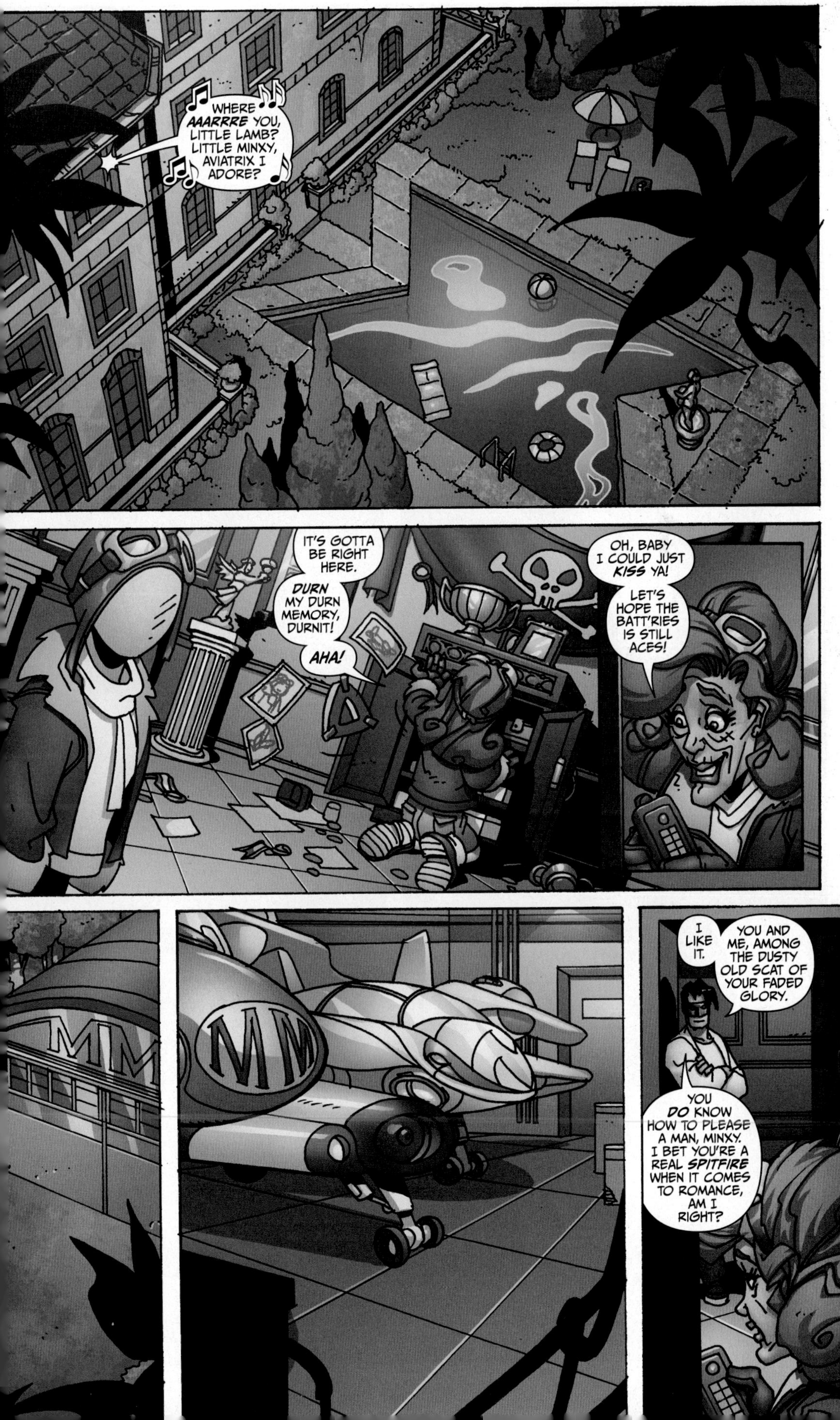
WHERE AAARRRE YOU, LITTLE LAMB? LITTLE MINXY, AVIATRIX I ADORE?
IT'S GOTTA BE RIGHT HERE.
DURN MY DURN MEMORY, DURNIT!
AHA!
OH, BABY I COULD JUST KISS YA!
LET'S HOPE THE BATT'RIES IS STILL ACES!
I LIKE IT.
YOU AND ME, AMONG THE DUSTY OLD SCAT OF YOUR FADED GLORY.
YOU DO KNOW HOW TO PLEASE A MAN, MINXY. I BET YOU'RE A REAL SPITFIRE WHEN IT COMES TO ROMANCE, AM I RIGHT?

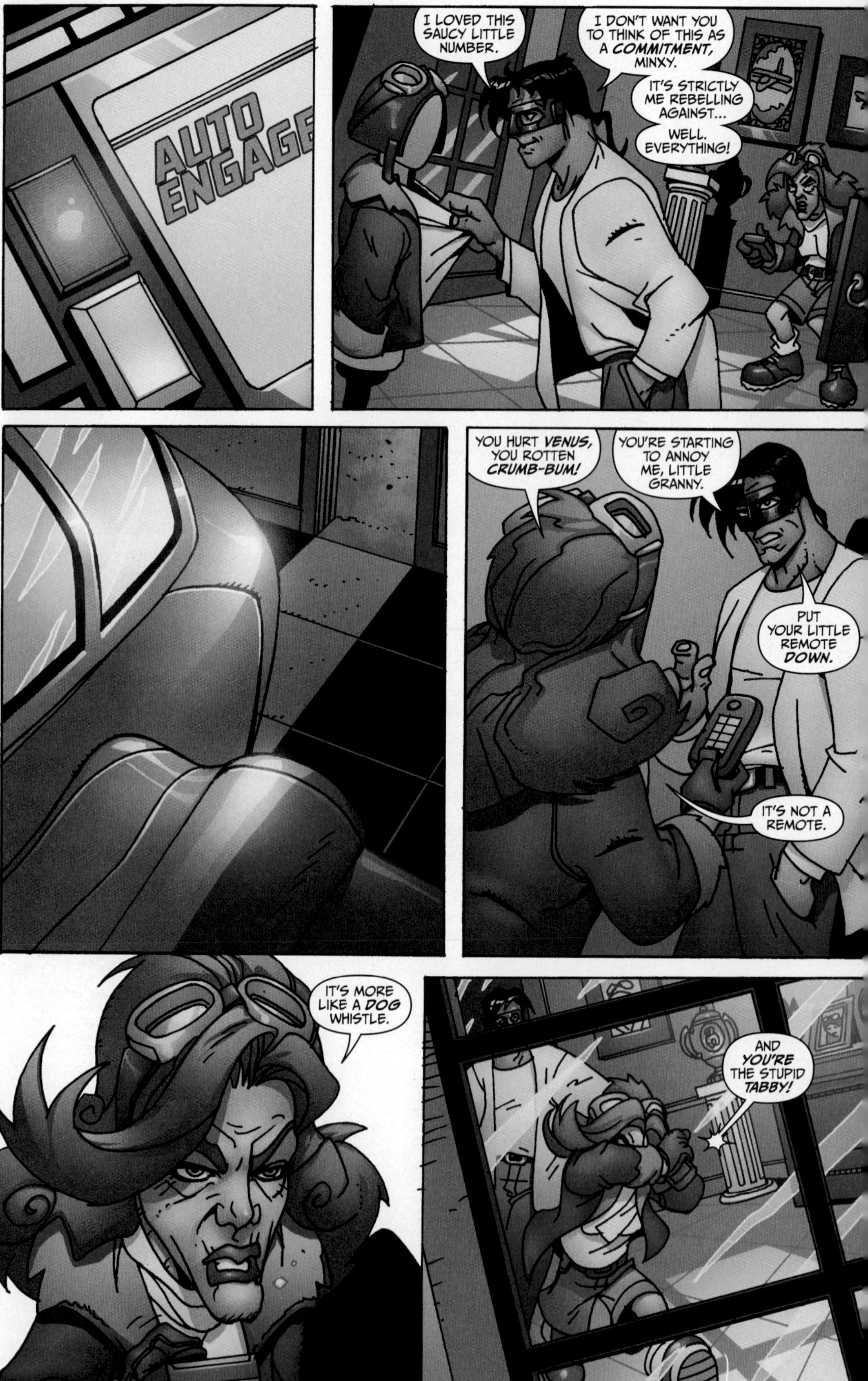
AUTO ENGAGE
I LOVED THIS SAUCY LITTLE NUMBER.
I DON'T WANT YOU TO THINK OF THIS AS A *COMMITMENT,* MINXY.
IT'S STRICTLY ME REBELLING AGAINST...
WELL. EVERYTHING!
YOU HURT *VENUS,* YOU ROTTEN *CRUMB-BUM!*
YOU'RE STARTING TO ANNOY ME, LITTLE GRANNY.
PUT YOUR LITTLE REMOTE *DOWN.*
IT'S NOT A REMOTE.
IT'S MORE LIKE A *DOG* WHISTLE.
AND *YOU'RE* THE STUPID *TABBY!*

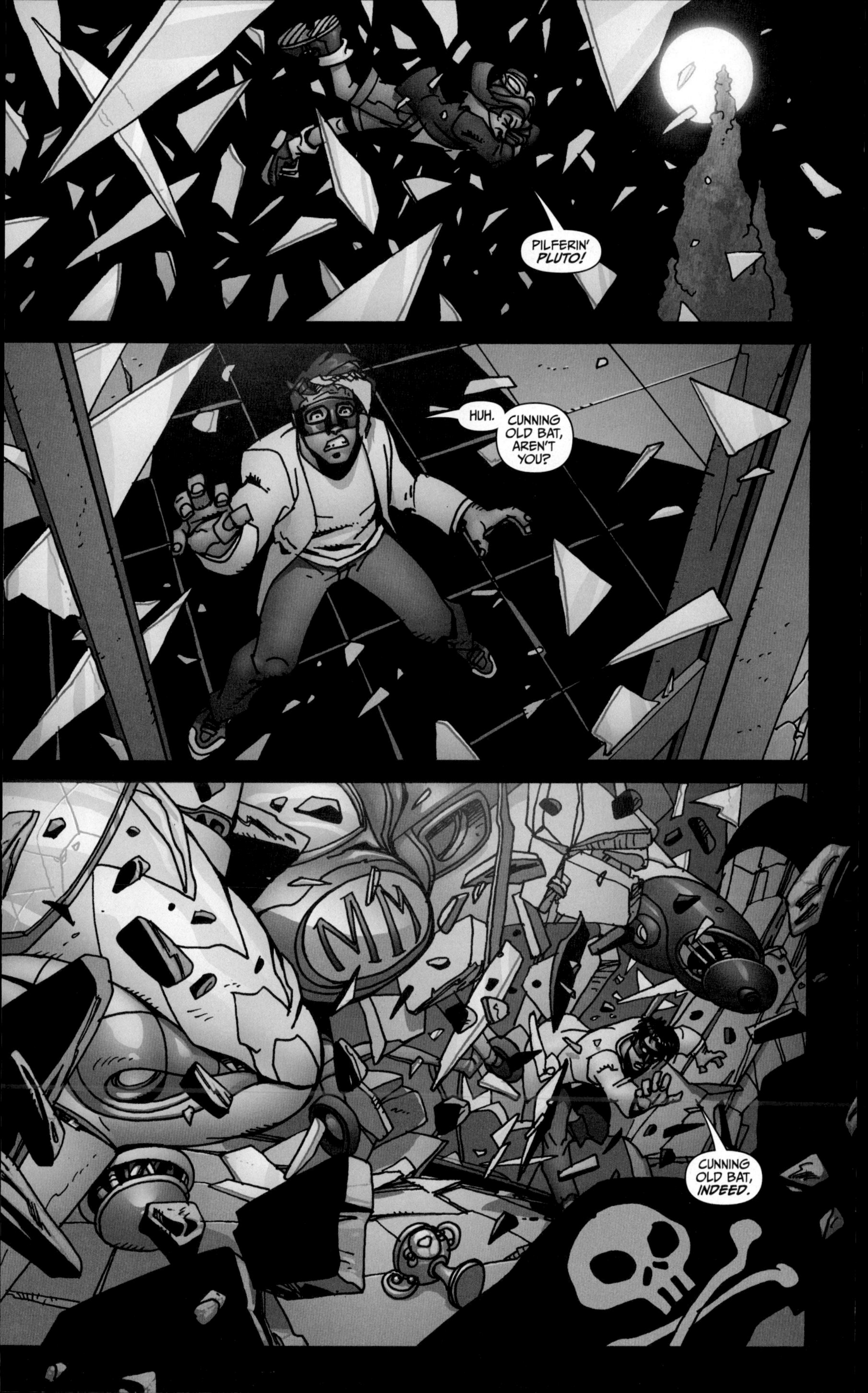
PILFERIN' *PLUTO!*
HUH.
CUNNING OLD BAT, AREN'T YOU?
CUNNING OLD BAT, *INDEED.*

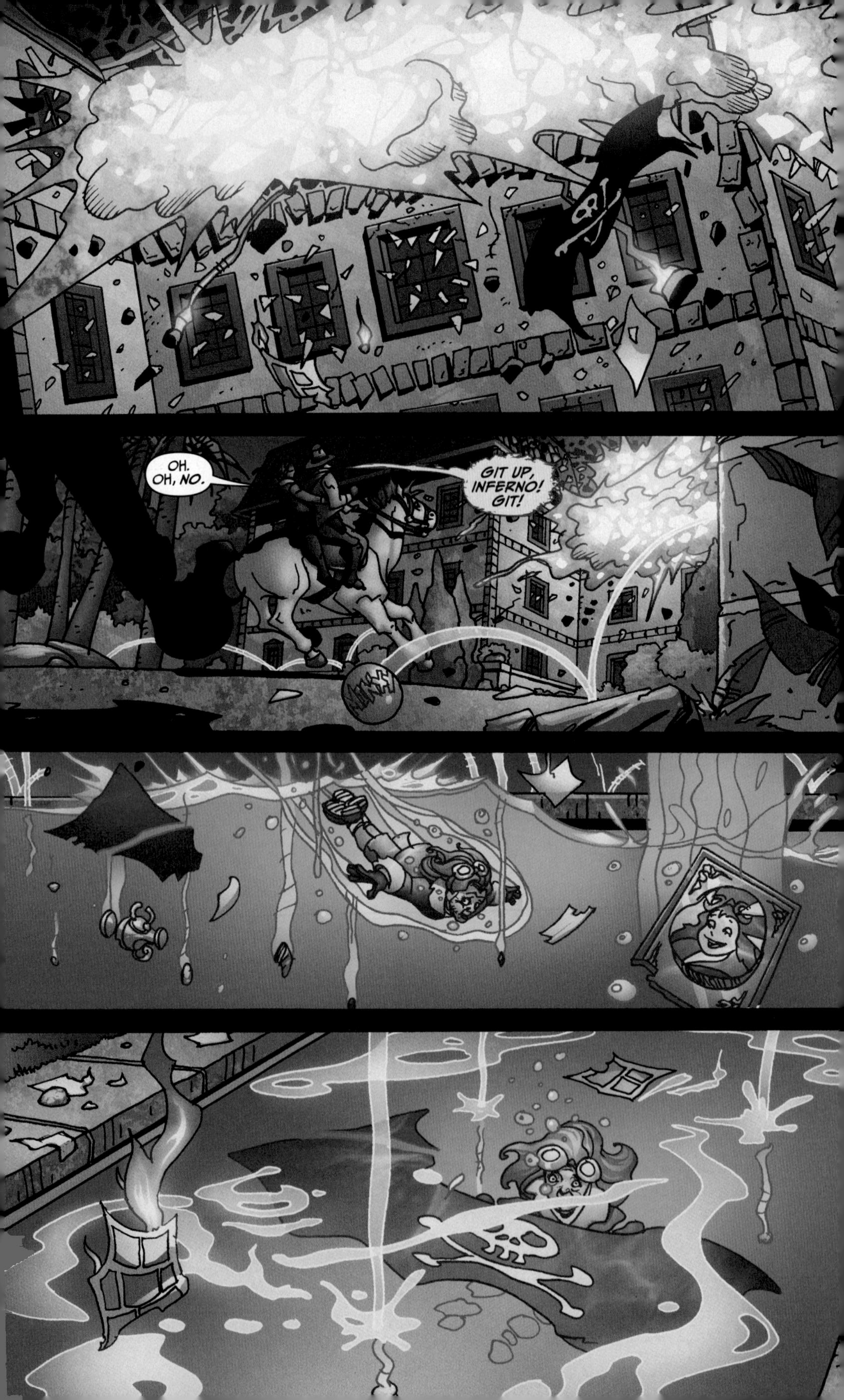
OH. OH, NO.
GIT UP, INFERNO! GIT!

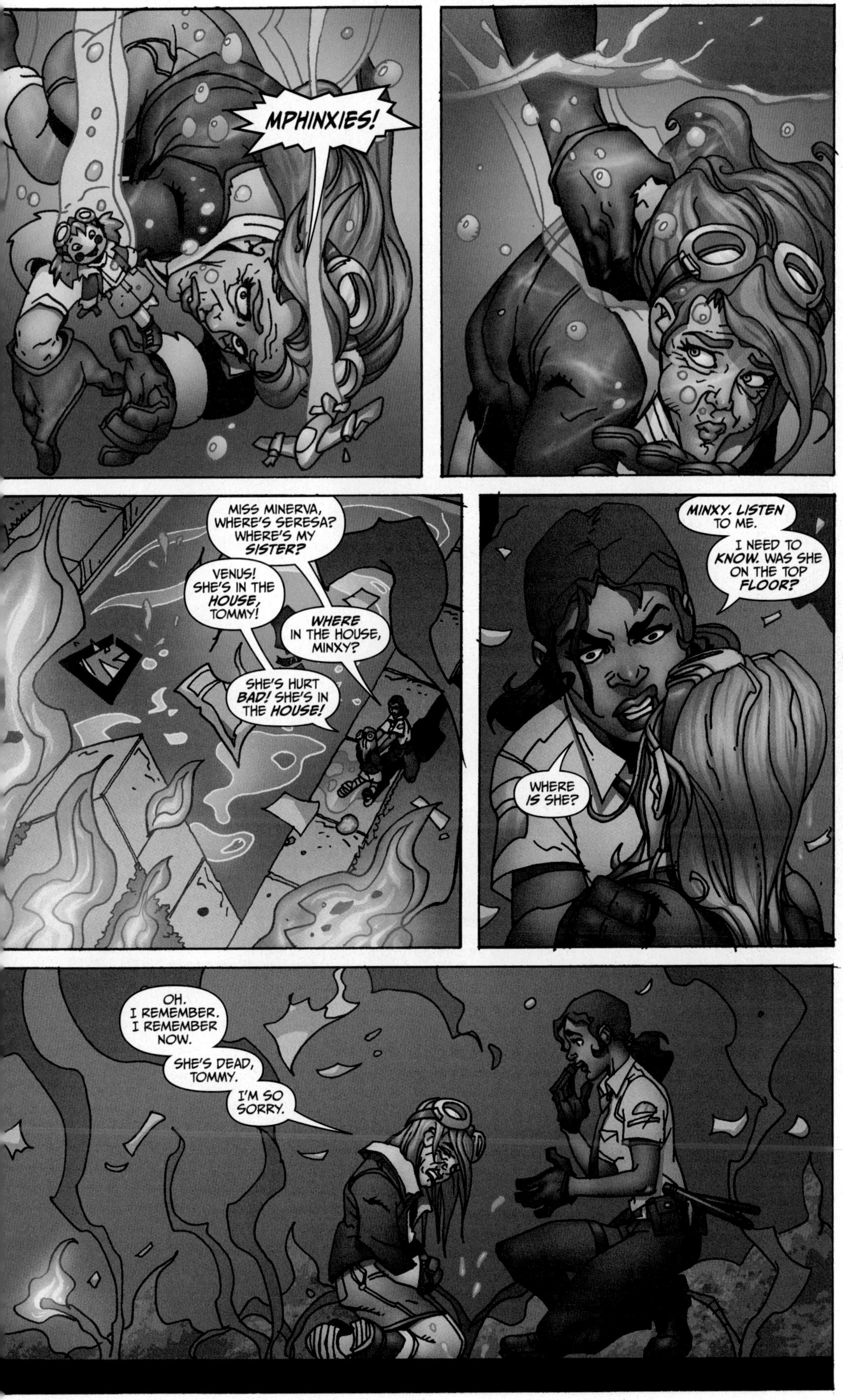
MPHINXIES!
MISS MINERVA, WHERE'S SERESA? WHERE'S MY SISTER?
VENUS! SHE'S IN THE HOUSE, TOMMY!
WHERE IN THE HOUSE, MINXY?
SHE'S HURT BAD! SHE'S IN THE HOUSE!
MINXY. LISTEN TO ME.
I NEED TO KNOW. WAS SHE ON THE TOP FLOOR?
WHERE IS SHE?
OH. I REMEMBER. I REMEMBER NOW.
SHE'S DEAD, TOMMY.
I'M SO SORRY.

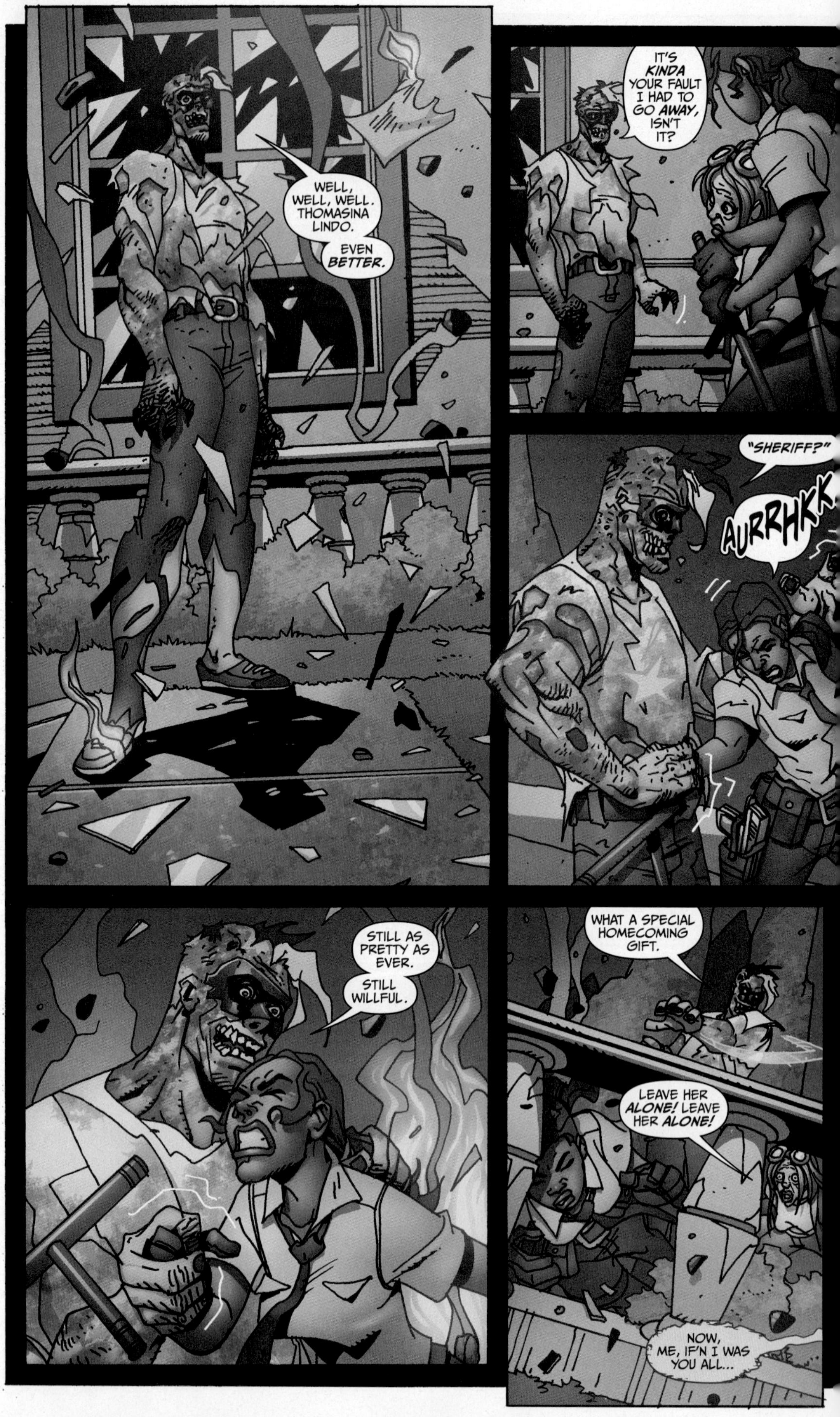
WELL, WELL, WELL. THOMASINA LINDO.
EVEN BETTER.
IT'S KINDA YOUR FAULT I HAD TO GO AWAY, ISN'T IT?
"SHERIFF?"
AURRHKK
STILL AS PRETTY AS EVER.
STILL WILLFUL.
WHAT A SPECIAL HOMECOMING GIFT.
LEAVE HER ALONE! LEAVE HER ALONE!
NOW, ME, IF'N I WAS YOU ALL...

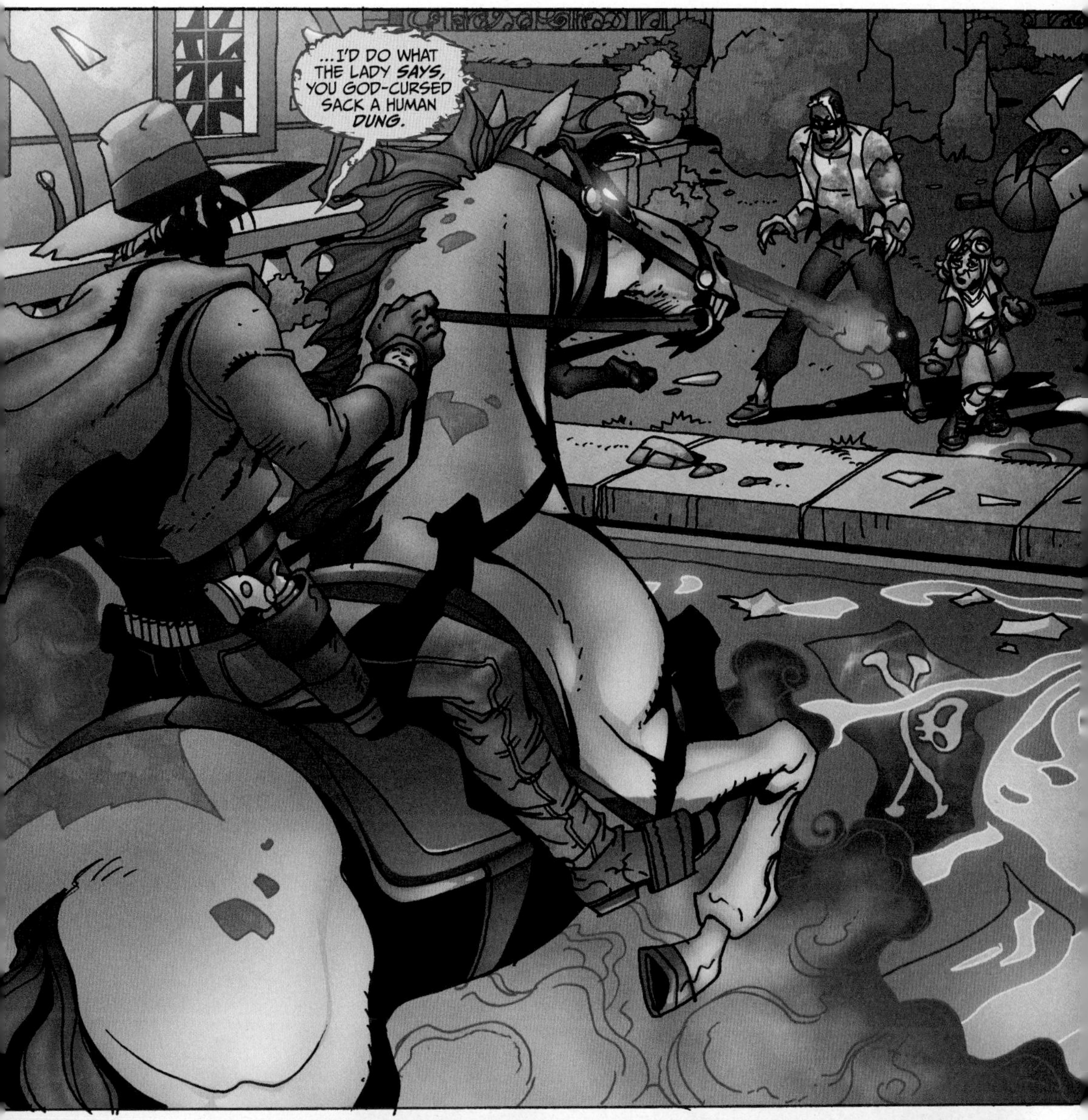
...I'D DO WHAT THE LADY SAYS, YOU GOD-CURSED SACK A HUMAN DUNG.

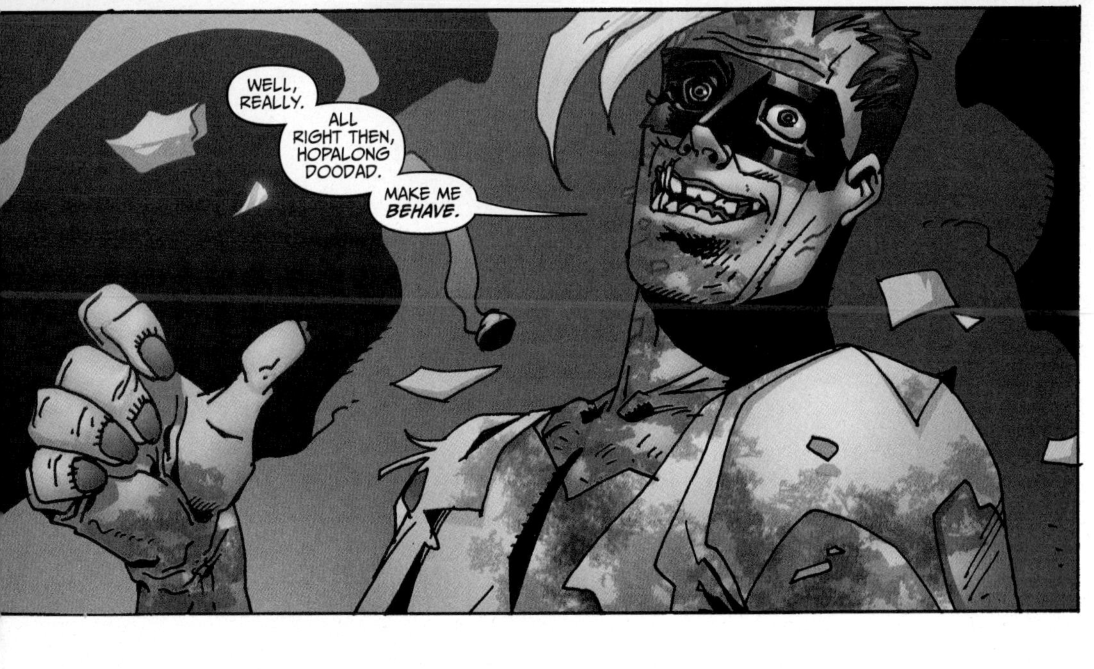
WELL, REALLY.
ALL RIGHT THEN, HOPALONG DOODAD.
MAKE ME BEHAVE.

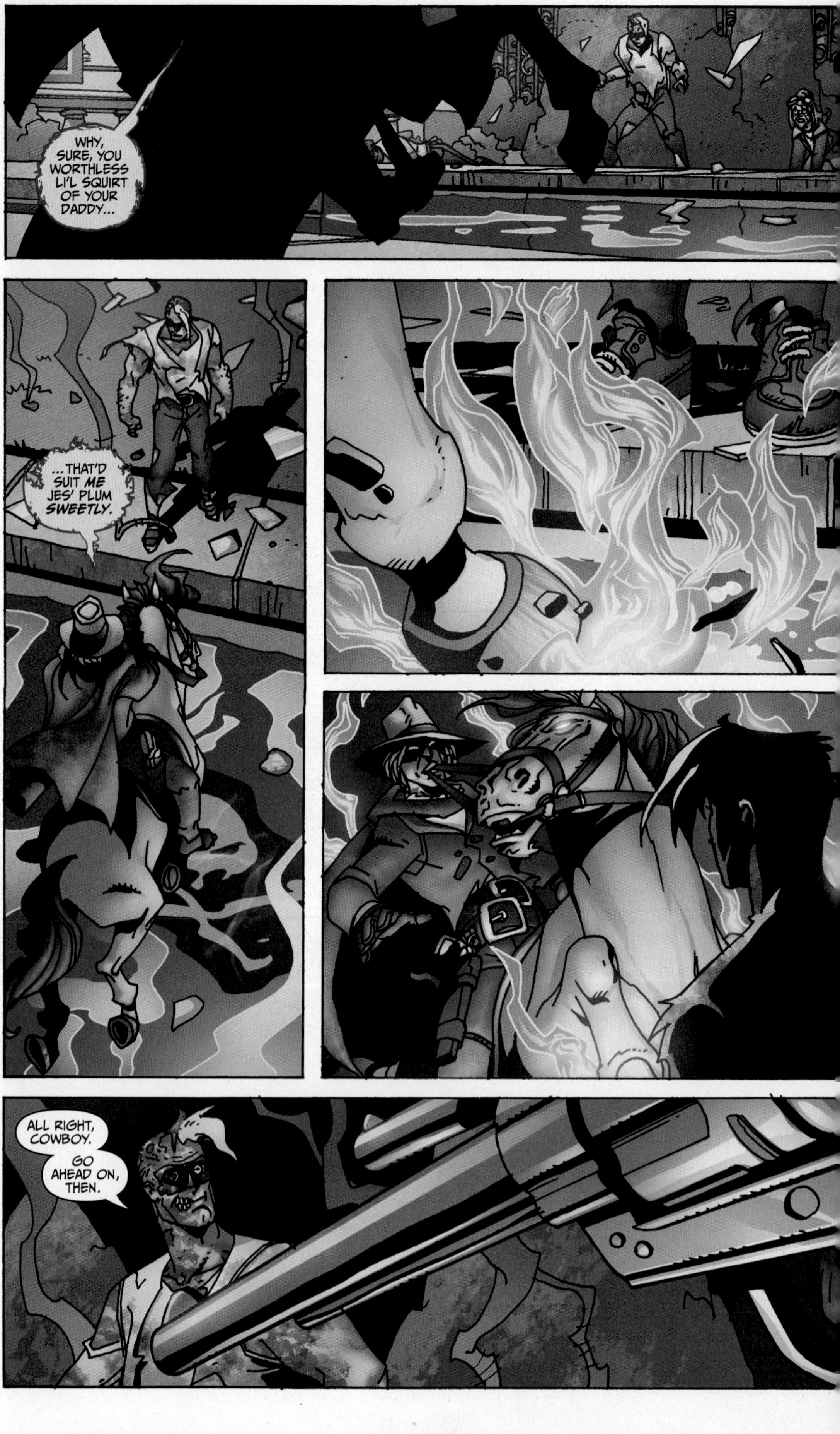
WHY, SURE, YOU WORTHLESS LI'L SQUIRT OF YOUR DADDY...
...THAT'D SUIT *ME* JES' PLUM *SWEETLY.*
ALL RIGHT, COWBOY.
GO AHEAD ON, THEN.

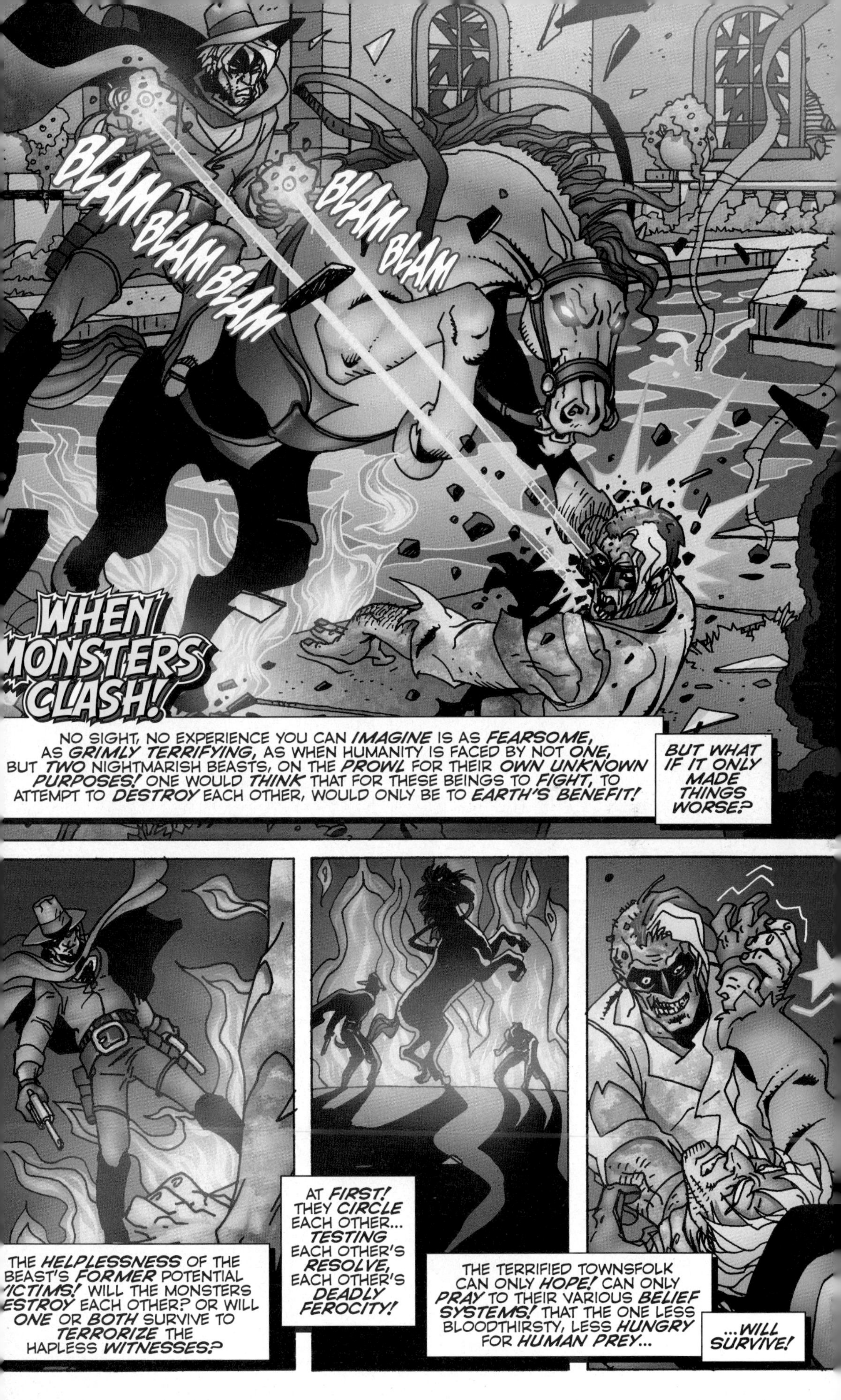

BLAM BLAM BLAM BLAM
BLAM BLAM
WHEN MONSTERS CLASH!
NO SIGHT, NO EXPERIENCE YOU CAN IMAGINE IS AS FEARSOME, AS GRIMLY TERRIFYING, AS WHEN HUMANITY IS FACED BY NOT ONE, BUT TWO NIGHTMARISH BEASTS, ON THE PROWL FOR THEIR OWN UNKNOWN PURPOSES! ONE WOULD THINK THAT FOR THESE BEINGS TO FIGHT, TO ATTEMPT TO DESTROY EACH OTHER, WOULD ONLY BE TO EARTH'S BENEFIT!
BUT WHAT IF IT ONLY MADE THINGS WORSE?
THE HELPLESSNESS OF THE BEAST'S FORMER POTENTIAL VICTIMS! WILL THE MONSTERS DESTROY EACH OTHER? OR WILL ONE OR BOTH SURVIVE TO TERRORIZE THE HAPLESS WITNESSES?
AT FIRST! THEY CIRCLE EACH OTHER... TESTING EACH OTHER'S RESOLVE, EACH OTHER'S DEADLY FEROCITY!
THE TERRIFIED TOWNSFOLK CAN ONLY HOPE! CAN ONLY PRAY TO THEIR VARIOUS BELIEF SYSTEMS! THAT THE ONE LESS BLOODTHIRSTY, LESS HUNGRY FOR HUMAN PREY...
...WILL SURVIVE!

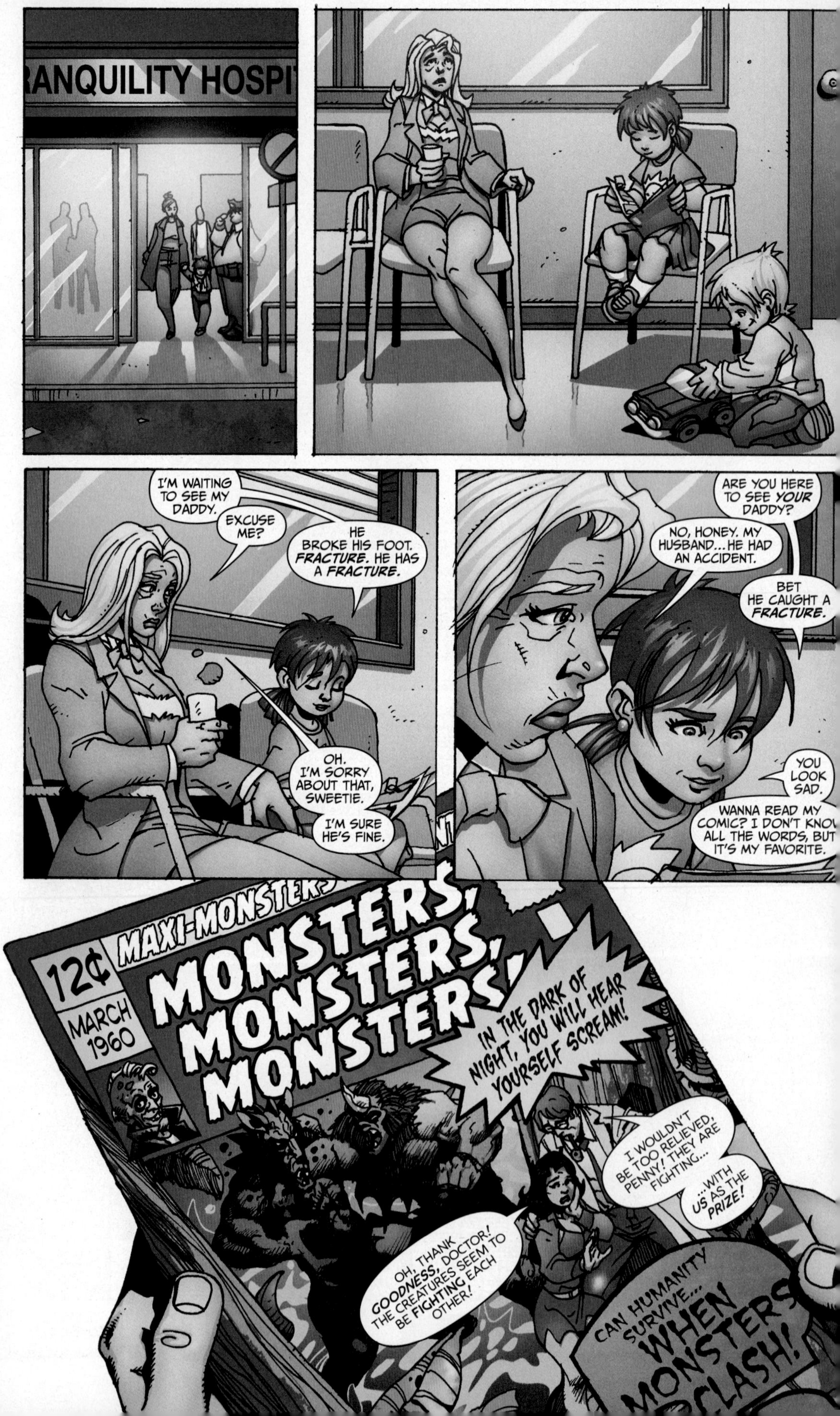
RANQUILITY HOSPI
I'M WAITING TO SEE MY DADDY.
EXCUSE ME?
HE BROKE HIS FOOT. FRACTURE. HE HAS A FRACTURE.
OH. I'M SORRY ABOUT THAT, SWEETIE.
I'M SURE HE'S FINE.
ARE YOU HERE TO SEE YOUR DADDY?
NO, HONEY. MY HUSBAND... HE HAD AN ACCIDENT.
BET HE CAUGHT A FRACTURE.
YOU LOOK SAD.
WANNA READ MY COMIC? I DON'T KNOW ALL THE WORDS, BUT IT'S MY FAVORITE.
MAXI-MONSTERS
12¢
MARCH 1960
MONSTERS, MONSTERS, MONSTERS!
IN THE DARK OF NIGHT, YOU WILL HEAR YOURSELF SCREAM!
OH, THANK GOODNESS, DOCTOR! THE CREATURES SEEM TO BE FIGHTING EACH OTHER!
I WOULDN'T BE TOO RELIEVED, PENNY! THEY ARE FIGHTING...
...WITH US AS THE PRIZE!
CAN HUMANITY SURVIVE... WHEN MONSTERS CLASH!

FANGS, I MEAN, *THANKS*, FOR JOINING US ONCE AGAIN, FEAR, I MEAN, *DEAR* READER!

I'M YOUR OL' PAL, ZOMBIE ZEKE, AND THIS IS MY FRIEND *HAMNET*, AND WE HAVE A SCARY, I MEAN A *FAIRY* TALE THAT'LL MAKE A CHILLING, I MEAN *THRILLING* BEDTIME TALE!

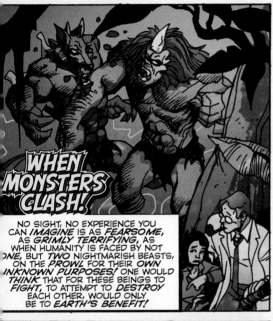

WHEN MONSTERS CLASH!

NO SIGHT, NO EXPERIENCE YOU CAN *IMAGINE* IS AS *FEARSOME*, AS *GRIMLY TERRIFYING*, AS WHEN HUMANITY IS FACED BY NOT *ONE*, BUT *TWO* NIGHTMARISH BEASTS, ON THE *PROWL* FOR THEIR *OWN UNKNOWN PURPOSES!* ONE WOULD *THINK* THAT FOR THESE BEINGS TO *FIGHT*, TO ATTEMPT TO *DESTROY* EACH OTHER, WOULD ONLY BE TO *EARTH'S BENEFIT!*

OH, DOCTOR... IT'S HORRIBLE. *HORRIBLE!* *TWO* SUCH ABOMINATIONS!

WE CAN ONLY PRAY THAT *NEITHER* SURVIVES THIS CONFLICT, PENNY!

THE *HELPLESSNESS* OF THE BEAST'S *FORMER* POTENTIAL *VICTIMS!* WILL THE MONSTERS *DESTROY* EACH OTHER? OR WILL *ONE* OR *BOTH* SURVIVE TO *TERRORIZE* THE HAPLESS *WITNESSES?*

AT *FIRST!* THEY *CIRCLE* EACH OTHER...*TESTING* EACH OTHER'S *RESOLVE*, EACH OTHER'S *DEADLY FEROCITY!*

THE TERRIFIED TOWNSFOLK CAN ONLY *HOPE!* CAN ONLY *PRAY* TO THEIR VARIOUS *BELIEF SYSTEMS!* THAT THE ONE LESS BLOODTHIRSTY, LESS *HUNGRY* FOR *HUMAN PREY*...

...*WILL SURVIVE!*

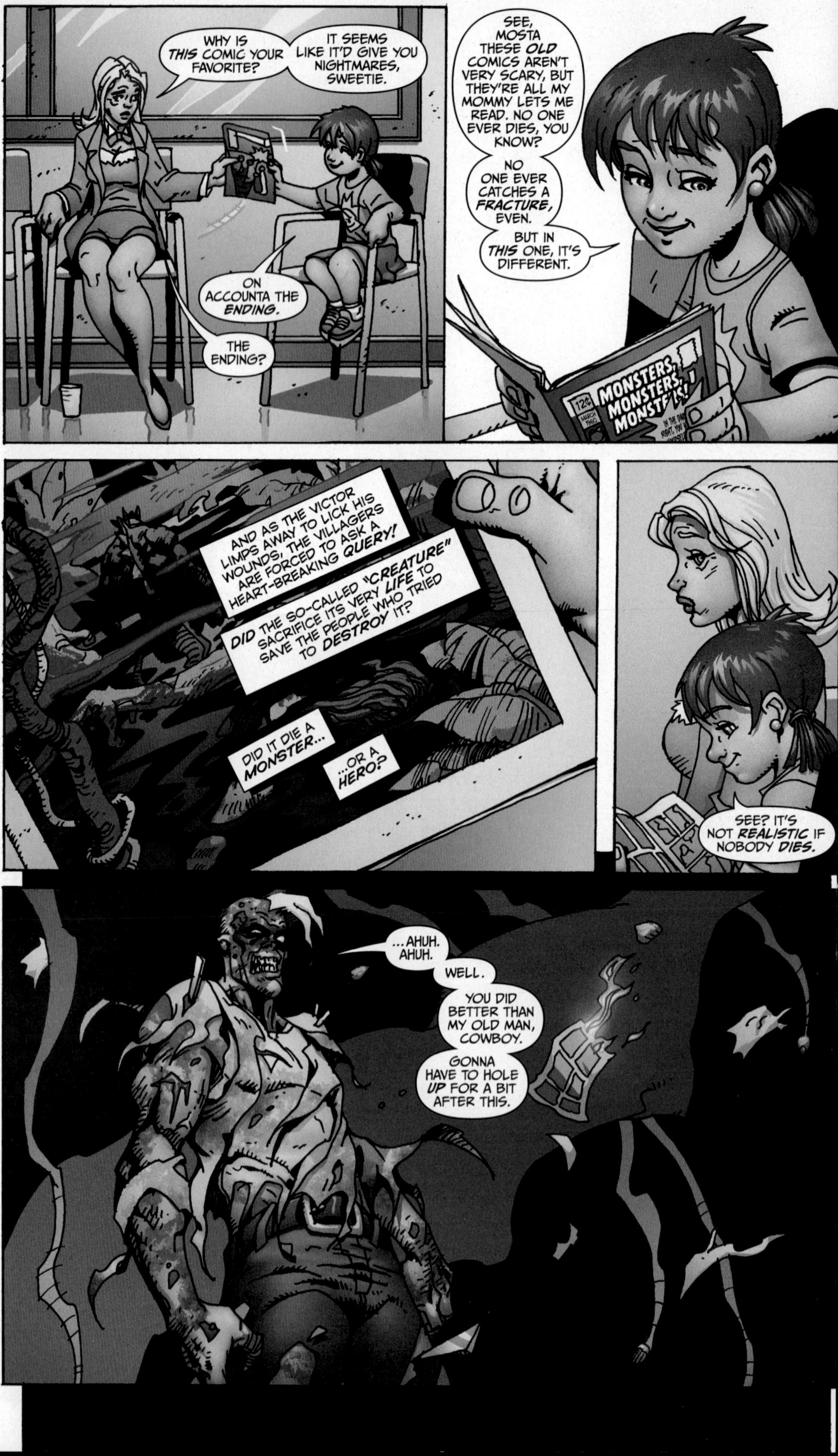
WHY IS THIS COMIC YOUR FAVORITE?
IT SEEMS LIKE IT'D GIVE YOU NIGHTMARES, SWEETIE.
ON ACCOUNTA THE ENDING.
THE ENDING?
SEE, MOSTA THESE OLD COMICS AREN'T VERY SCARY, BUT THEY'RE ALL MY MOMMY LETS ME READ. NO ONE EVER DIES, YOU KNOW?
NO ONE EVER CATCHES A FRACTURE, EVEN.
BUT IN THIS ONE, IT'S DIFFERENT.
MONSTERS, MONSTERS, MONSTERS!
12¢
AND AS THE VICTOR LIMPS AWAY TO LICK HIS WOUNDS, THE VILLAGERS ARE FORCED TO ASK A HEART-BREAKING QUERY!
DID THE SO-CALLED "CREATURE" SACRIFICE ITS VERY LIFE TO SAVE THE PEOPLE WHO TRIED TO DESTROY IT?
DID IT DIE A MONSTER...
...OR A HERO?
SEE? IT'S NOT REALISTIC IF NOBODY DIES.
...AHUH. AHUH.
WELL.
YOU DID BETTER THAN MY OLD MAN, COWBOY.
GONNA HAVE TO HOLE UP FOR A BIT AFTER THIS.

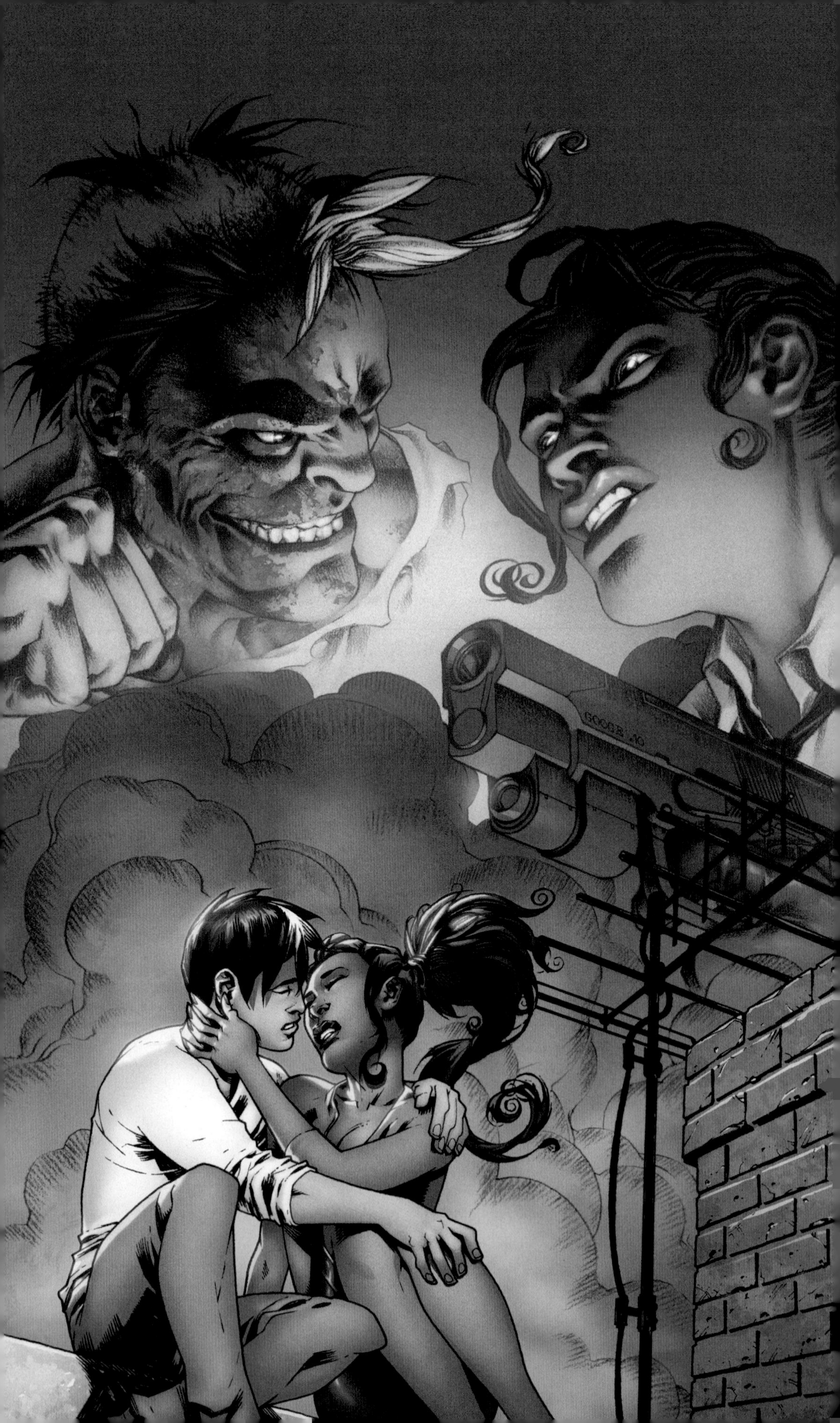

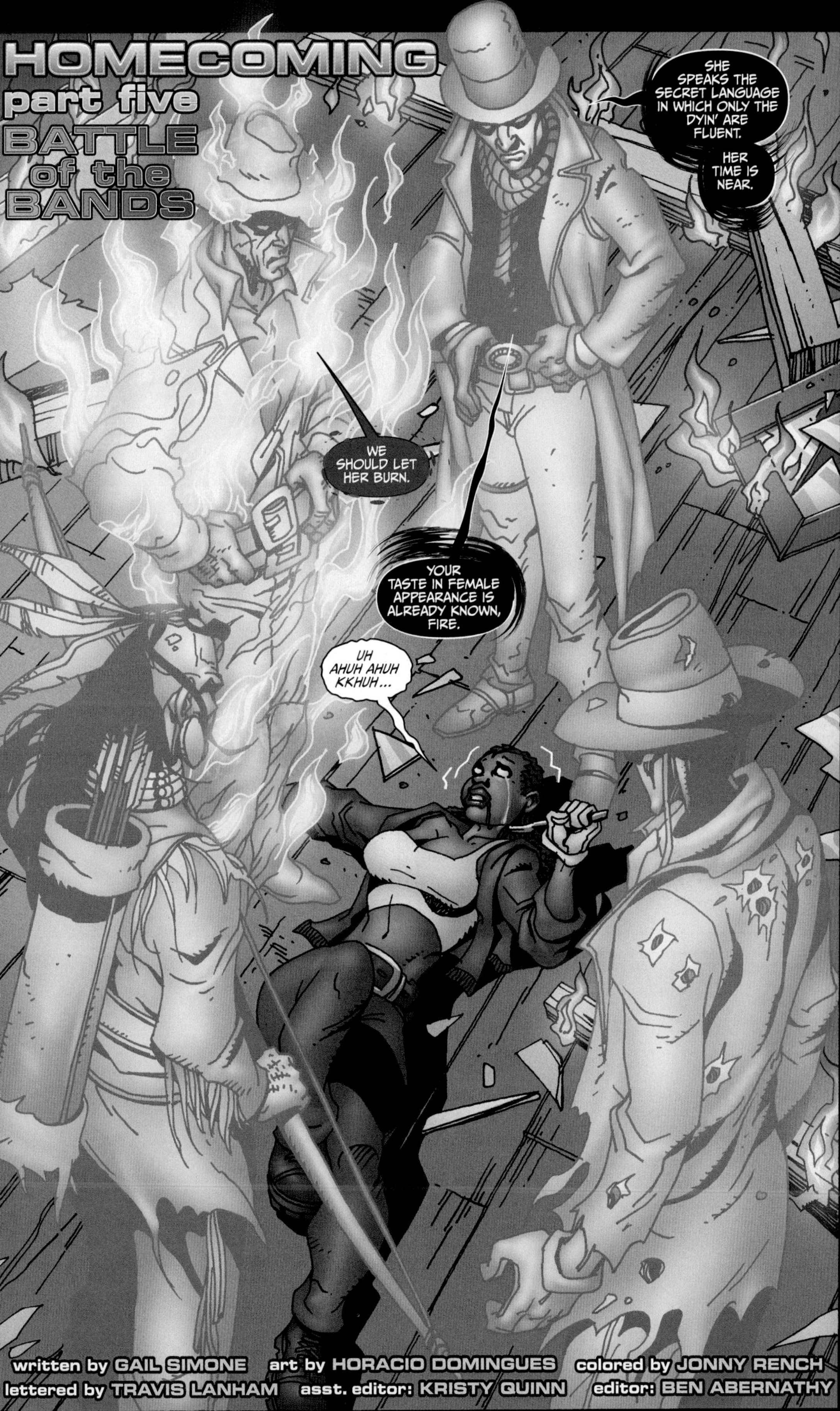

HOMECOMING
part five
BATTLE of the BANDS
SHE SPEAKS THE SECRET LANGUAGE IN WHICH ONLY THE DYIN' ARE FLUENT.
HER TIME IS NEAR.
WE SHOULD LET HER BURN.
YOUR TASTE IN FEMALE APPEARANCE IS ALREADY KNOWN, FIRE.
UH AHUH AHUH KKHUH...
written by GAIL SIMONE art by HORACIO DOMINGUES colored by JONNY RENCH
lettered by TRAVIS LANHAM asst. editor: KRISTY QUINN editor: BEN ABERNATHY

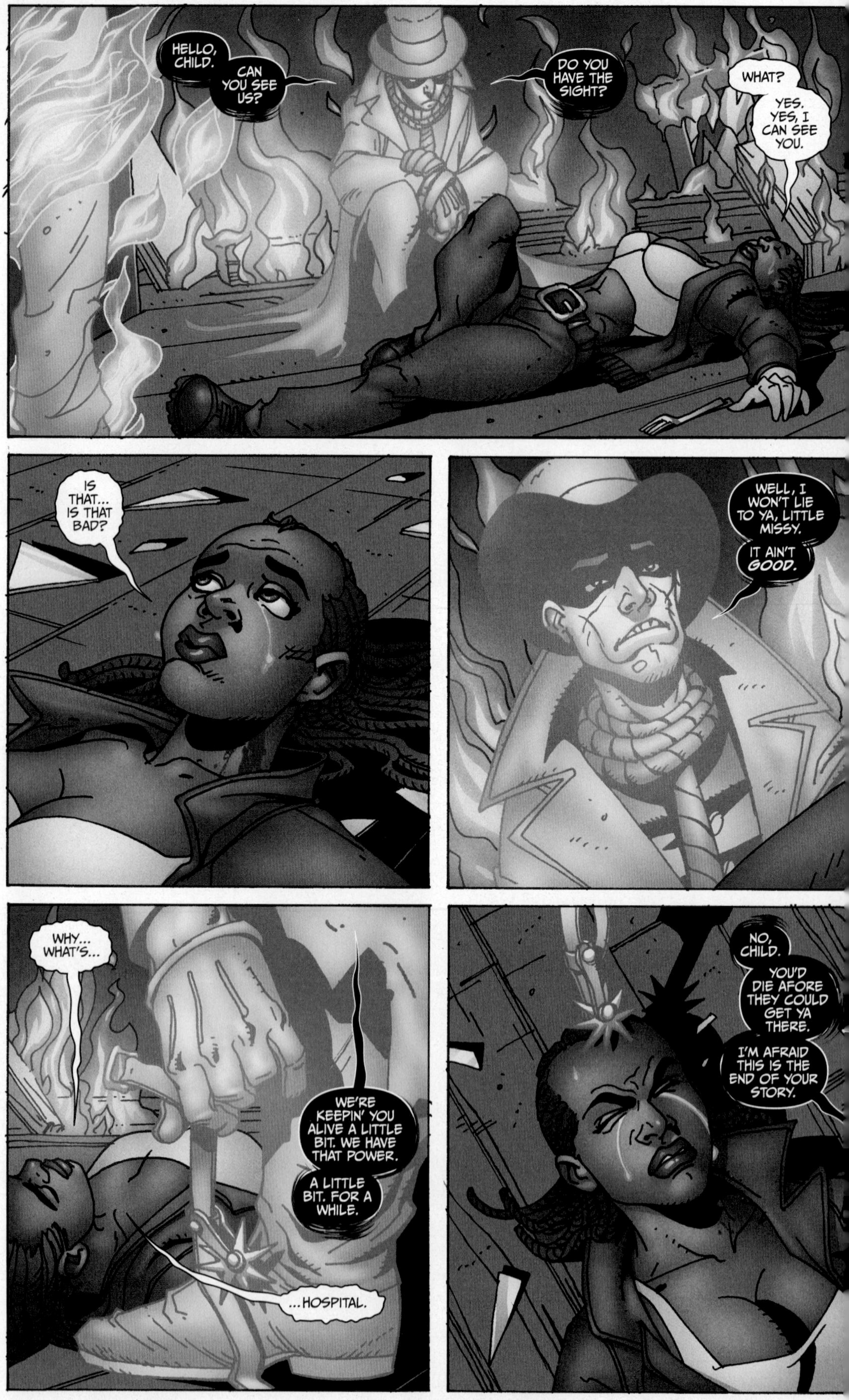
HELLO, CHILD.
CAN YOU SEE US?
DO YOU HAVE THE SIGHT?
WHAT?
YES. YES, I CAN SEE YOU.
IS THAT... IS THAT BAD?
WELL, I WON'T LIE TO YA, LITTLE MISSY.
IT AIN'T *GOOD.*
WHY... WHAT'S...
...HOSPITAL.
WE'RE KEEPIN' YOU ALIVE A LITTLE BIT. WE HAVE THAT POWER.
A LITTLE BIT. FOR A WHILE.
NO, CHILD.
YOU'D DIE AFORE THEY COULD GET YA THERE.
I'M AFRAID THIS IS THE END OF YOUR STORY.

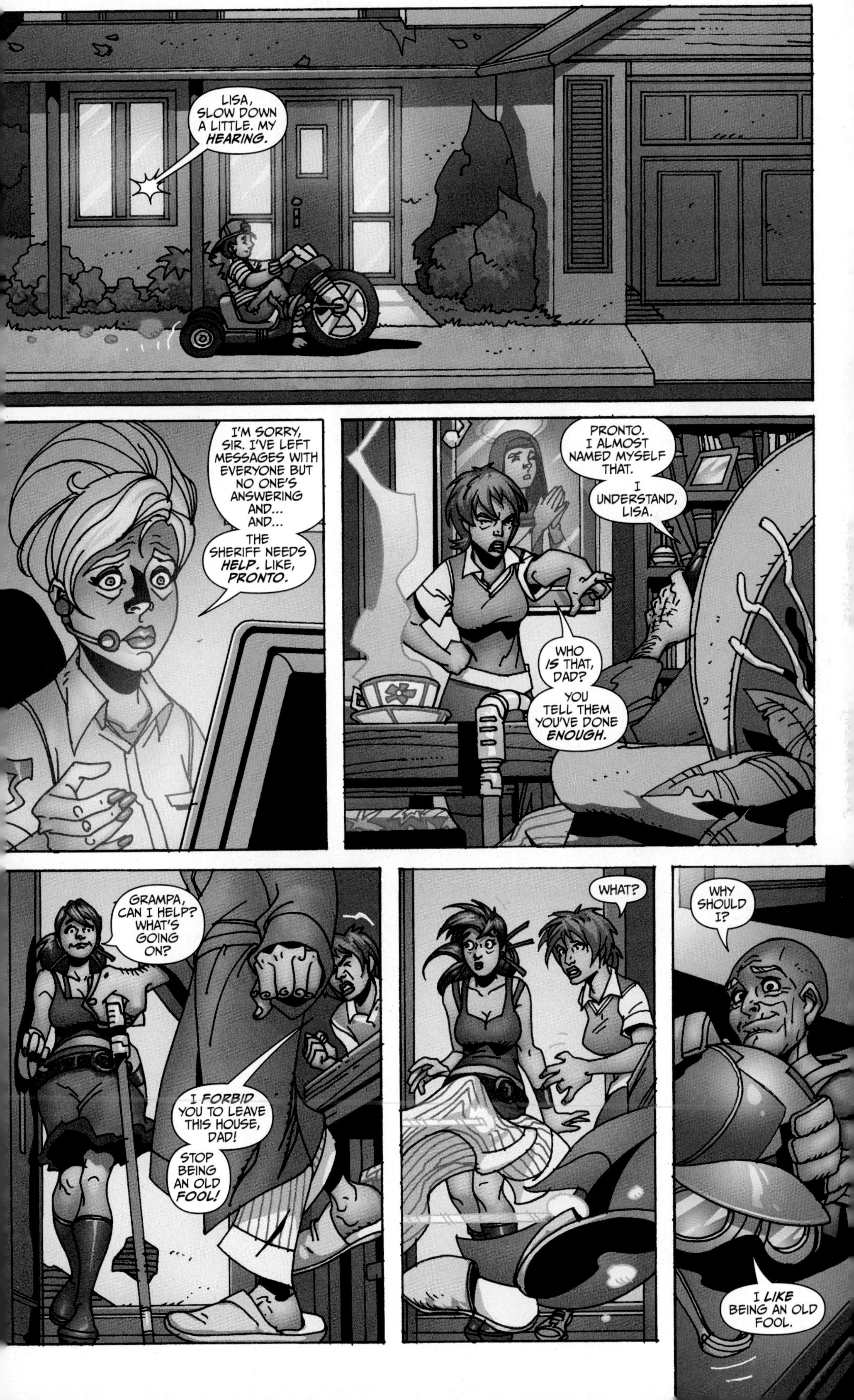
LISA, SLOW DOWN A LITTLE. MY *HEARING.*
I'M SORRY, SIR. I'VE LEFT MESSAGES WITH EVERYONE BUT NO ONE'S ANSWERING AND... AND...
THE SHERIFF NEEDS *HELP*. LIKE, *PRONTO.*
PRONTO. I ALMOST NAMED MYSELF THAT.
I UNDERSTAND, LISA.
WHO *IS* THAT, DAD?
YOU TELL THEM YOU'VE DONE *ENOUGH.*
GRAMPA, CAN I HELP? WHAT'S GOING ON?
I *FORBID* YOU TO LEAVE THIS HOUSE, DAD!
STOP BEING AN OLD *FOOL!*
WHAT?
WHY SHOULD I?
I *LIKE* BEING AN OLD FOOL.

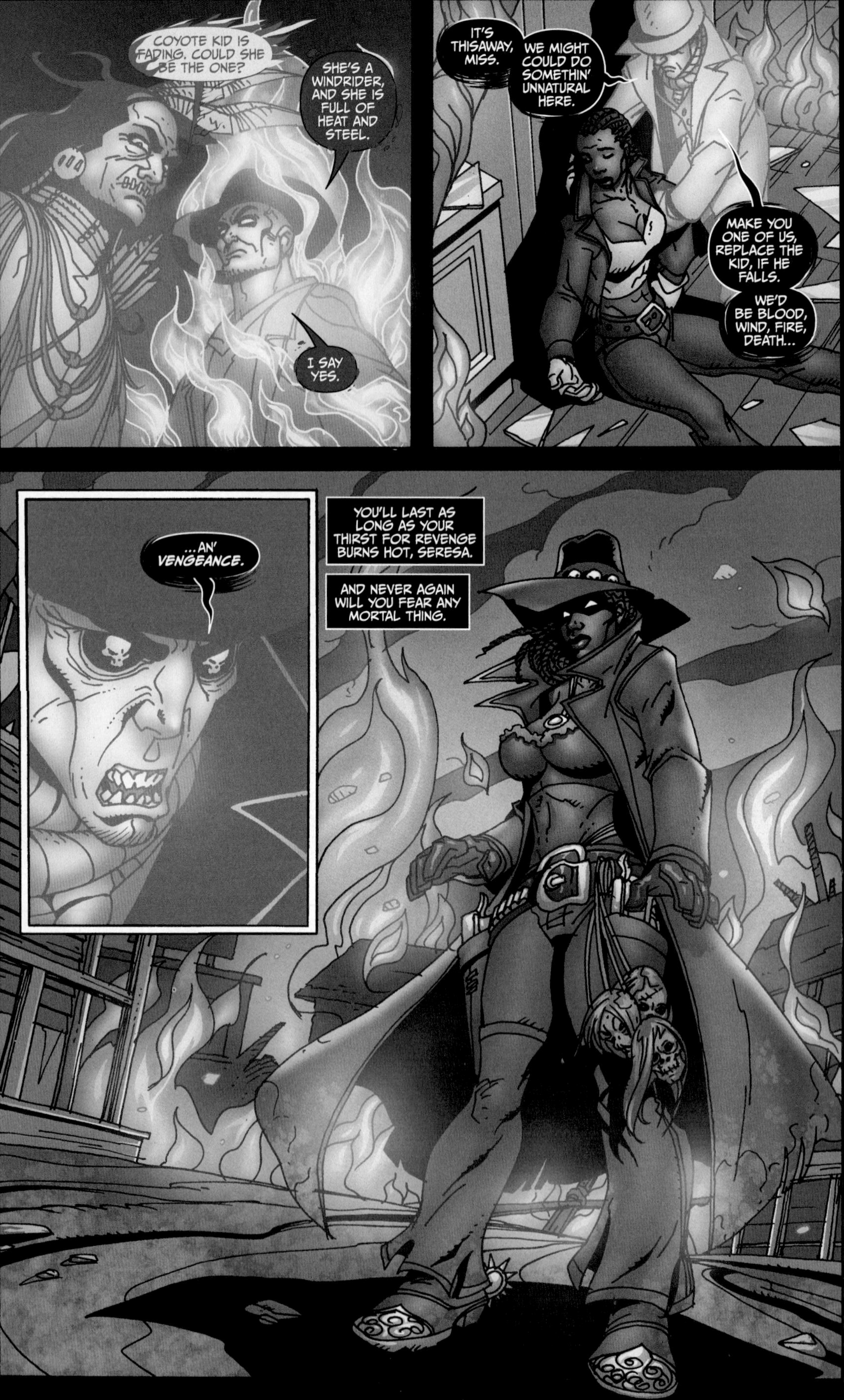
COYOTE KID IS FADING. COULD SHE BE THE ONE?
SHE'S A WINDRIDER, AND SHE IS FULL OF HEAT AND STEEL.
I SAY YES.
IT'S THISAWAY, MISS.
WE MIGHT COULD DO SOMETHIN' UNNATURAL HERE.
MAKE YOU ONE OF US, REPLACE THE KID, IF HE FALLS.
WE'D BE BLOOD, WIND, FIRE, DEATH...
...AN' *VENGEANCE.*
YOU'LL LAST AS LONG AS YOUR THIRST FOR REVENGE BURNS HOT, SERESA.
AND NEVER AGAIN WILL YOU FEAR ANY MORTAL THING.

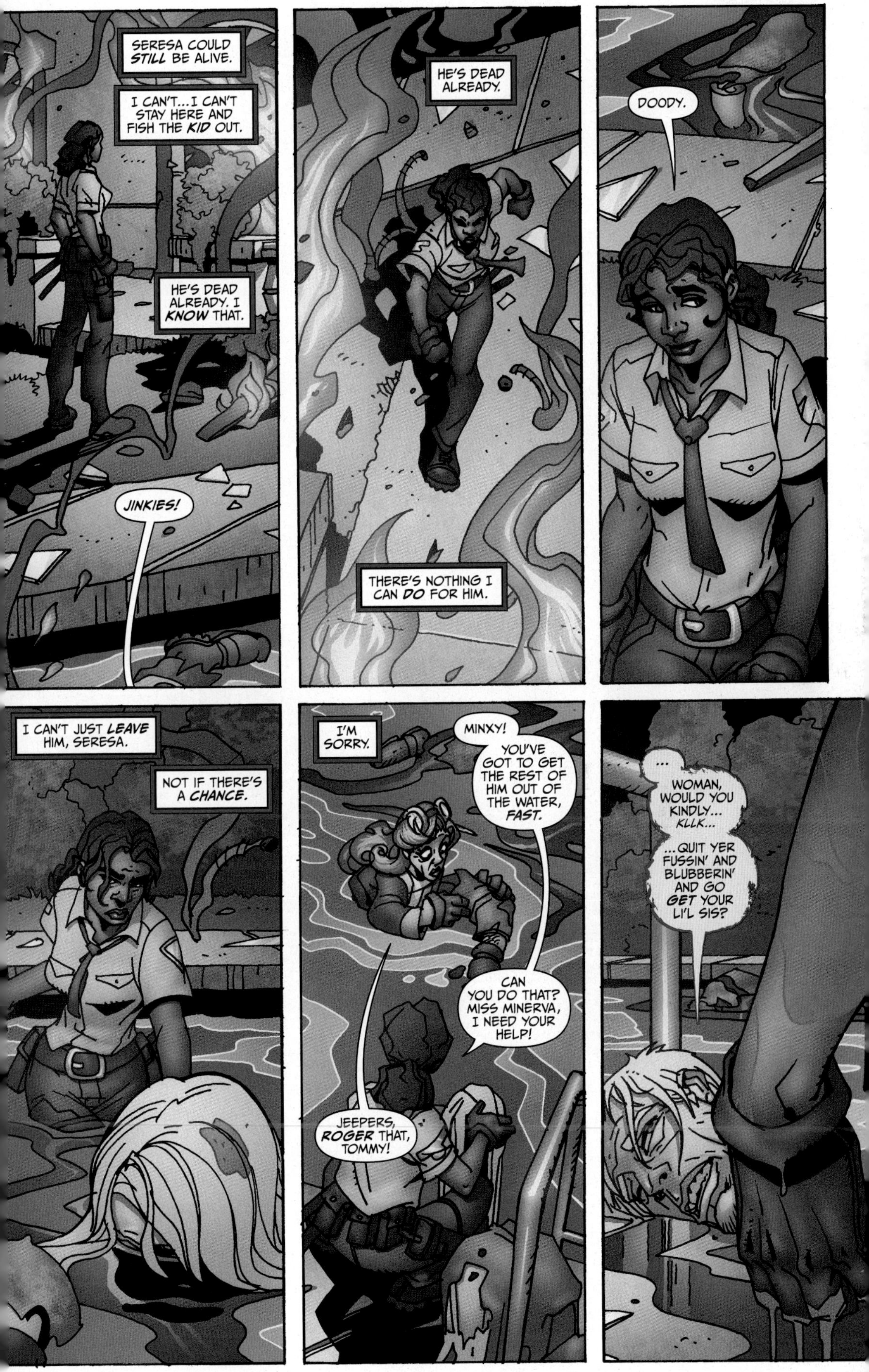

SERESA COULD STILL BE ALIVE.
I CAN'T...I CAN'T STAY HERE AND FISH THE KID OUT.
HE'S DEAD ALREADY. I KNOW THAT.
JINKIES!
HE'S DEAD ALREADY.
THERE'S NOTHING I CAN DO FOR HIM.
DOODY.
I CAN'T JUST LEAVE HIM, SERESA.
NOT IF THERE'S A CHANCE.
I'M SORRY.
MINXY!
YOU'VE GOT TO GET THE REST OF HIM OUT OF THE WATER, FAST.
CAN YOU DO THAT? MISS MINERVA, I NEED YOUR HELP!
JEEPERS, ROGER THAT, TOMMY!
...
WOMAN, WOULD YOU KINDLY... KLLK...
...QUIT YER FUSSIN' AND BLUBBERIN' AND GO GET YOUR LI'L SIS?

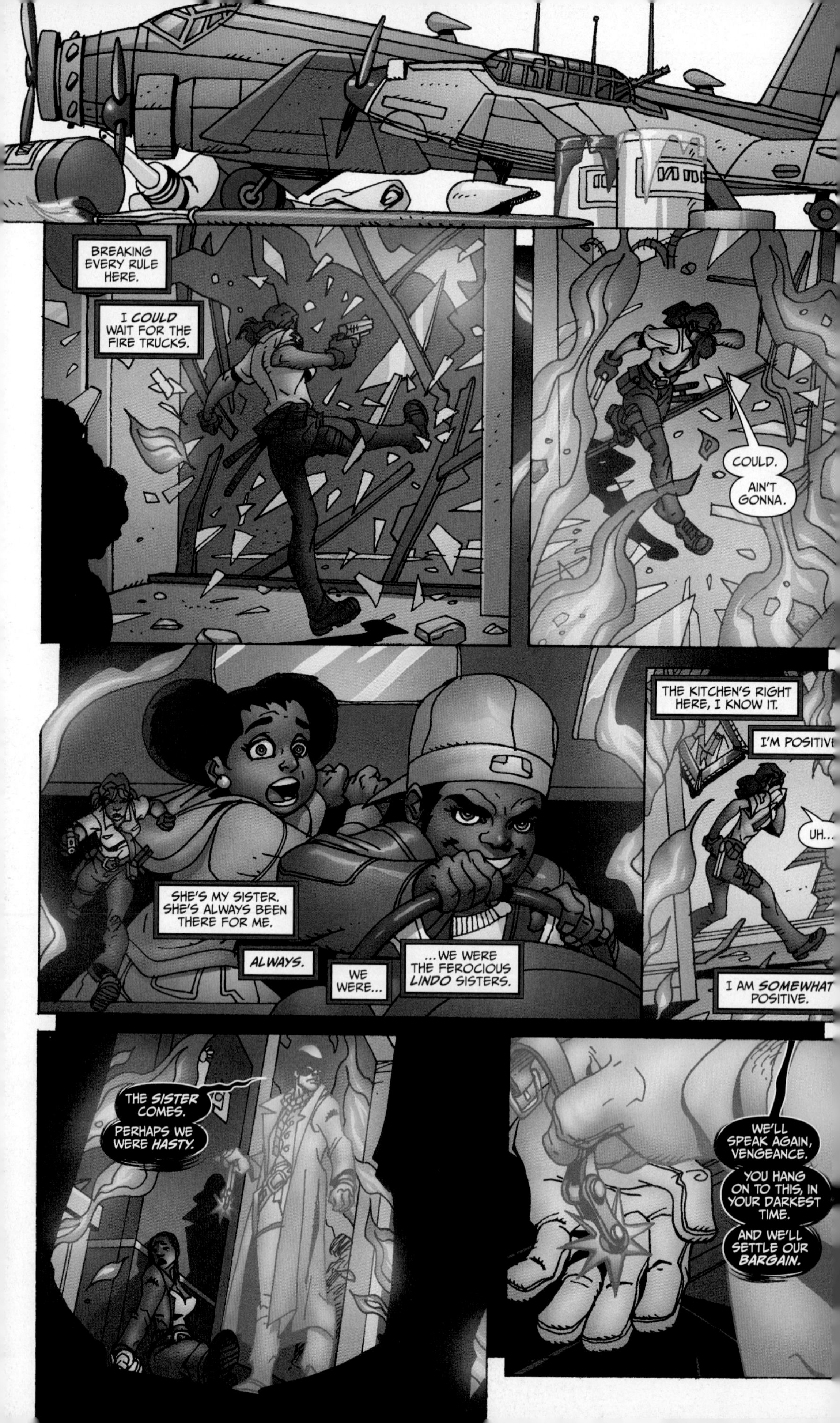

BREAKING EVERY RULE HERE.
I *COULD* WAIT FOR THE FIRE TRUCKS.
COULD.
AIN'T GONNA.
SHE'S MY SISTER. SHE'S ALWAYS BEEN THERE FOR ME.
ALWAYS.
WE WERE...
...WE WERE THE FEROCIOUS *LINDO* SISTERS.
THE KITCHEN'S RIGHT HERE, I KNOW IT.
I'M POSITIVE
UH...
I AM *SOMEWHAT* POSITIVE.
THE *SISTER* COMES.
PERHAPS WE WERE *HASTY.*
WE'LL SPEAK AGAIN, VENGEANCE.
YOU HANG ON TO THIS, IN YOUR DARKEST TIME.
AND WE'LL SETTLE OUR *BARGAIN.*

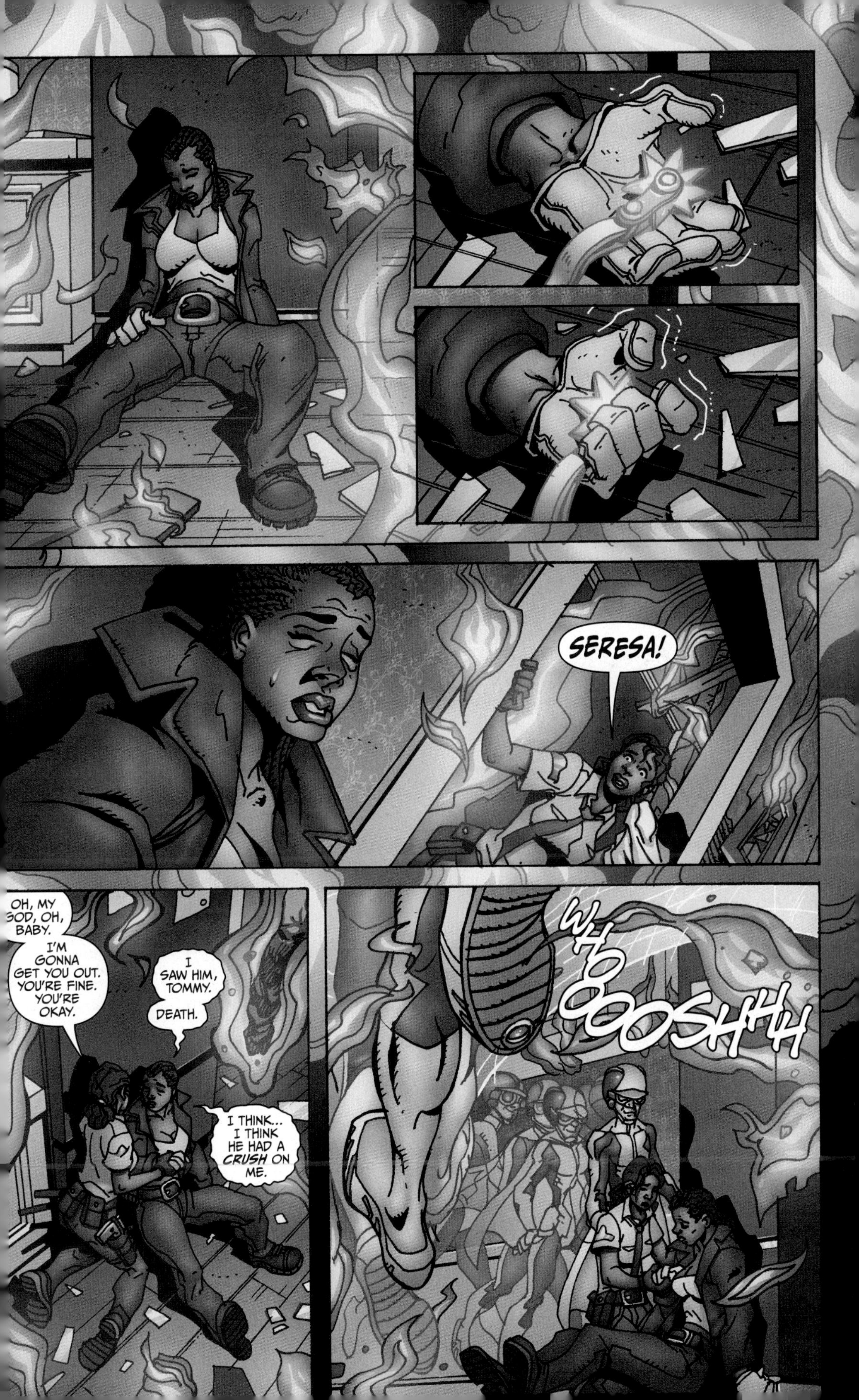
SERESA!
OH, MY GOD, OH, BABY.
I'M GONNA GET YOU OUT. YOU'RE FINE. YOU'RE OKAY.
I SAW HIM, TOMMY.
DEATH.
I THINK... I THINK HE HAD A CRUSH ON ME.
WHOOOOOSHHH

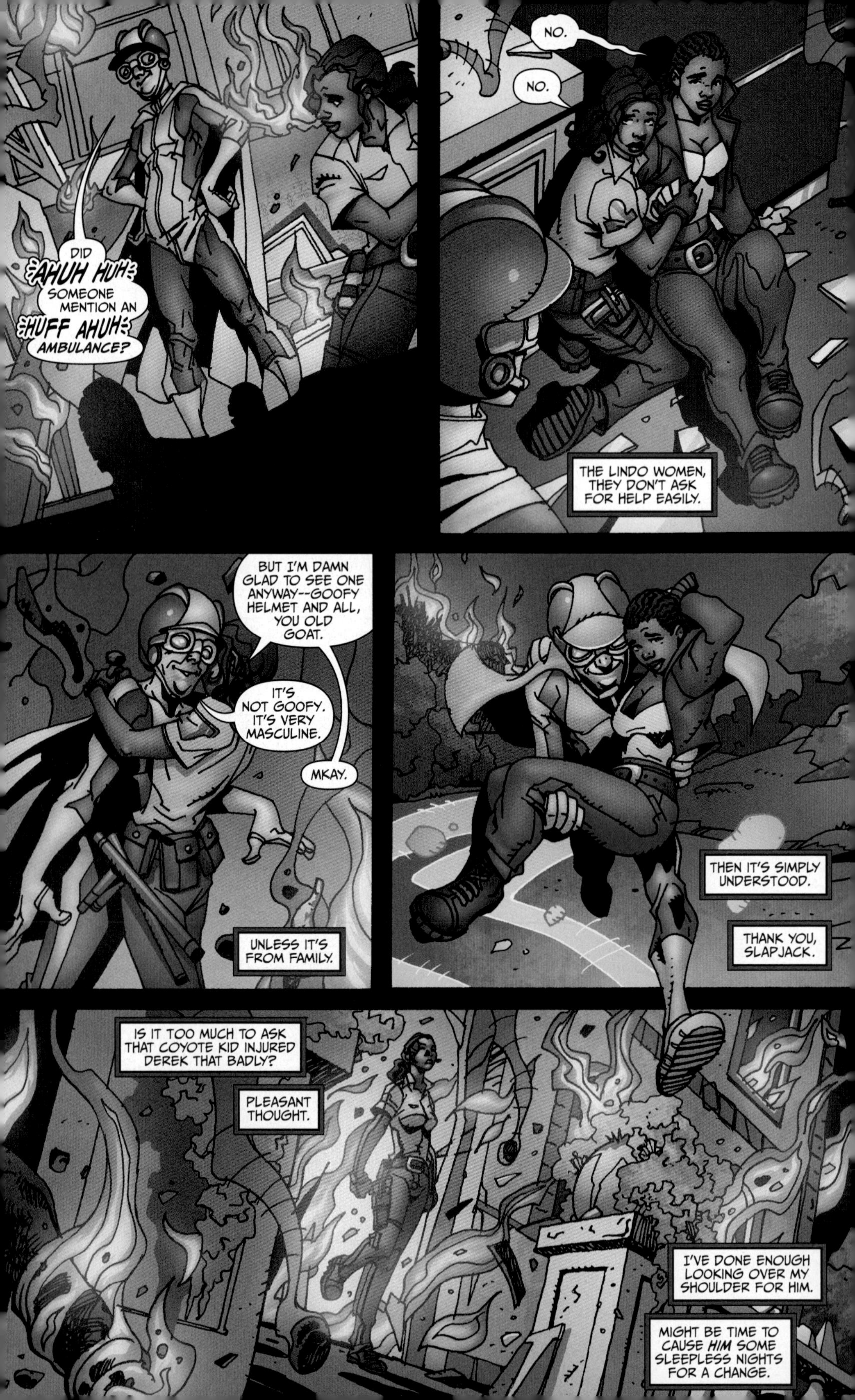
DID AHUH HUH SOMEONE MENTION AN HUFF AHUH AMBULANCE?
NO.
NO.
THE LINDO WOMEN, THEY DON'T ASK FOR HELP EASILY.
BUT I'M DAMN GLAD TO SEE ONE ANYWAY--GOOFY HELMET AND ALL, YOU OLD GOAT.
IT'S NOT GOOFY. IT'S VERY MASCULINE.
MKAY.
UNLESS IT'S FROM FAMILY.
THEN IT'S SIMPLY UNDERSTOOD.
THANK YOU, SLAPJACK.
IS IT TOO MUCH TO ASK THAT COYOTE KID INJURED DEREK THAT BADLY?
PLEASANT THOUGHT.
I'VE DONE ENOUGH LOOKING OVER MY SHOULDER FOR HIM.
MIGHT BE TIME TO CAUSE HIM SOME SLEEPLESS NIGHTS FOR A CHANGE.

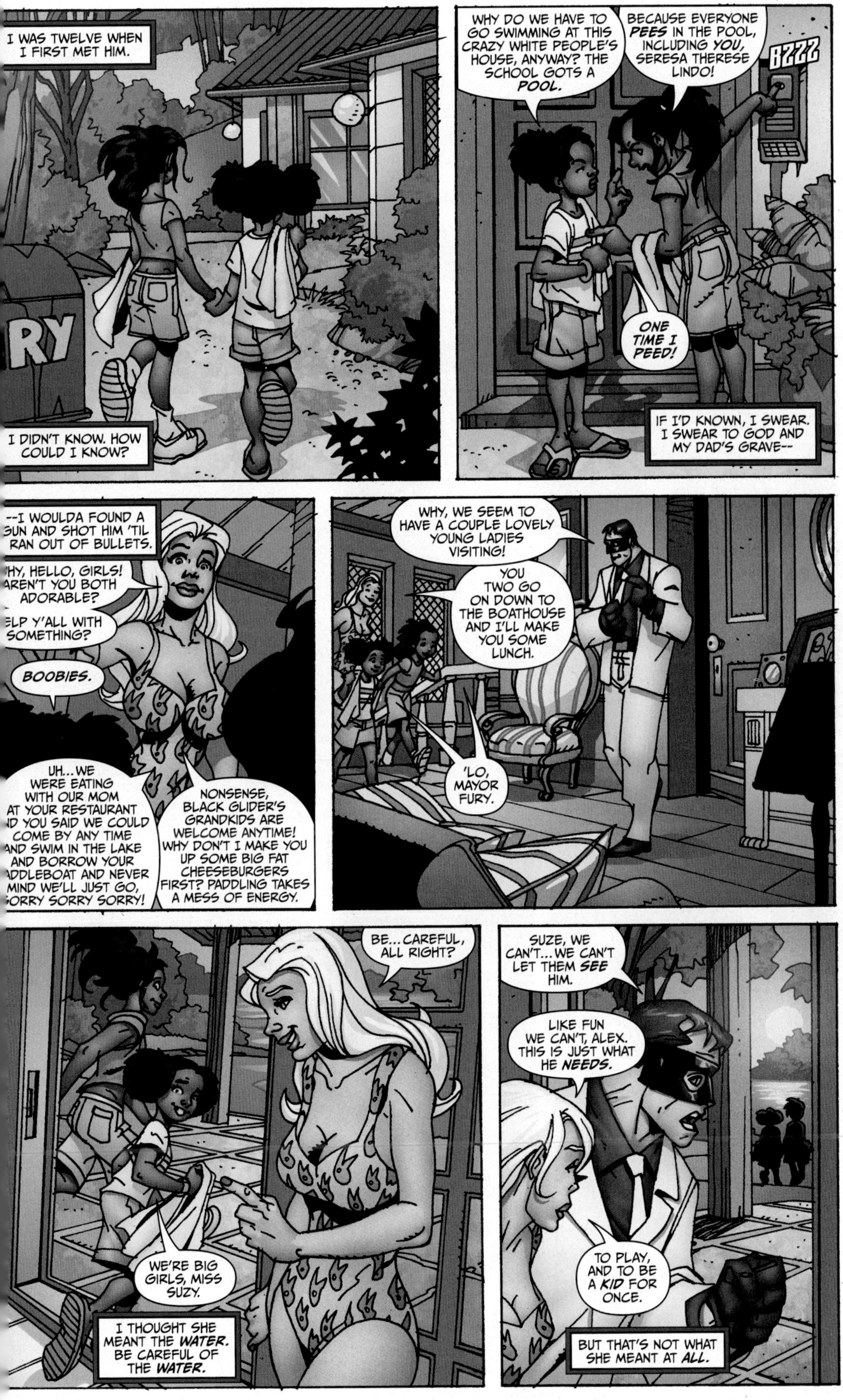
I WAS TWELVE WHEN I FIRST MET HIM.
RY
I DIDN'T KNOW. HOW COULD I KNOW?
WHY DO WE HAVE TO GO SWIMMING AT THIS CRAZY WHITE PEOPLE'S HOUSE, ANYWAY? THE SCHOOL GOTS A POOL.
BECAUSE EVERYONE PEES IN THE POOL, INCLUDING YOU, SERESA THERESE LINDO!
BZZZ
ONE TIME I PEED!
IF I'D KNOWN, I SWEAR. I SWEAR TO GOD AND MY DAD'S GRAVE--
--I WOULDA FOUND A GUN AND SHOT HIM 'TIL RAN OUT OF BULLETS.
HY, HELLO, GIRLS! AREN'T YOU BOTH ADORABLE?
ELP Y'ALL WITH SOMETHING?
BOOBIES.
UH...WE WERE EATING WITH OUR MOM AT YOUR RESTAURANT D YOU SAID WE COULD COME BY ANY TIME AND SWIM IN THE LAKE AND BORROW YOUR ADDLEBOAT AND NEVER MIND WE'LL JUST GO, ORRY SORRY SORRY!
NONSENSE, BLACK GLIDER'S GRANDKIDS ARE WELCOME ANYTIME! WHY DON'T I MAKE YOU UP SOME BIG FAT CHEESEBURGERS FIRST? PADDLING TAKES A MESS OF ENERGY.
WHY, WE SEEM TO HAVE A COUPLE LOVELY YOUNG LADIES VISITING!
YOU TWO GO ON DOWN TO THE BOATHOUSE AND I'LL MAKE YOU SOME LUNCH.
'LO, MAYOR FURY.
BE...CAREFUL, ALL RIGHT?
WE'RE BIG GIRLS, MISS SUZY.
I THOUGHT SHE MEANT THE WATER. BE CAREFUL OF THE WATER.
SUZE, WE CAN'T...WE CAN'T LET THEM SEE HIM.
LIKE FUN WE CAN'T, ALEX. THIS IS JUST WHAT HE NEEDS.
TO PLAY, AND TO BE A KID FOR ONCE.
BUT THAT'S NOT WHAT SHE MEANT AT ALL.

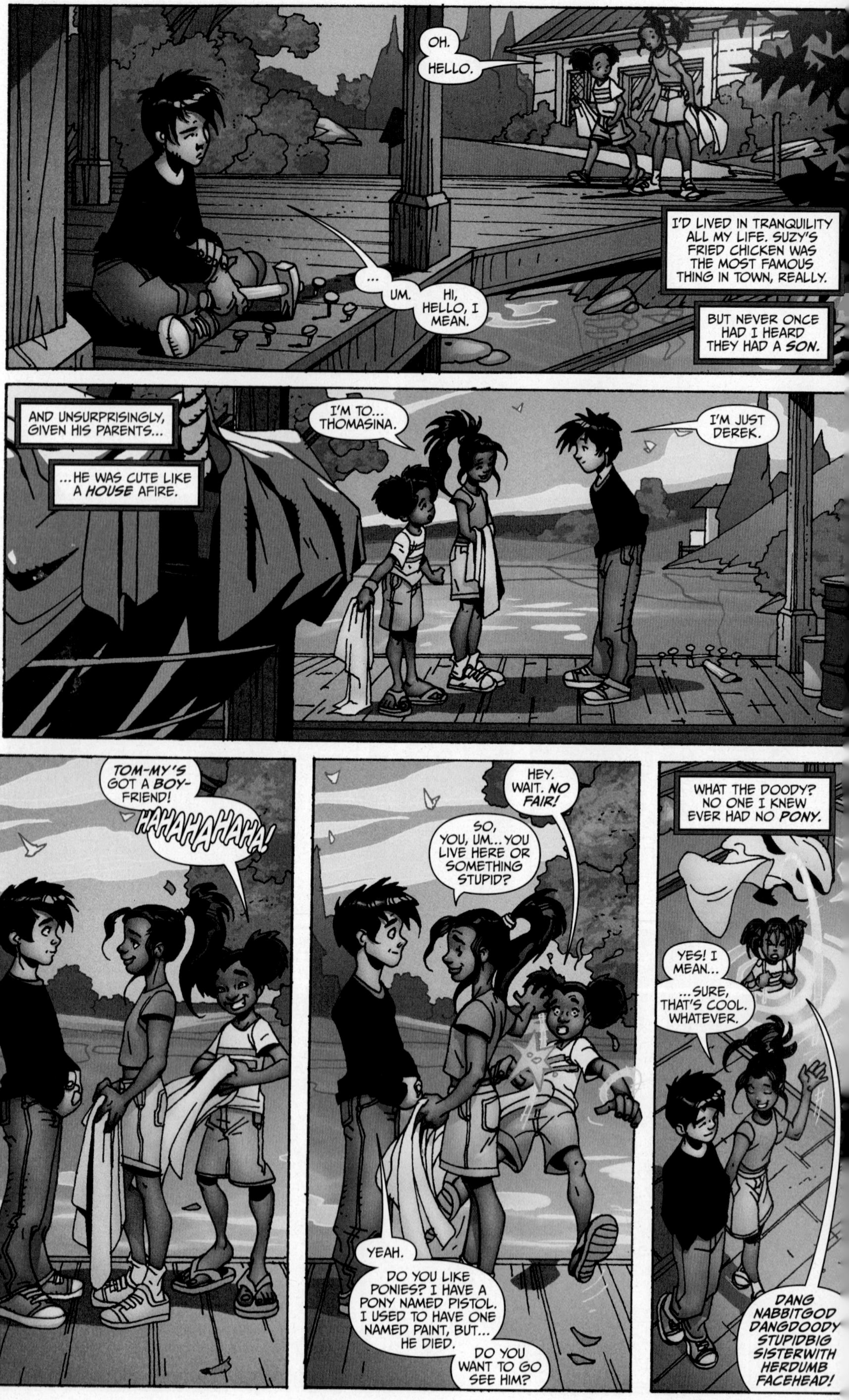

OH.
HELLO.
...
UM.
HI, HELLO, I MEAN.
I'D LIVED IN TRANQUILITY ALL MY LIFE. SUZY'S FRIED CHICKEN WAS THE MOST FAMOUS THING IN TOWN, REALLY.
BUT NEVER ONCE HAD I HEARD THEY HAD A *SON*.
AND UNSURPRISINGLY, GIVEN HIS PARENTS...
...HE WAS CUTE LIKE A *HOUSE* AFIRE.
I'M TO... THOMASINA.
I'M JUST DEREK.
TOM-MY'S GOT A *BOY-*FRIEND!
HAHAHAHAHAHA!
HEY. WAIT. *NO FAIR!*
SO, YOU, UM... YOU LIVE HERE OR SOMETHING STUPID?
YEAH.
DO YOU LIKE PONIES? I HAVE A PONY NAMED PISTOL. I USED TO HAVE ONE NAMED PAINT, BUT... HE DIED.
DO YOU WANT TO GO SEE HIM?
WHAT THE DOODY? NO ONE I KNEW EVER HAD NO *PONY*.
YES! I MEAN...
...SURE, THAT'S COOL. WHATEVER.
DANG NABBITGOD DANGDOODY STUPIDBIG SISTERWITH HERDUMB FACEHEAD!

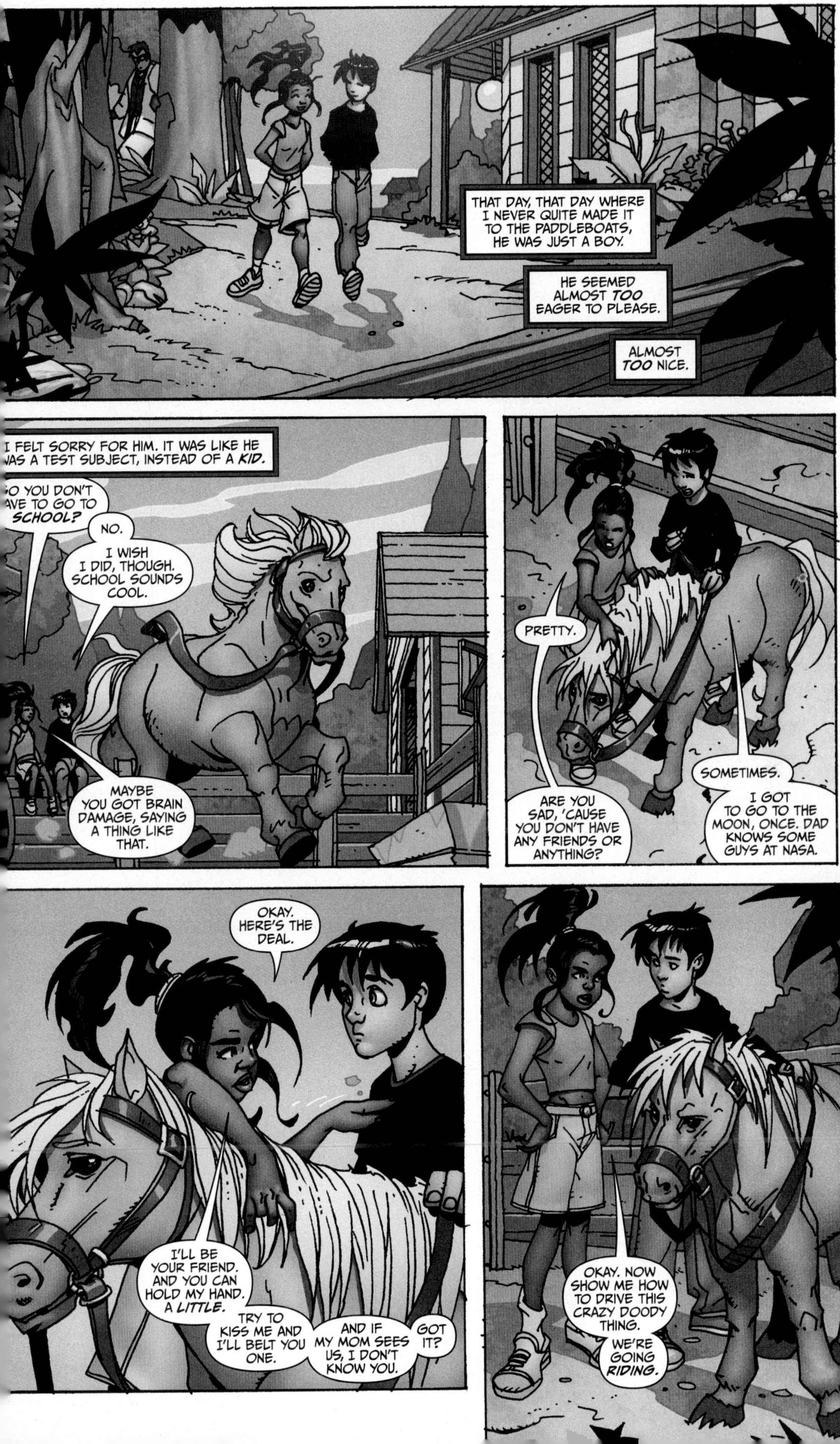
THAT DAY, THAT DAY WHERE I NEVER QUITE MADE IT TO THE PADDLEBOATS, HE WAS JUST A BOY.
HE SEEMED ALMOST *TOO* EAGER TO PLEASE.
ALMOST *TOO* NICE.
I FELT SORRY FOR HIM. IT WAS LIKE HE WAS A TEST SUBJECT, INSTEAD OF A *KID.*
SO YOU DON'T HAVE TO GO TO *SCHOOL?*
NO.
I WISH I DID, THOUGH. SCHOOL SOUNDS COOL.
MAYBE YOU GOT BRAIN DAMAGE, SAYING A THING LIKE THAT.
PRETTY.
ARE YOU SAD, 'CAUSE YOU DON'T HAVE ANY FRIENDS OR ANYTHING?
SOMETIMES.
I GOT TO GO TO THE MOON, ONCE. DAD KNOWS SOME GUYS AT NASA.
OKAY. HERE'S THE DEAL.
I'LL BE YOUR FRIEND. AND YOU CAN HOLD MY HAND. A *LITTLE.*
TRY TO KISS ME AND I'LL BELT YOU ONE.
AND IF MY MOM SEES US, I DON'T KNOW YOU.
GOT IT?
OKAY. NOW SHOW ME HOW TO DRIVE THIS CRAZY DOODY THING.
WE'RE GOING *RIDING.*

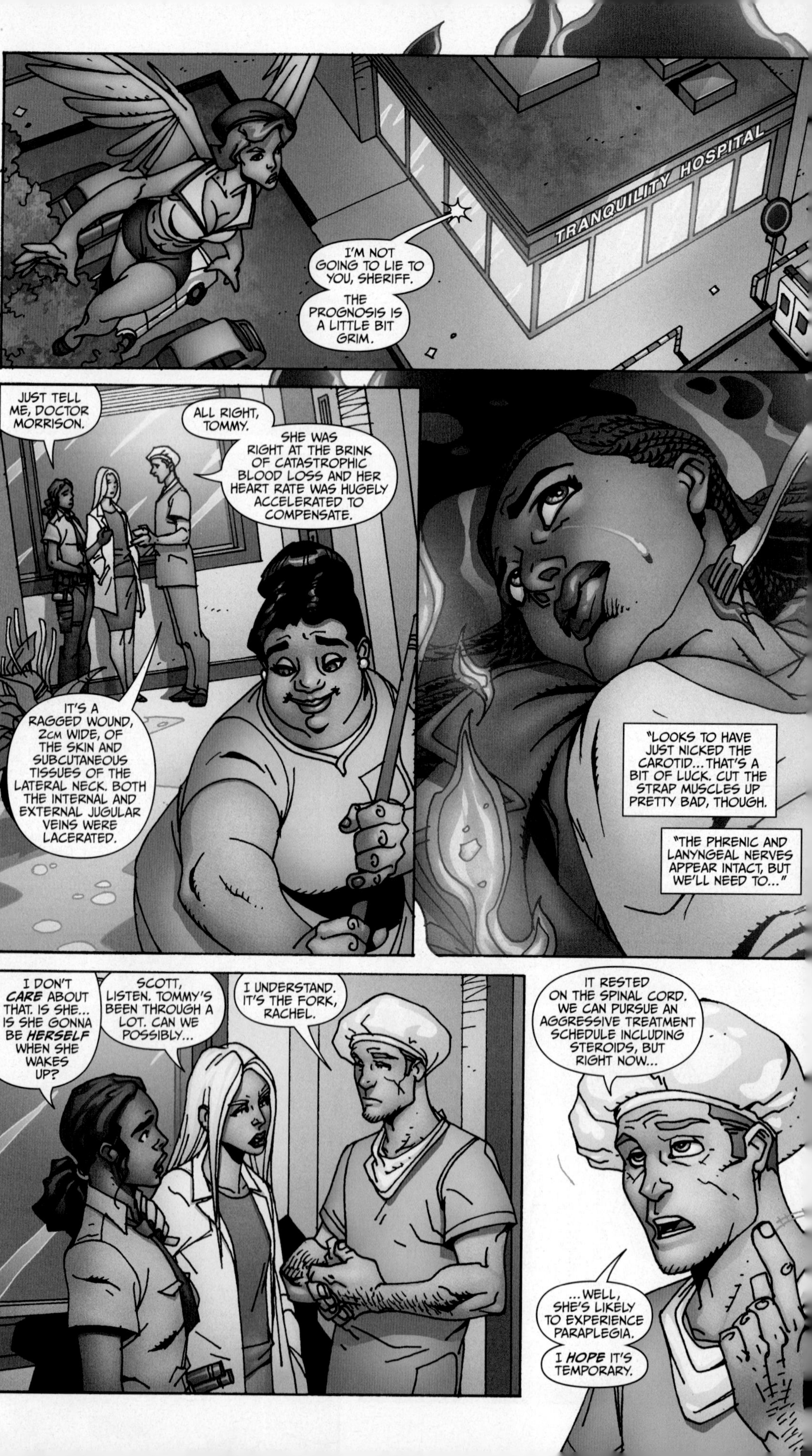
TRANQUILITY HOSPITAL
I'M NOT GOING TO LIE TO YOU, SHERIFF.
THE PROGNOSIS IS A LITTLE BIT GRIM.
JUST TELL ME, DOCTOR MORRISON.
ALL RIGHT, TOMMY.
SHE WAS RIGHT AT THE BRINK OF CATASTROPHIC BLOOD LOSS AND HER HEART RATE WAS HUGELY ACCELERATED TO COMPENSATE.
IT'S A RAGGED WOUND, 2CM WIDE, OF THE SKIN AND SUBCUTANEOUS TISSUES OF THE LATERAL NECK. BOTH THE INTERNAL AND EXTERNAL JUGULAR VEINS WERE LACERATED.
"LOOKS TO HAVE JUST NICKED THE CAROTID... THAT'S A BIT OF LUCK. CUT THE STRAP MUSCLES UP PRETTY BAD, THOUGH.
"THE PHRENIC AND LANYNGEAL NERVES APPEAR INTACT, BUT WE'LL NEED TO..."
I DON'T *CARE* ABOUT THAT. IS SHE... IS SHE GONNA BE *HERSELF* WHEN SHE WAKES UP?
SCOTT, LISTEN. TOMMY'S BEEN THROUGH A LOT. CAN WE POSSIBLY...
I UNDERSTAND. IT'S THE FORK, RACHEL.
IT RESTED ON THE SPINAL CORD. WE CAN PURSUE AN AGGRESSIVE TREATMENT SCHEDULE INCLUDING STEROIDS, BUT RIGHT NOW...
...WELL, SHE'S LIKELY TO EXPERIENCE PARAPLEGIA.
I *HOPE* IT'S TEMPORARY.

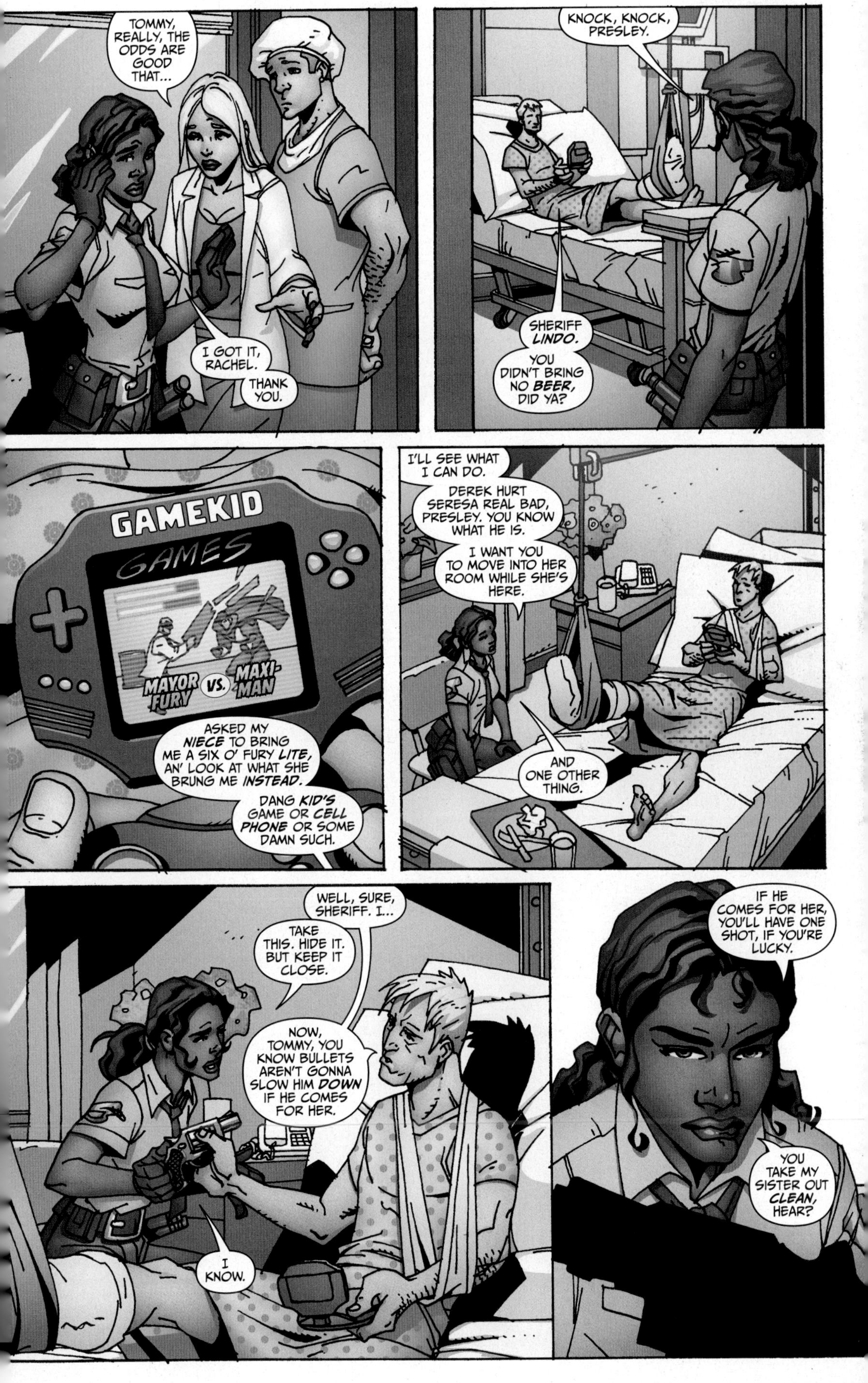
TOMMY, REALLY, THE ODDS ARE GOOD THAT...
I GOT IT, RACHEL.
THANK YOU.
KNOCK, KNOCK, PRESLEY.
SHERIFF LINDO.
YOU DIDN'T BRING NO BEER, DID YA?
GAMEKID
GAMES
MAYOR FURY
VS.
MAXI-MAN
ASKED MY NIECE TO BRING ME A SIX O' FURY LITE, AN' LOOK AT WHAT SHE BRUNG ME INSTEAD.
DANG KID'S GAME OR CELL PHONE OR SOME DAMN SUCH.
I'LL SEE WHAT I CAN DO.
DEREK HURT SERESA REAL BAD, PRESLEY. YOU KNOW WHAT HE IS.
I WANT YOU TO MOVE INTO HER ROOM WHILE SHE'S HERE.
AND ONE OTHER THING.
WELL, SURE, SHERIFF. I...
TAKE THIS. HIDE IT. BUT KEEP IT CLOSE.
NOW, TOMMY, YOU KNOW BULLETS AREN'T GONNA SLOW HIM DOWN IF HE COMES FOR HER.
I KNOW.
IF HE COMES FOR HER, YOU'LL HAVE ONE SHOT, IF YOU'RE LUCKY.
YOU TAKE MY SISTER OUT CLEAN, HEAR?

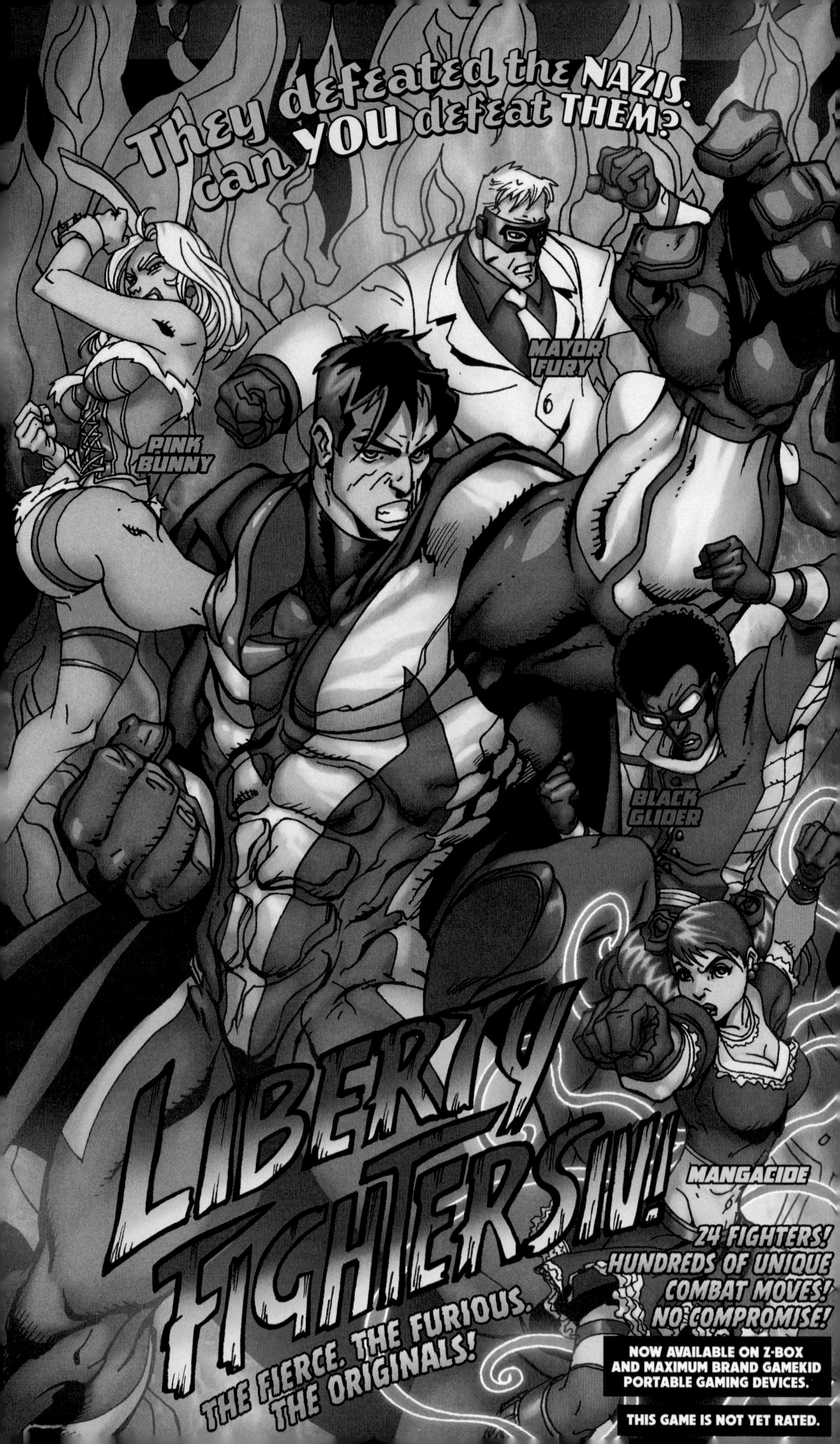

They defeated the NAZIS.
can YOU defeat THEM?
MAYOR FURY
PINK BUNNY
BLACK GLIDER
MANGACIDE
LIBERTY FIGHTERS IV!
THE FIERCE. THE FURIOUS. THE ORIGINALS!
24 FIGHTERS!
HUNDREDS OF UNIQUE COMBAT MOVES!
NO COMPROMISE!
NOW AVAILABLE ON Z-BOX AND MAXIMUM BRAND GAMEKID PORTABLE GAMING DEVICES.
THIS GAME IS NOT YET RATED.

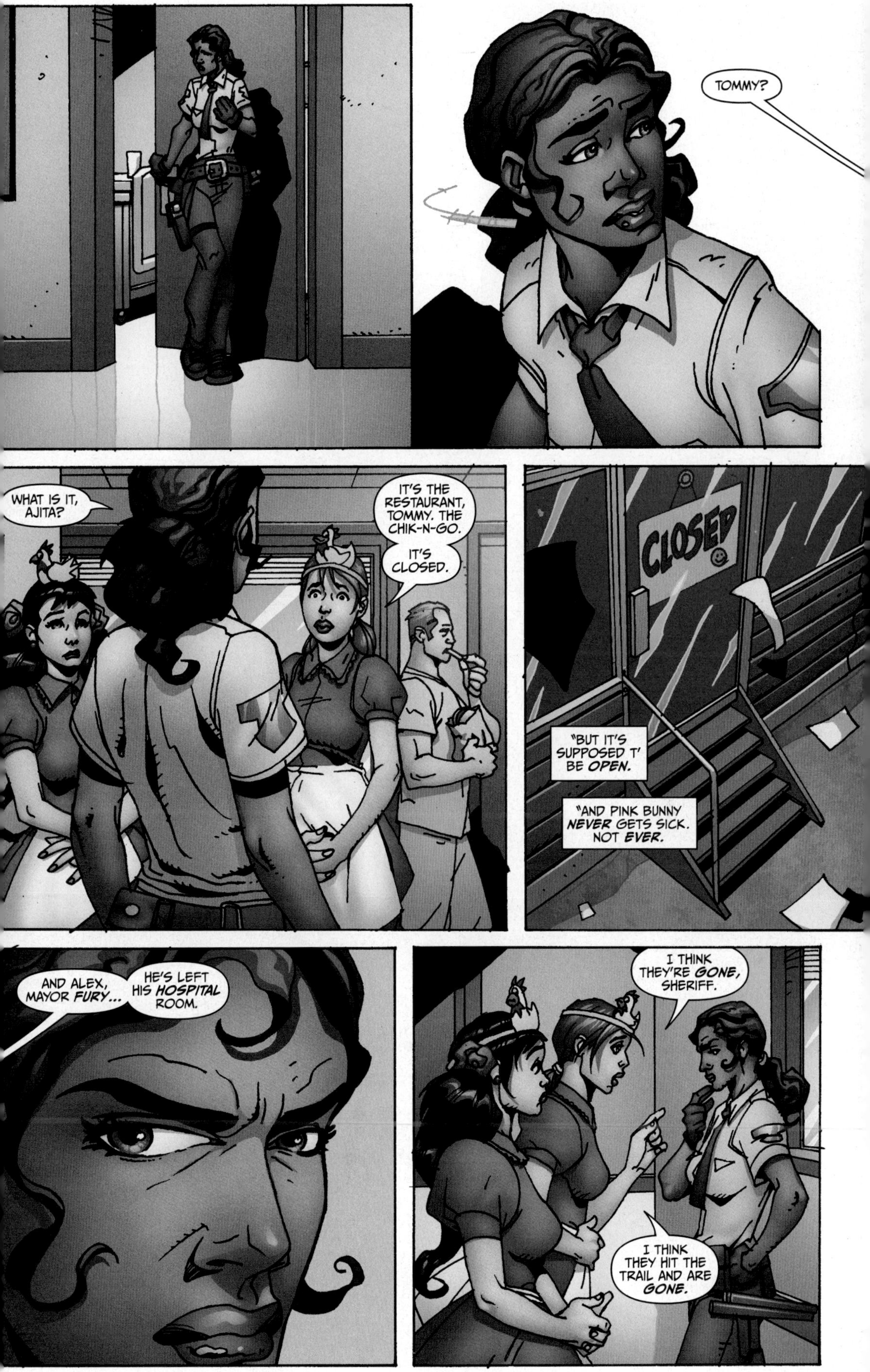
TOMMY?
WHAT IS IT, AJITA?
IT'S THE RESTAURANT, TOMMY. THE CHIK-N-GO.
IT'S CLOSED.
CLOSED
"BUT IT'S SUPPOSED T' BE *OPEN*.
"AND PINK BUNNY *NEVER* GETS SICK. NOT *EVER*.
AND ALEX, MAYOR *FURY*...
HE'S LEFT HIS *HOSPITAL* ROOM.
I THINK THEY'RE *GONE*, SHERIFF.
I THINK THEY HIT THE TRAIL AND ARE *GONE*.

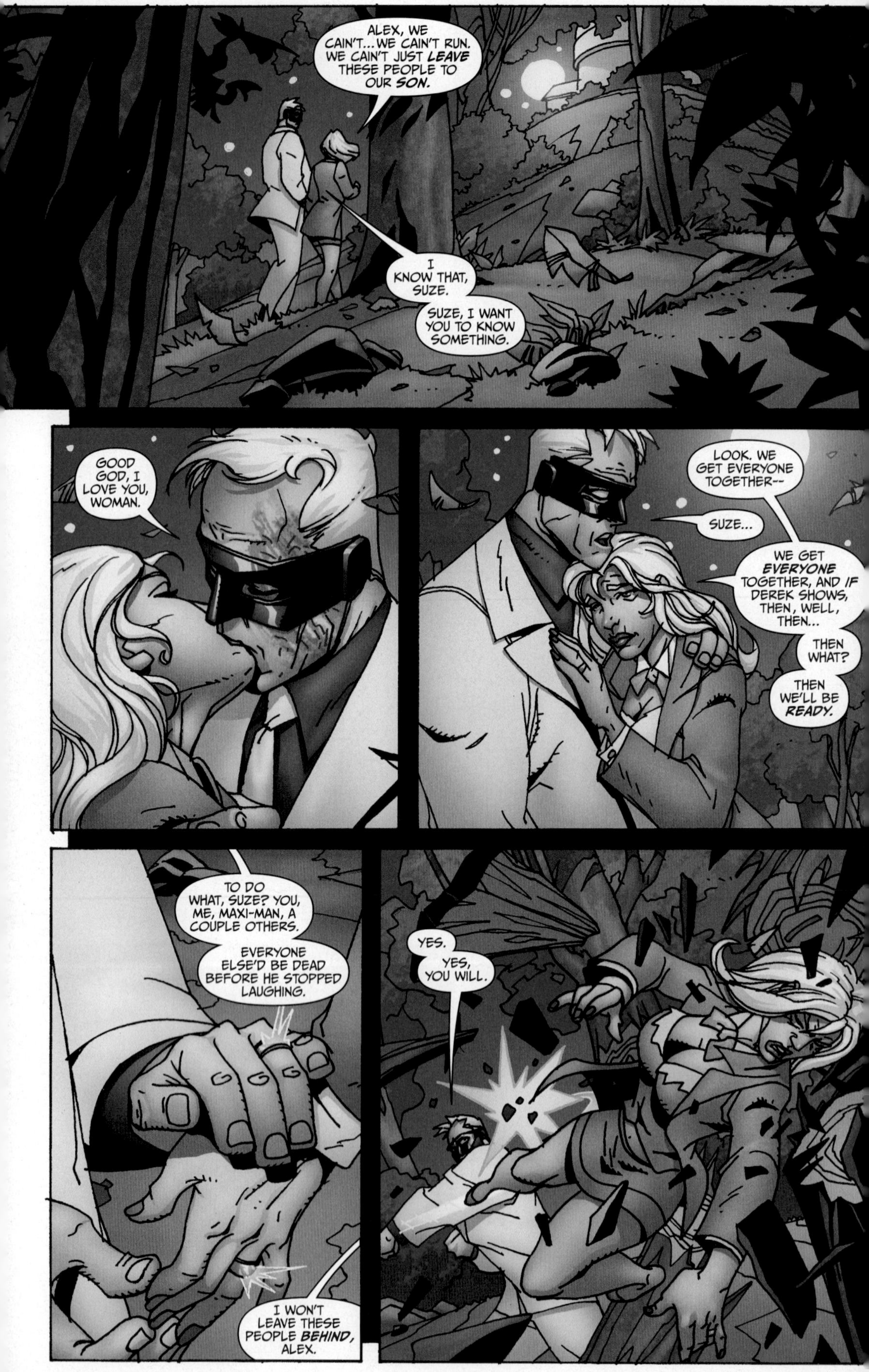
ALEX, WE CAIN'T... WE CAIN'T RUN. WE CAIN'T JUST *LEAVE* THESE PEOPLE TO OUR *SON.*
I KNOW THAT, SUZE.
SUZE, I WANT YOU TO KNOW SOMETHING.
GOOD GOD, I LOVE YOU, WOMAN.
LOOK. WE GET EVERYONE TOGETHER--
SUZE...
WE GET *EVERYONE* TOGETHER, AND *IF* DEREK SHOWS, THEN, WELL, THEN...
THEN WHAT?
THEN WE'LL BE *READY.*
TO DO WHAT, SUZE? YOU, ME, MAXI-MAN, A COUPLE OTHERS.
EVERYONE ELSE'D BE DEAD BEFORE HE STOPPED LAUGHING.
I WON'T LEAVE THESE PEOPLE *BEHIND,* ALEX.
YES.
YES, YOU WILL.

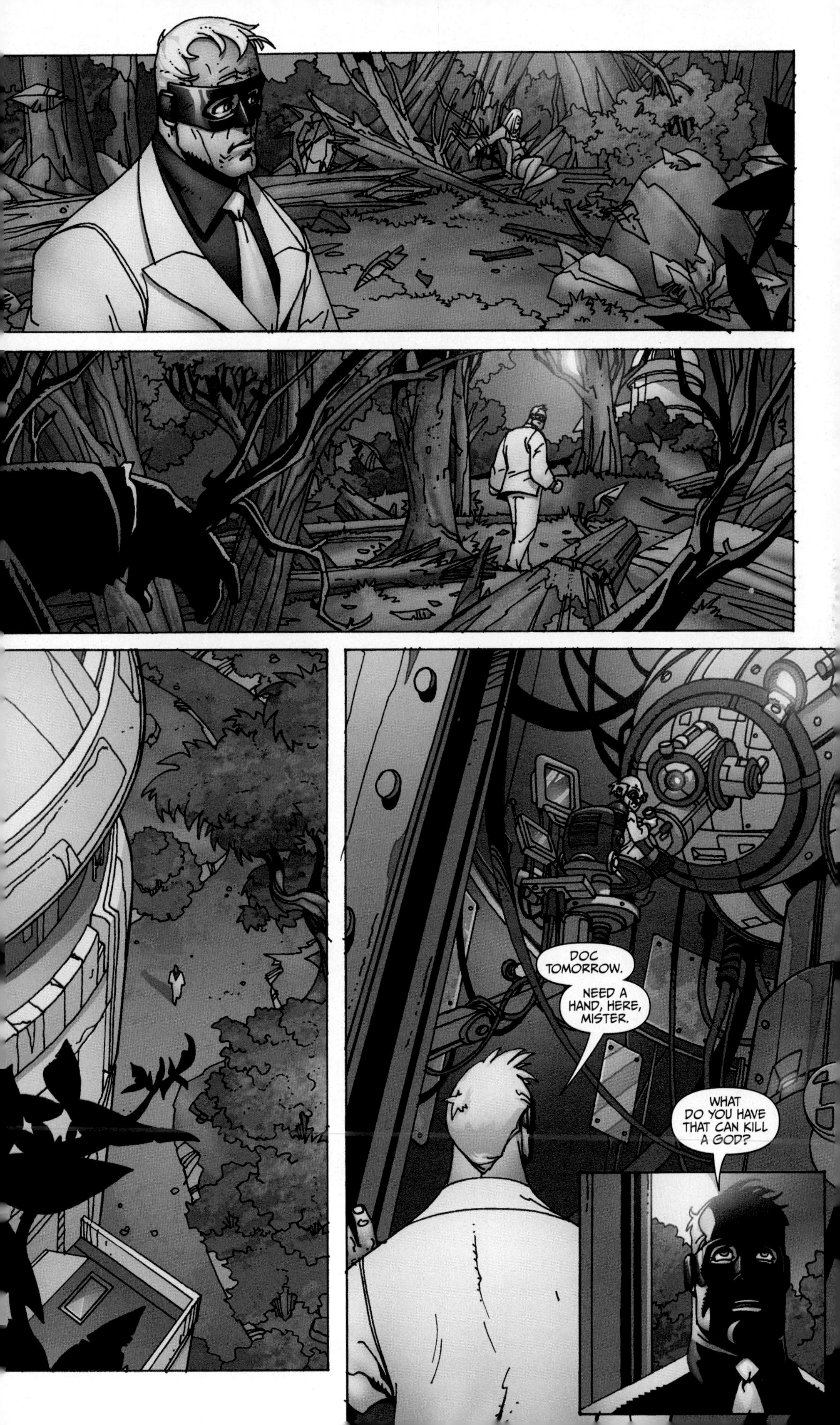
DOC TOMORROW.
NEED A HAND, HERE, MISTER.
WHAT DO YOU HAVE THAT CAN KILL A GOD?

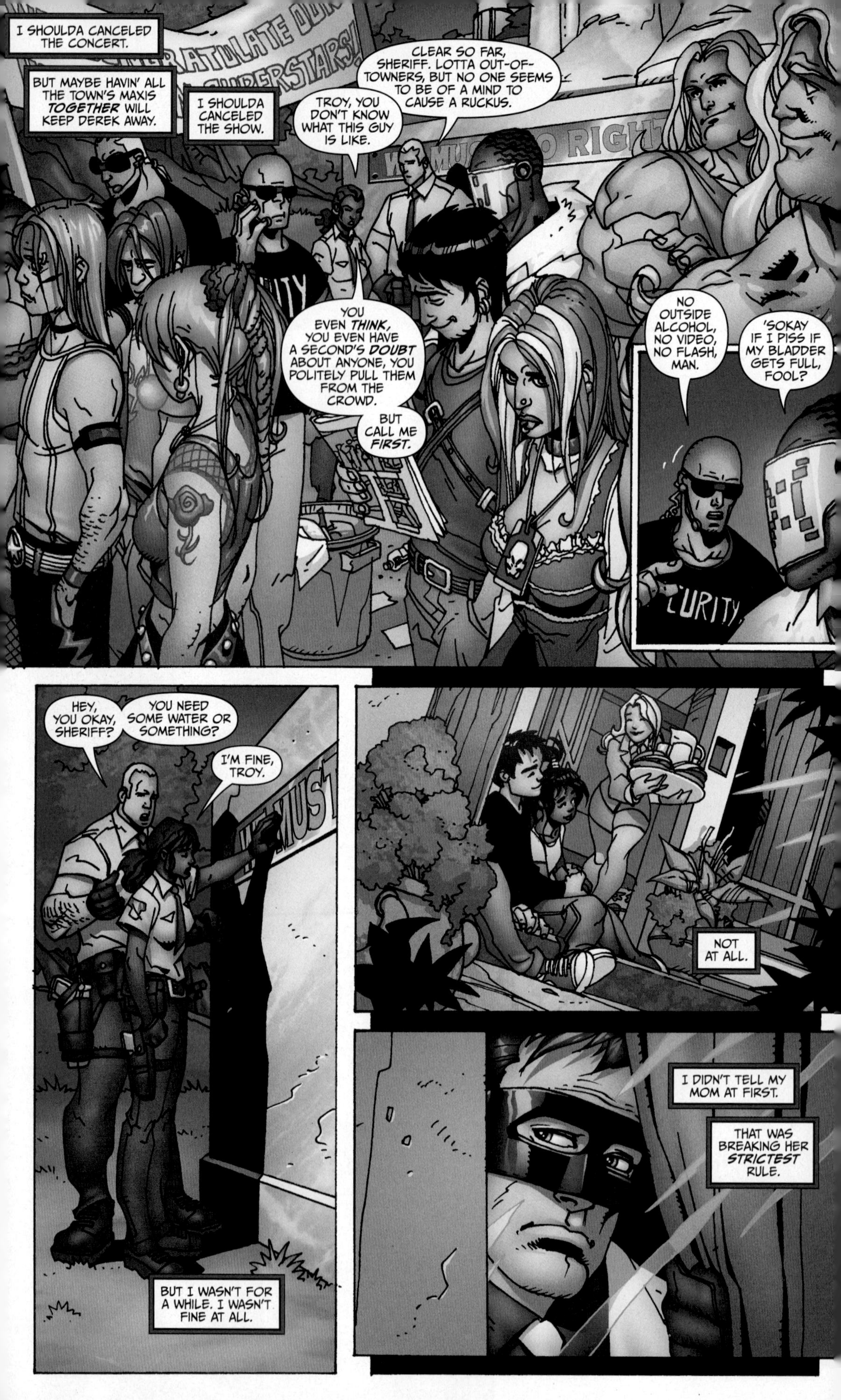
I SHOULDA CANCELED THE CONCERT.
BUT MAYBE HAVIN' ALL THE TOWN'S MAXIS TOGETHER WILL KEEP DEREK AWAY.
I SHOULDA CANCELED THE SHOW.
TROY, YOU DON'T KNOW WHAT THIS GUY IS LIKE.
CLEAR SO FAR, SHERIFF. LOTTA OUT-OF-TOWNERS, BUT NO ONE SEEMS TO BE OF A MIND TO CAUSE A RUCKUS.
YOU EVEN THINK, YOU EVEN HAVE A SECOND'S DOUBT ABOUT ANYONE, YOU POLITELY PULL THEM FROM THE CROWD.
BUT CALL ME FIRST.
NO OUTSIDE ALCOHOL, NO VIDEO, NO FLASH, MAN.
'SOKAY IF I PISS IF MY BLADDER GETS FULL, FOOL?
HEY, YOU OKAY, SHERIFF?
YOU NEED SOME WATER OR SOMETHING?
I'M FINE, TROY.
BUT I WASN'T FOR A WHILE. I WASN'T FINE AT ALL.
NOT AT ALL.
I DIDN'T TELL MY MOM AT FIRST.
THAT WAS BREAKING HER STRICTEST RULE.

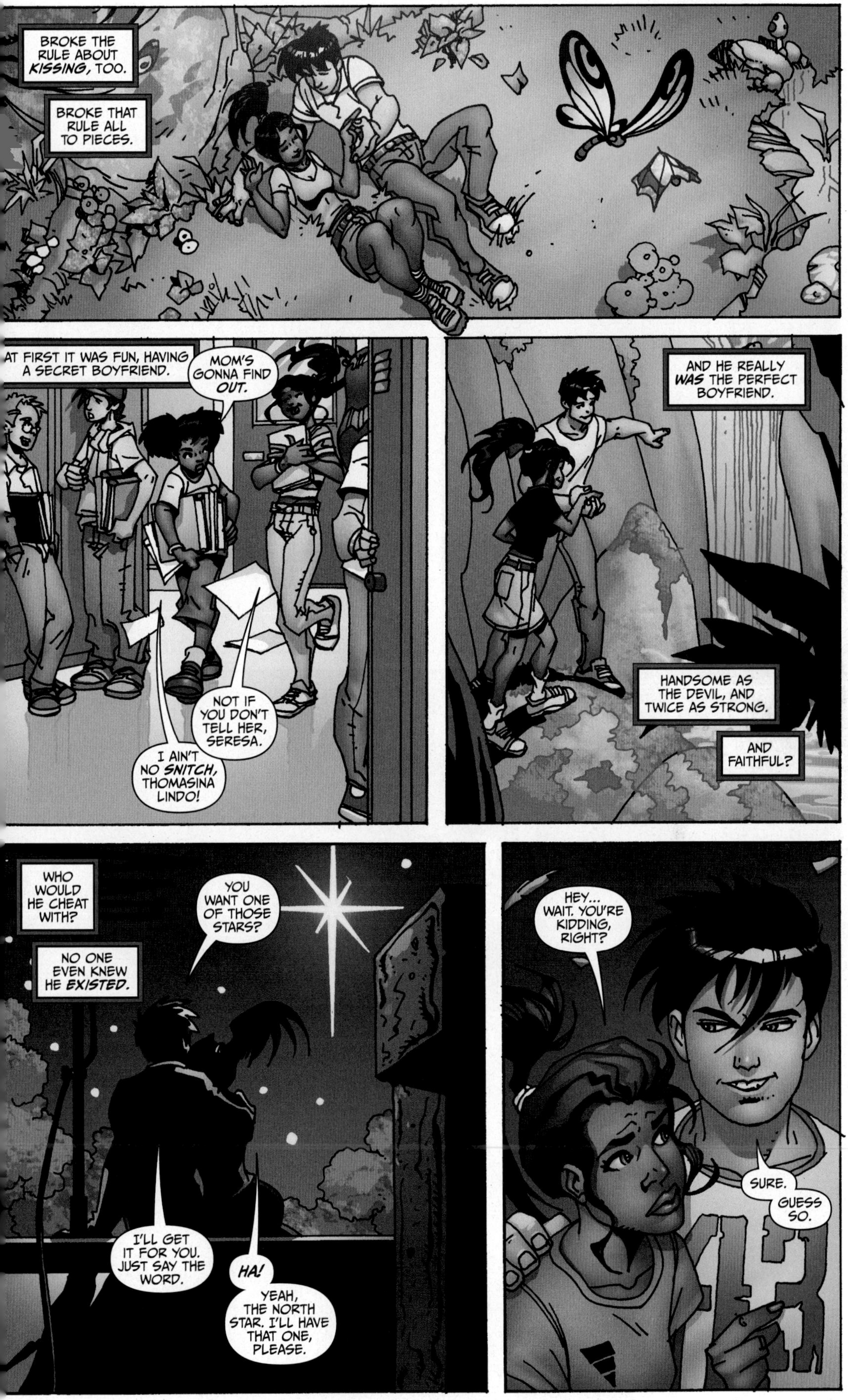
BROKE THE RULE ABOUT KISSING, TOO.
BROKE THAT RULE ALL TO PIECES.
AT FIRST IT WAS FUN, HAVING A SECRET BOYFRIEND.
MOM'S GONNA FIND OUT.
NOT IF YOU DON'T TELL HER, SERESA.
I AIN'T NO SNITCH, THOMASINA LINDO!
AND HE REALLY WAS THE PERFECT BOYFRIEND.
HANDSOME AS THE DEVIL, AND TWICE AS STRONG.
AND FAITHFUL?
WHO WOULD HE CHEAT WITH?
NO ONE EVEN KNEW HE EXISTED.
YOU WANT ONE OF THOSE STARS?
I'LL GET IT FOR YOU. JUST SAY THE WORD.
HA!
YEAH, THE NORTH STAR. I'LL HAVE THAT ONE, PLEASE.
HEY... WAIT. YOU'RE KIDDING, RIGHT?
SURE.
GUESS SO.

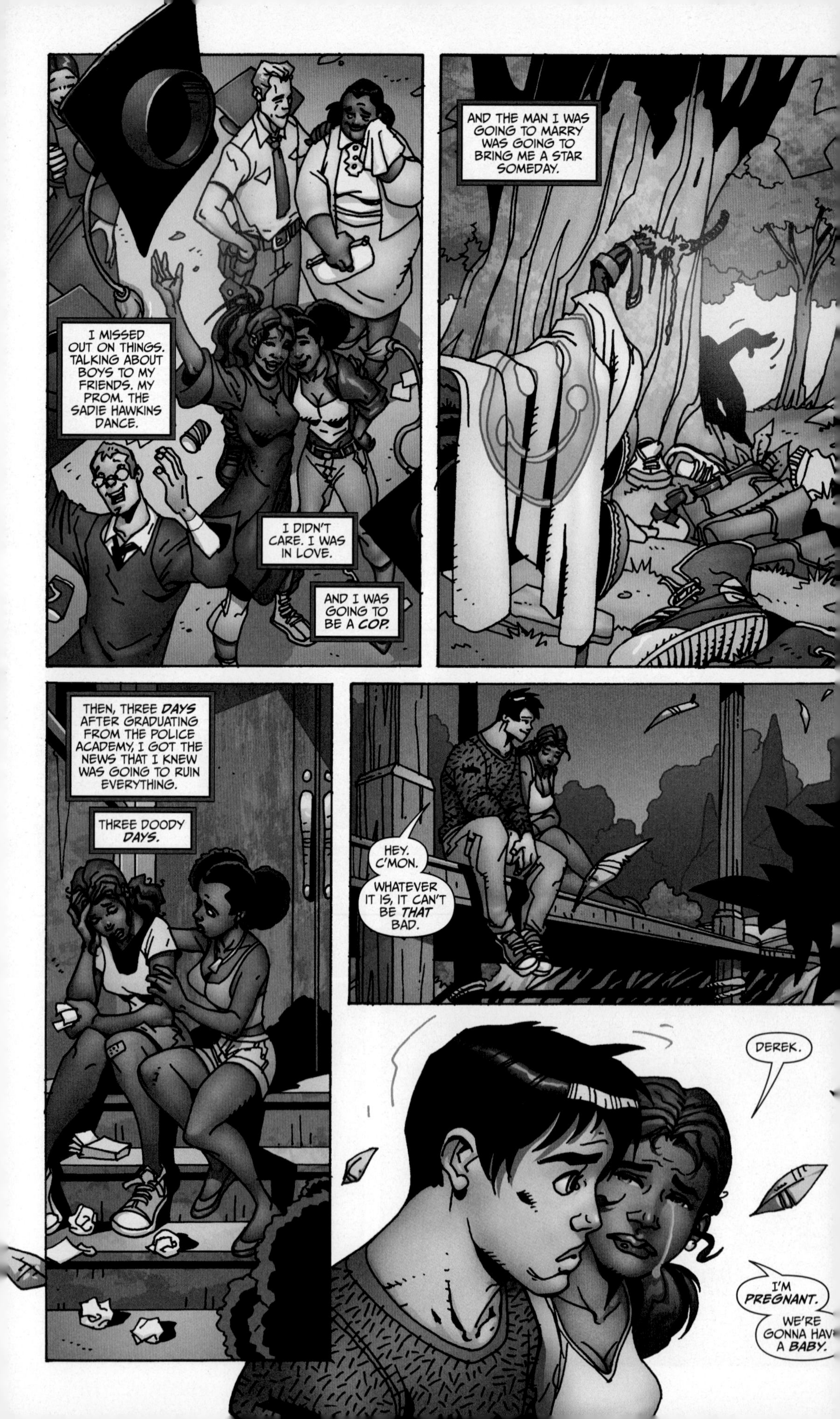
I MISSED OUT ON THINGS. TALKING ABOUT BOYS TO MY FRIENDS. MY PROM. THE SADIE HAWKINS DANCE.
I DIDN'T CARE. I WAS IN LOVE.
AND I WAS GOING TO BE A *COP*.
AND THE MAN I WAS GOING TO MARRY WAS GOING TO BRING ME A STAR SOMEDAY.
THEN, THREE *DAYS* AFTER GRADUATING FROM THE POLICE ACADEMY, I GOT THE NEWS THAT I KNEW WAS GOING TO RUIN EVERYTHING.
THREE DOODY *DAYS*.
HEY. C'MON.
WHATEVER IT IS, IT CAN'T BE *THAT* BAD.
DEREK.
I'M *PREGNANT*.

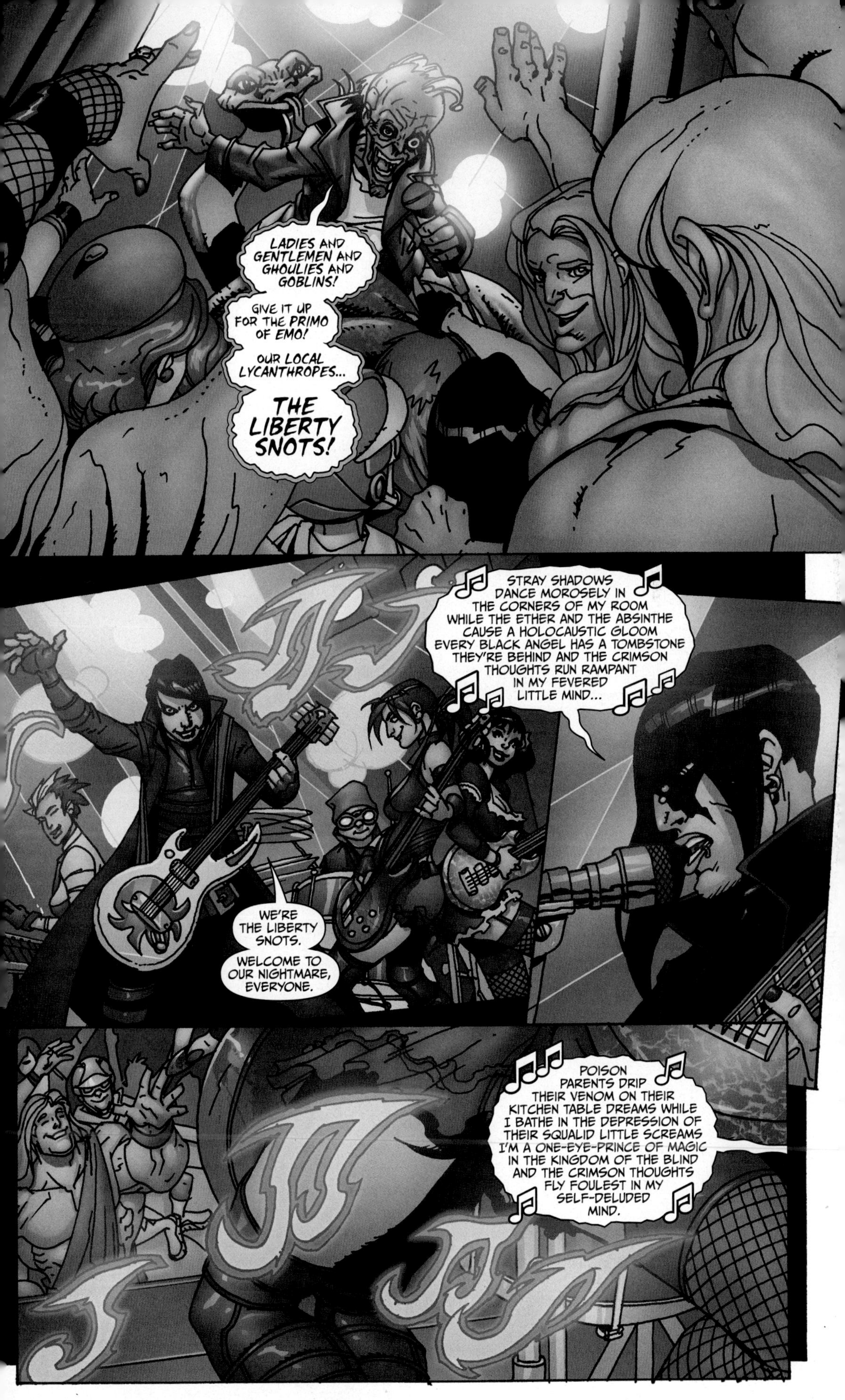
LADIES AND GENTLEMEN AND GHOULIES AND GOBLINS!
GIVE IT UP FOR THE PRIMO OF EMO!
OUR LOCAL LYCANTHROPES...
THE LIBERTY SNOTS!
STRAY SHADOWS DANCE MOROSELY IN THE CORNERS OF MY ROOM WHILE THE ETHER AND THE ABSINTHE CAUSE A HOLOCAUSTIC GLOOM EVERY BLACK ANGEL HAS A TOMBSTONE THEY'RE BEHIND AND THE CRIMSON THOUGHTS RUN RAMPANT IN MY FEVERED LITTLE MIND...
WE'RE THE LIBERTY SNOTS.
WELCOME TO OUR NIGHTMARE, EVERYONE.
POISON PARENTS DRIP THEIR VENOM ON THEIR KITCHEN TABLE DREAMS WHILE I BATHE IN THE DEPRESSION OF THEIR SQUALID LITTLE SCREAMS I'M A ONE-EYE-PRINCE OF MAGIC IN THE KINGDOM OF THE BLIND AND THE CRIMSON THOUGHTS FLY FOULEST IN MY SELF-DELUDED MIND.

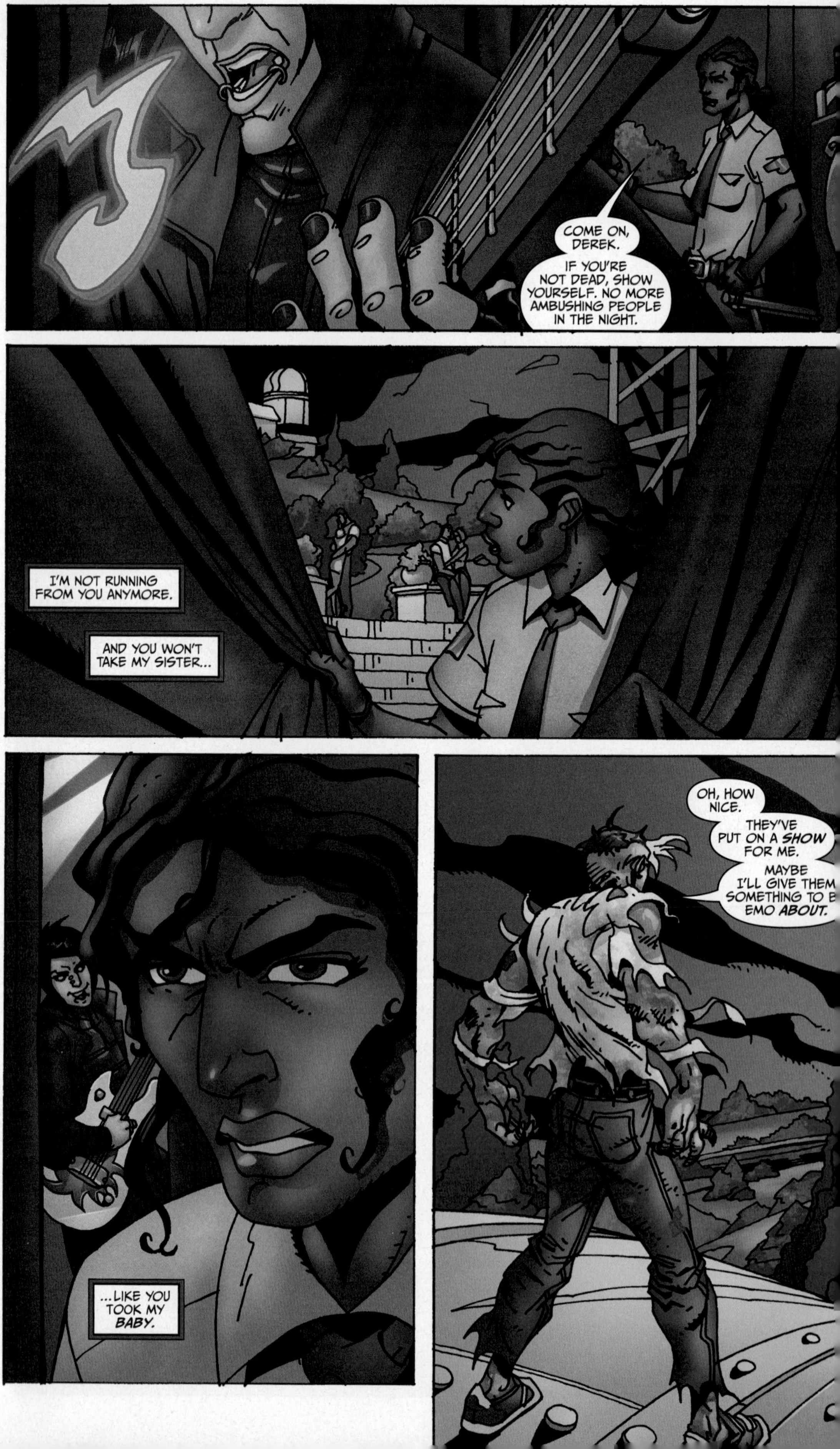
COME ON, DEREK.
IF YOU'RE NOT DEAD, SHOW YOURSELF. NO MORE AMBUSHING PEOPLE IN THE NIGHT.
I'M NOT RUNNING FROM YOU ANYMORE.
AND YOU WON'T TAKE MY SISTER...
...LIKE YOU TOOK MY BABY.
OH, HOW NICE.
THEY'VE PUT ON A SHOW FOR ME.
MAYBE I'LL GIVE THEM SOMETHING TO B EMO ABOUT.

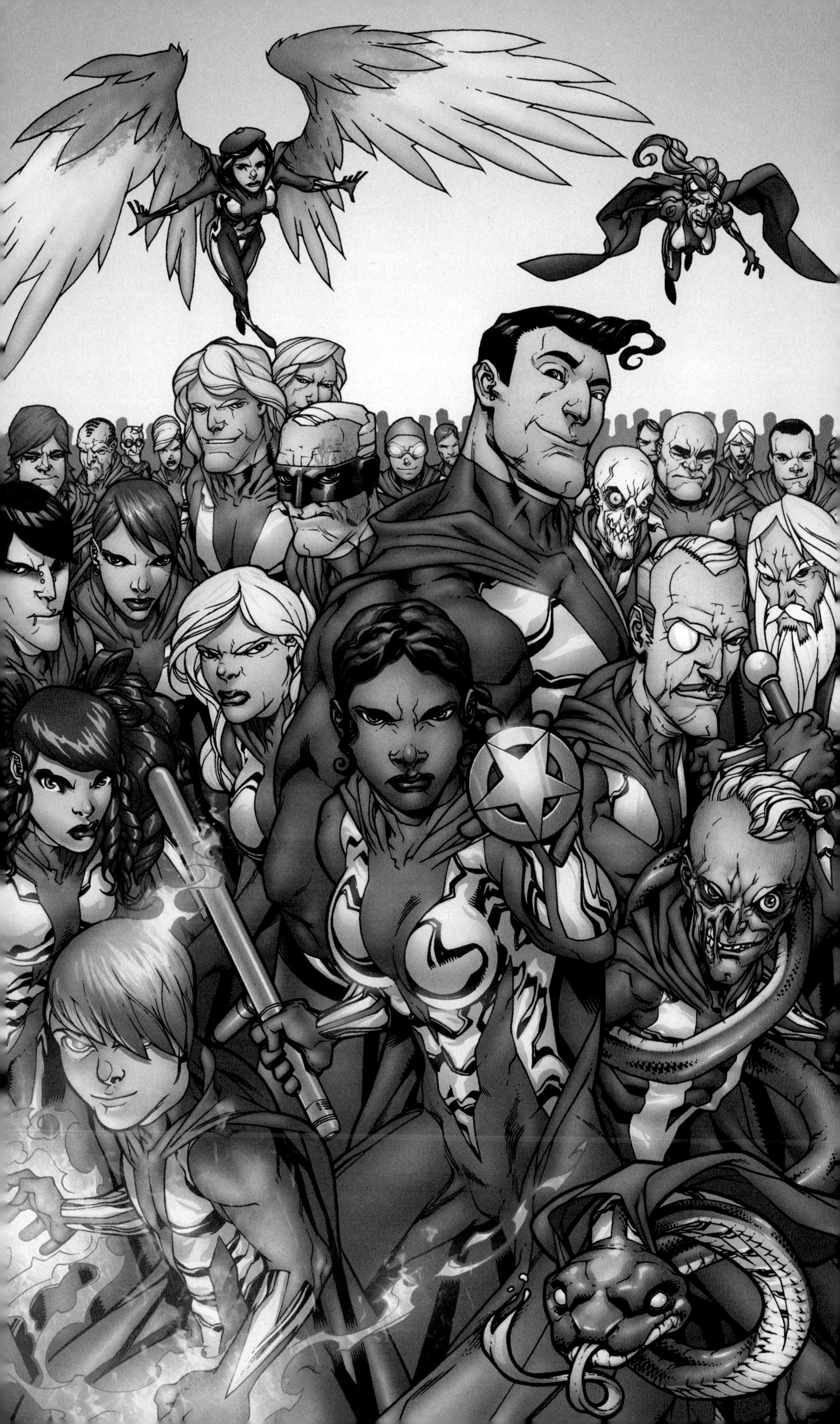

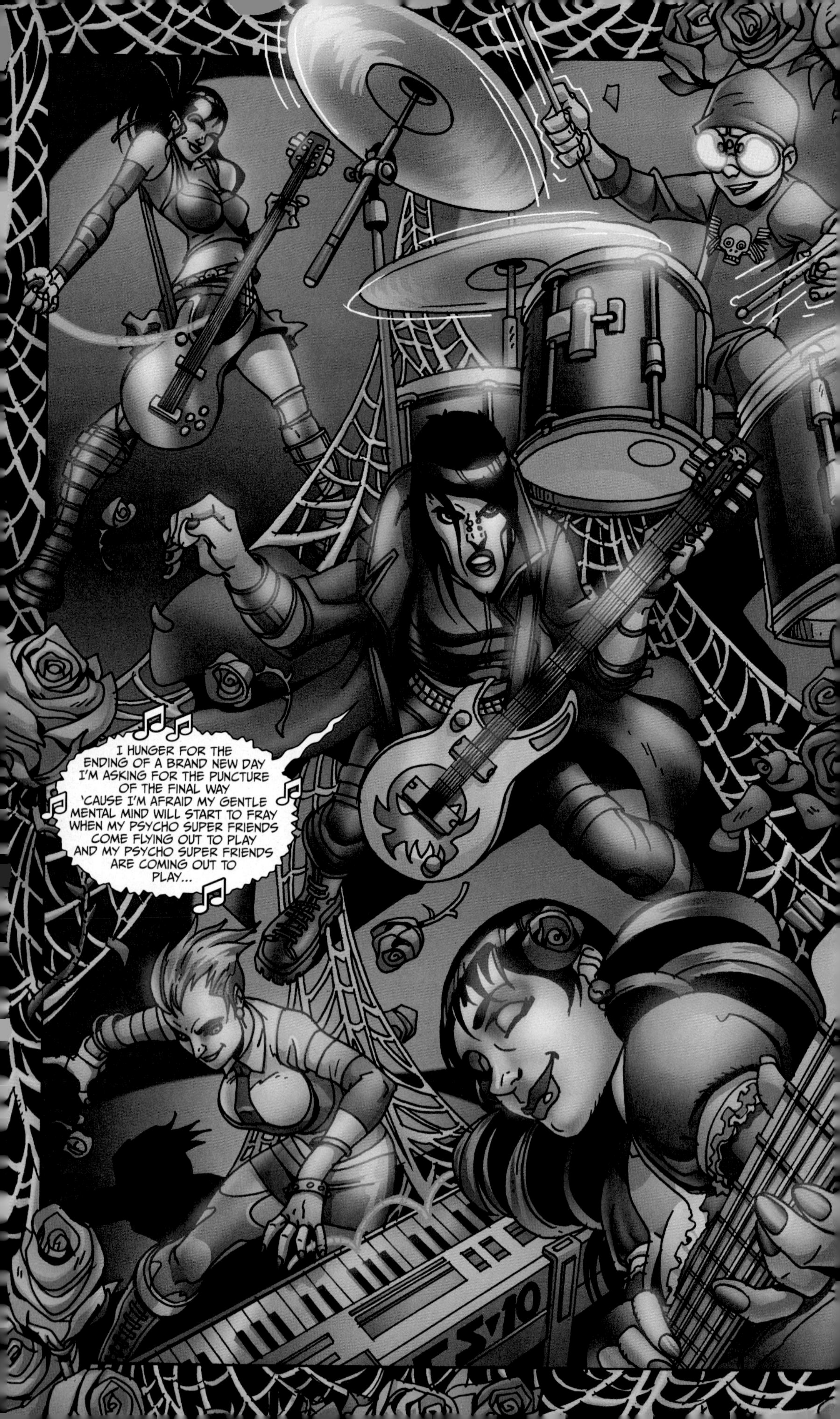
I HUNGER FOR THE ENDING OF A BRAND NEW DAY I'M ASKING FOR THE PUNCTURE OF THE FINAL WAY 'CAUSE I'M AFRAID MY GENTLE MENTAL MIND WILL START TO FRAY WHEN MY PSYCHO SUPER FRIENDS COME FLYING OUT TO PLAY AND MY PSYCHO SUPER FRIENDS ARE COMING OUT TO PLAY...
S-10

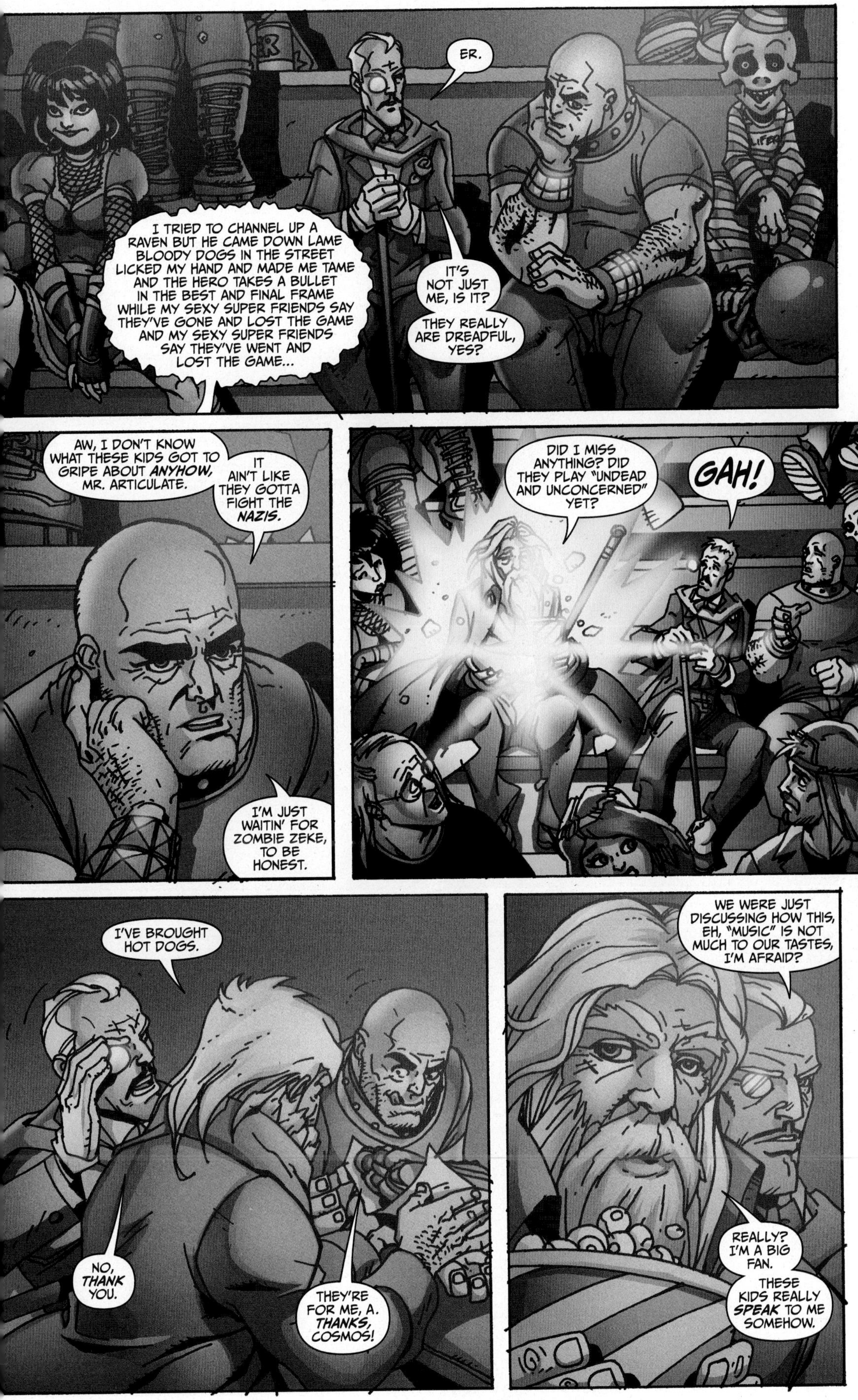
ER.
I TRIED TO CHANNEL UP A RAVEN BUT HE CAME DOWN LAME BLOODY DOGS IN THE STREET LICKED MY HAND AND MADE ME TAME AND THE HERO TAKES A BULLET IN THE BEST AND FINAL FRAME WHILE MY SEXY SUPER FRIENDS SAY THEY'VE GONE AND LOST THE GAME AND MY SEXY SUPER FRIENDS SAY THEY'VE WENT AND LOST THE GAME...
IT'S NOT JUST ME, IS IT?
THEY REALLY ARE DREADFUL, YES?
AW, I DON'T KNOW WHAT THESE KIDS GOT TO GRIPE ABOUT *ANYHOW*, MR. ARTICULATE.
IT AIN'T LIKE THEY GOTTA FIGHT THE *NAZIS*.
I'M JUST WAITIN' FOR ZOMBIE ZEKE, TO BE HONEST.
DID I MISS ANYTHING? DID THEY PLAY "UNDEAD AND UNCONCERNED" YET?
GAH!
I'VE BROUGHT HOT DOGS.
NO, *THANK* YOU.
THEY'RE FOR ME, A. *THANKS*, COSMOS!
WE WERE JUST DISCUSSING HOW THIS, EH, "MUSIC" IS NOT MUCH TO OUR TASTES, I'M AFRAID?
REALLY? I'M A BIG FAN.
THESE KIDS REALLY *SPEAK* TO ME SOMEHOW.

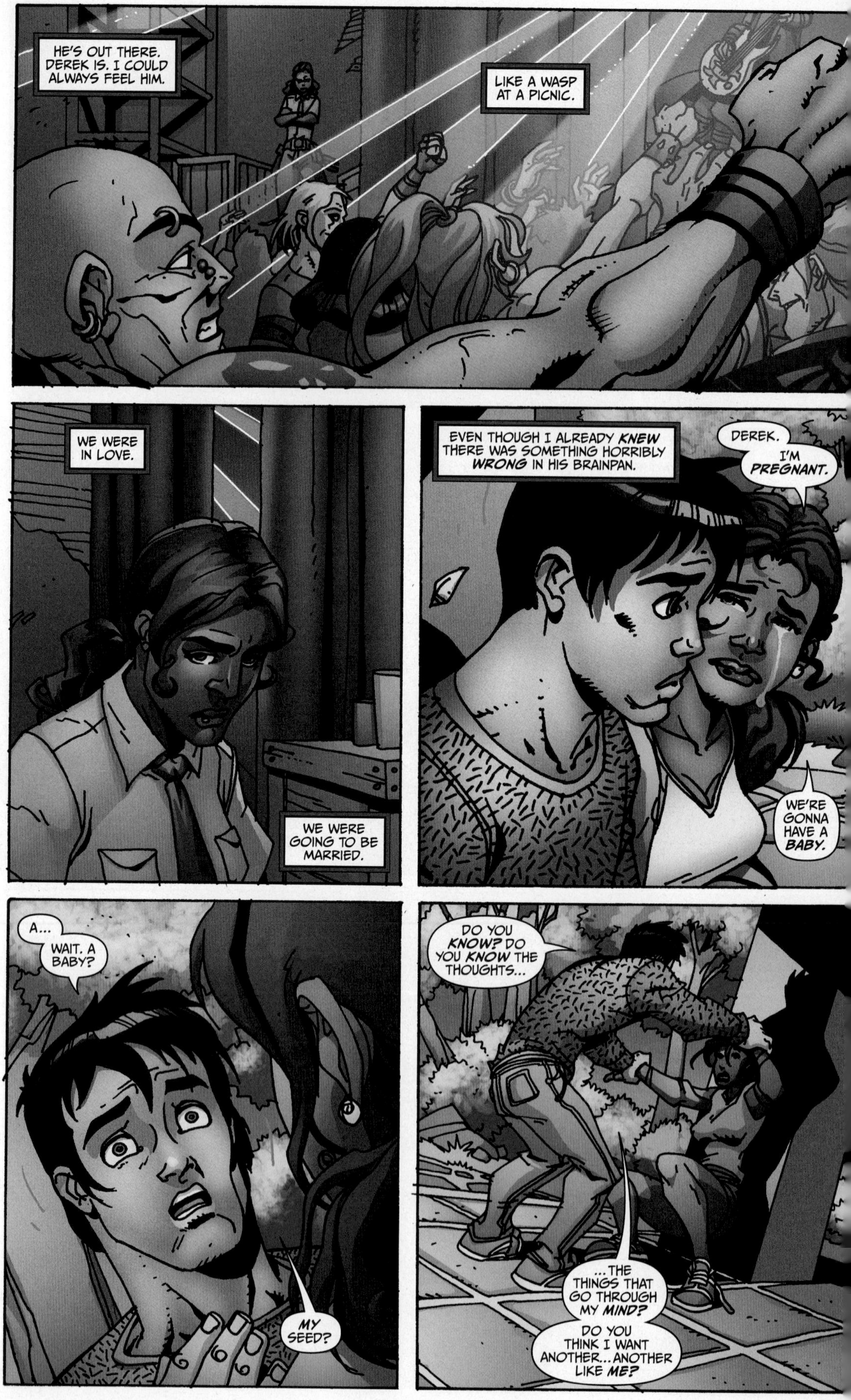
HE'S OUT THERE. DEREK IS. I COULD ALWAYS FEEL HIM.
LIKE A WASP AT A PICNIC.
WE WERE IN LOVE.
WE WERE GOING TO BE MARRIED.
EVEN THOUGH I ALREADY KNEW THERE WAS SOMETHING HORRIBLY WRONG IN HIS BRAINPAN.
DEREK. I'M PREGNANT.
WE'RE GONNA HAVE A BABY.
A... WAIT. A BABY?
MY SEED?
DO YOU KNOW? DO YOU KNOW THE THOUGHTS...
...THE THINGS THAT GO THROUGH MY MIND?
DO YOU THINK I WANT ANOTHER... ANOTHER LIKE ME?

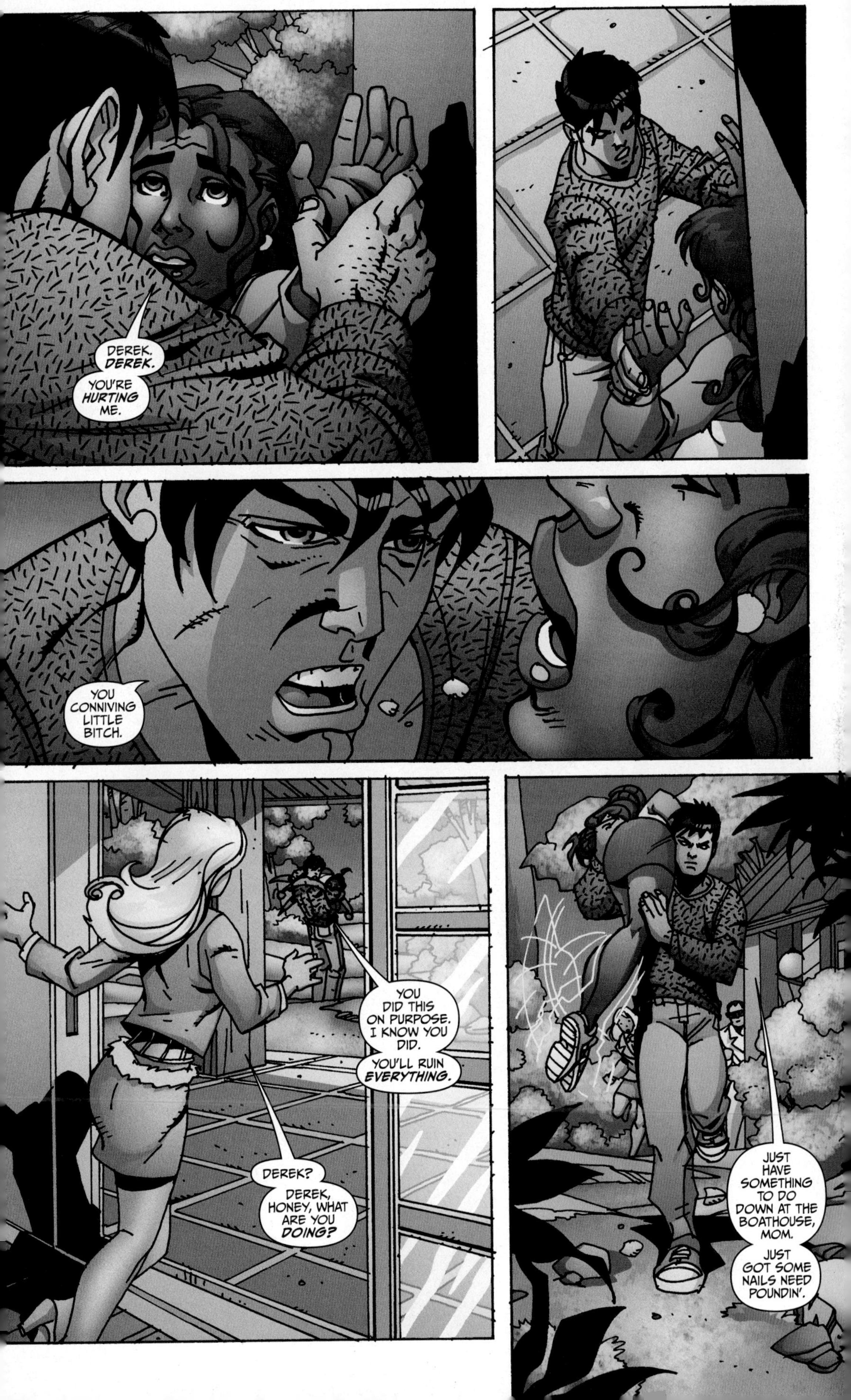
DEREK. DEREK.
YOU'RE HURTING ME.
YOU CONNIVING LITTLE BITCH.
YOU DID THIS ON PURPOSE. I KNOW YOU DID.
YOU'LL RUIN EVERYTHING.
DEREK?
DEREK, HONEY, WHAT ARE YOU DOING?
JUST HAVE SOMETHING TO DO DOWN AT THE BOATHOUSE, MOM.
JUST GOT SOME NAILS NEED POUNDIN'.

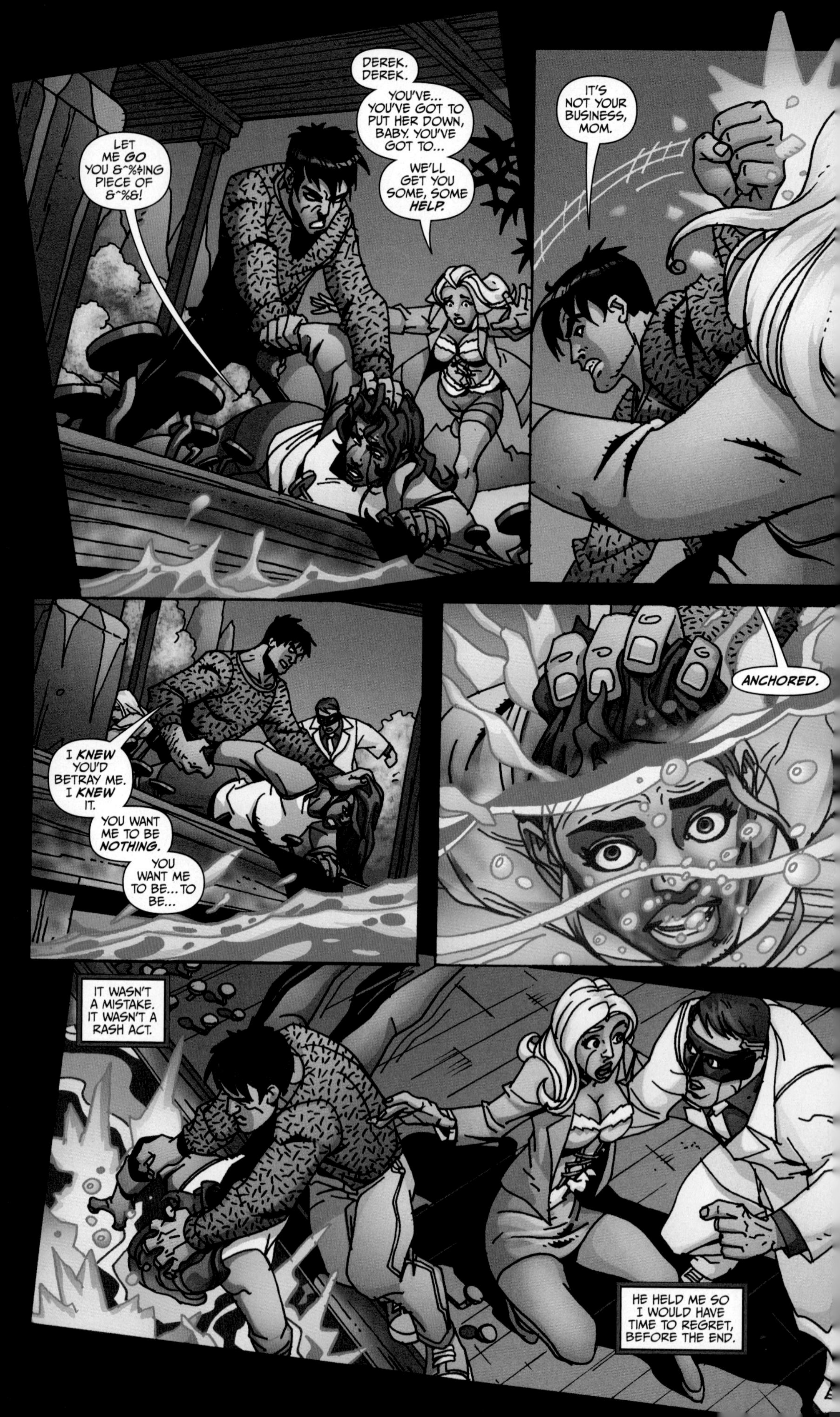
DEREK. DEREK.
YOU'VE... YOU'VE GOT TO PUT HER DOWN, BABY. YOU'VE GOT TO...
WE'LL GET YOU SOME, SOME HELP.
LET ME GO YOU &^%$ING PIECE OF &^%&!
IT'S NOT YOUR BUSINESS, MOM.
I KNEW YOU'D BETRAY ME. I KNEW IT.
YOU WANT ME TO BE NOTHING.
YOU WANT ME TO BE... TO BE...
ANCHORED.
IT WASN'T A MISTAKE. IT WASN'T A RASH ACT.
HE HELD ME SO I WOULD HAVE TIME TO REGRET, BEFORE THE END.

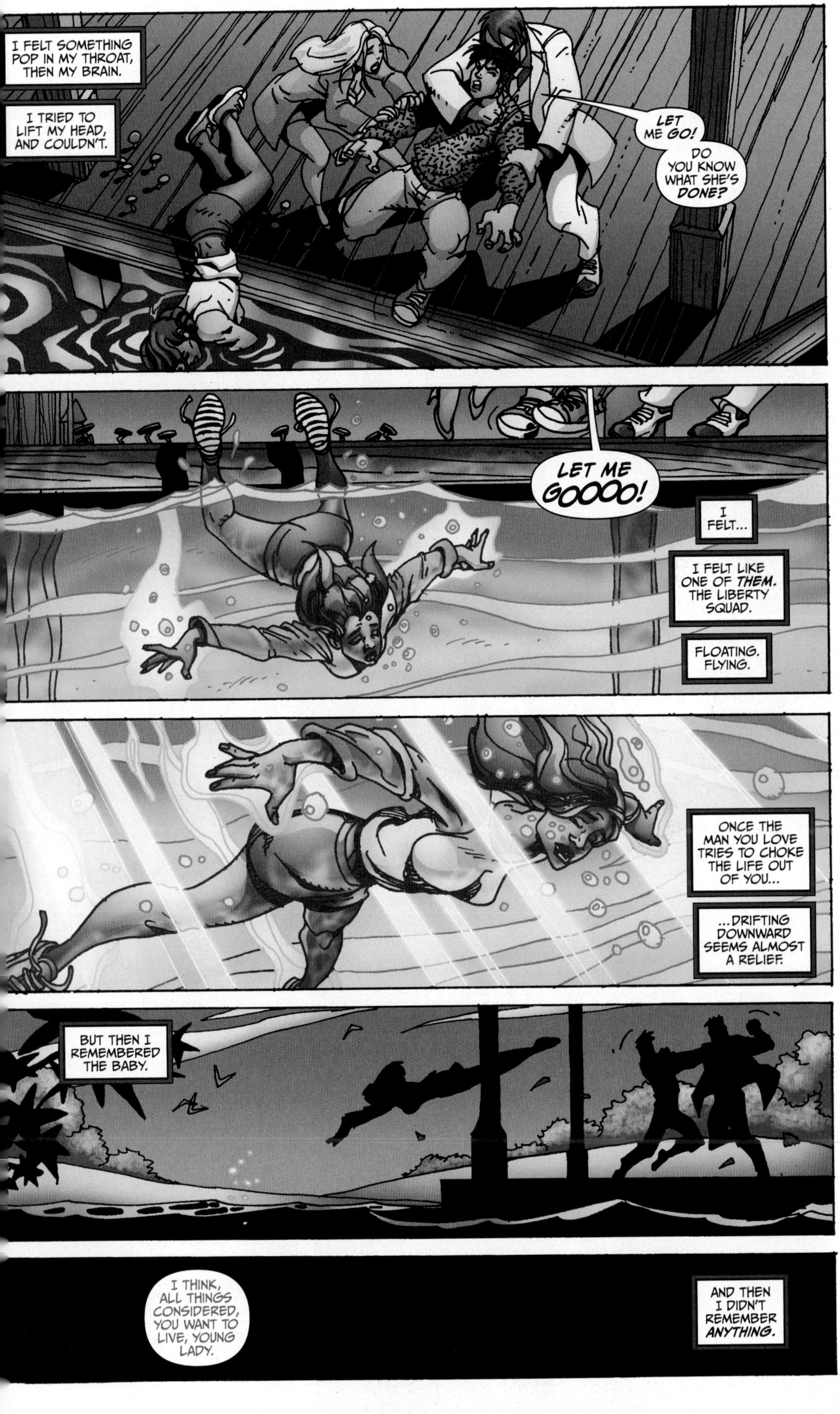
I FELT SOMETHING POP IN MY THROAT, THEN MY BRAIN.
I TRIED TO LIFT MY HEAD, AND COULDN'T.
LET ME GO! DO YOU KNOW WHAT SHE'S DONE?
LET ME GOOOO!
I FELT...
I FELT LIKE ONE OF THEM. THE LIBERTY SQUAD.
FLOATING. FLYING.
ONCE THE MAN YOU LOVE TRIES TO CHOKE THE LIFE OUT OF YOU...
...DRIFTING DOWNWARD SEEMS ALMOST A RELIEF.
BUT THEN I REMEMBERED THE BABY.
I THINK, ALL THINGS CONSIDERED, YOU WANT TO LIVE, YOUNG LADY.
AND THEN I DIDN'T REMEMBER ANYTHING.

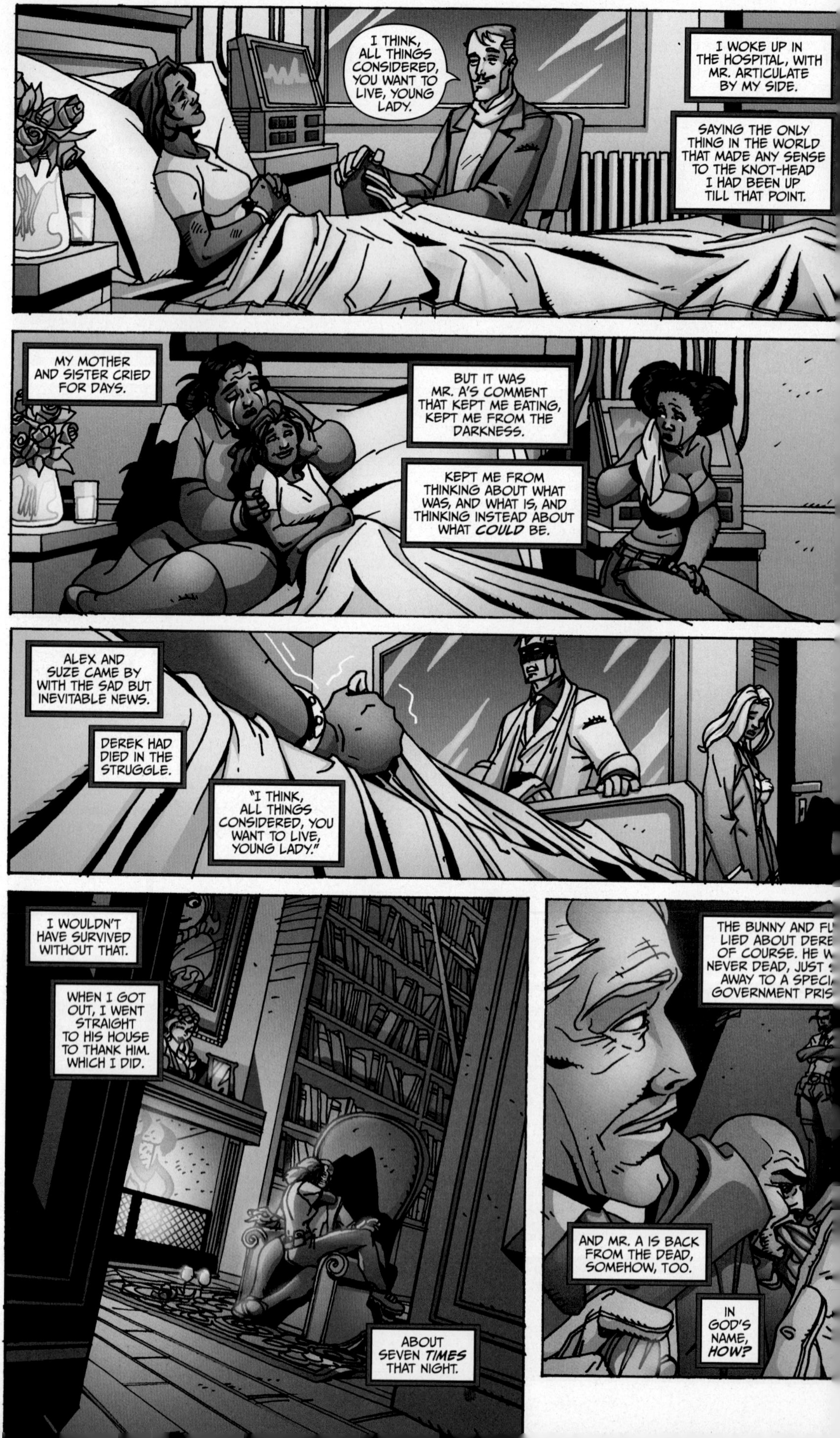
I WOKE UP IN THE HOSPITAL, WITH MR. ARTICULATE BY MY SIDE.
I THINK, ALL THINGS CONSIDERED, YOU WANT TO LIVE, YOUNG LADY.
SAYING THE ONLY THING IN THE WORLD THAT MADE ANY SENSE TO THE KNOT-HEAD I HAD BEEN UP TILL THAT POINT.
MY MOTHER AND SISTER CRIED FOR DAYS.
BUT IT WAS MR. A'S COMMENT THAT KEPT ME EATING, KEPT ME FROM THE DARKNESS.
KEPT ME FROM THINKING ABOUT WHAT WAS, AND WHAT IS, AND THINKING INSTEAD ABOUT WHAT *COULD* BE.
ALEX AND SUZE CAME BY WITH THE SAD BUT INEVITABLE NEWS.
DEREK HAD DIED IN THE STRUGGLE.
"I THINK, ALL THINGS CONSIDERED, YOU WANT TO LIVE, YOUNG LADY."
I WOULDN'T HAVE SURVIVED WITHOUT THAT.
WHEN I GOT OUT, I WENT STRAIGHT TO HIS HOUSE TO THANK HIM. WHICH I DID.
ABOUT SEVEN *TIMES* THAT NIGHT.
THE BUNNY AND FU LIED ABOUT DERE OF COURSE. HE W NEVER DEAD, JUST AWAY TO A SPECI GOVERNMENT PRIS
AND MR. A IS BACK FROM THE DEAD, SOMEHOW, TOO.
IN GOD'S NAME, *HOW?*

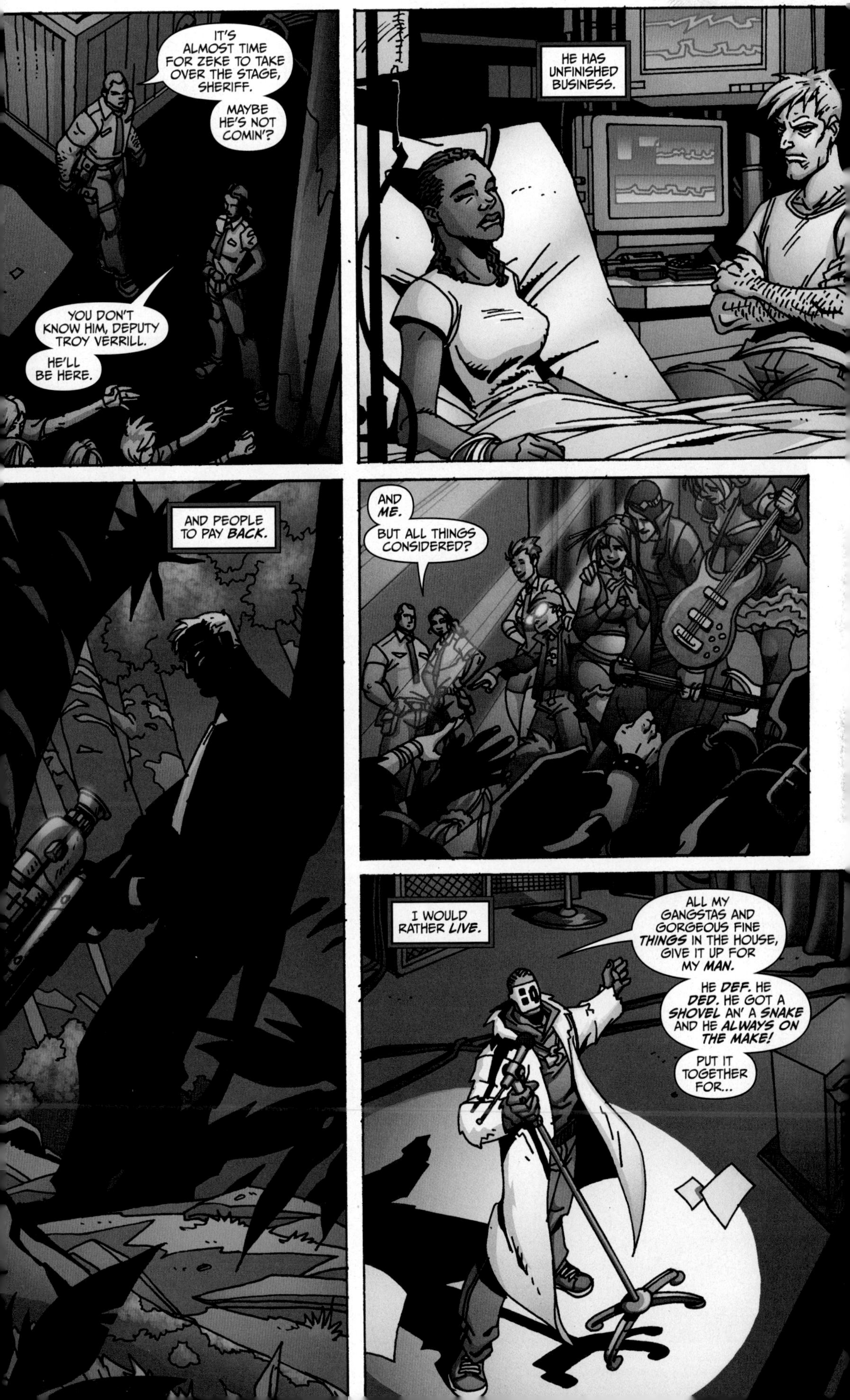
IT'S ALMOST TIME FOR ZEKE TO TAKE OVER THE STAGE, SHERIFF.
MAYBE HE'S NOT COMIN'?
YOU DON'T KNOW HIM, DEPUTY TROY VERRILL.
HE'LL BE HERE.
HE HAS UNFINISHED BUSINESS.
AND PEOPLE TO PAY *BACK.*
AND *ME.*
BUT ALL THINGS CONSIDERED?
I WOULD RATHER *LIVE.*
ALL MY GANGSTAS AND GORGEOUS FINE *THINGS* IN THE HOUSE, GIVE IT UP FOR MY *MAN.*
HE *DEF.* HE *DED.* HE GOT A *SHOVEL* AN' A *SNAKE* AND HE *ALWAYS ON THE MAKE!*
PUT IT TOGETHER FOR...

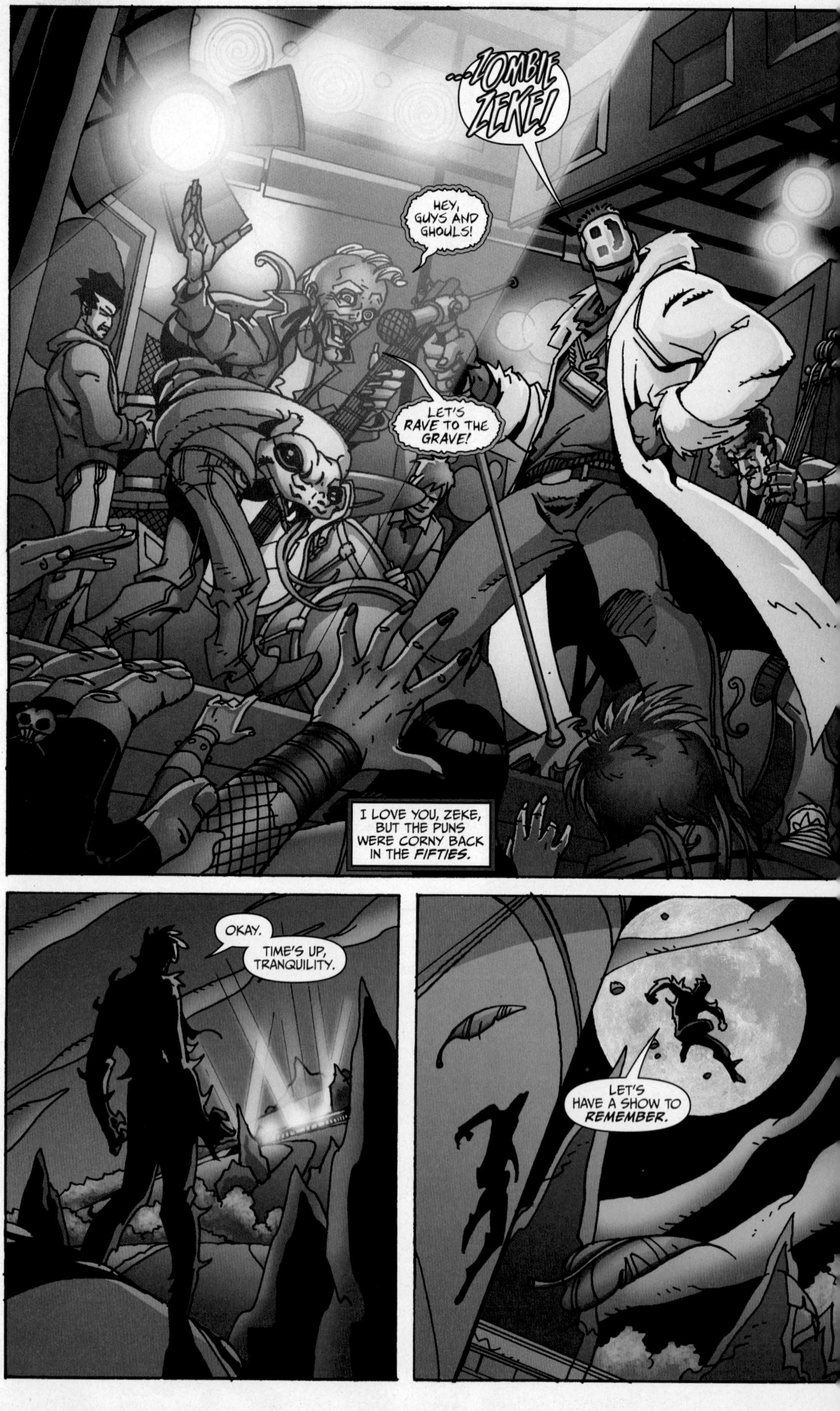
HEY, GUYS AND GHOULS!
...ZOMBIE ZEKE!
LET'S RAVE TO THE GRAVE!
I LOVE YOU, ZEKE, BUT THE PUNS WERE CORNY BACK IN THE FIFTIES.
OKAY.
TIME'S UP, TRANQUILITY.
LET'S HAVE A SHOW TO REMEMBER.

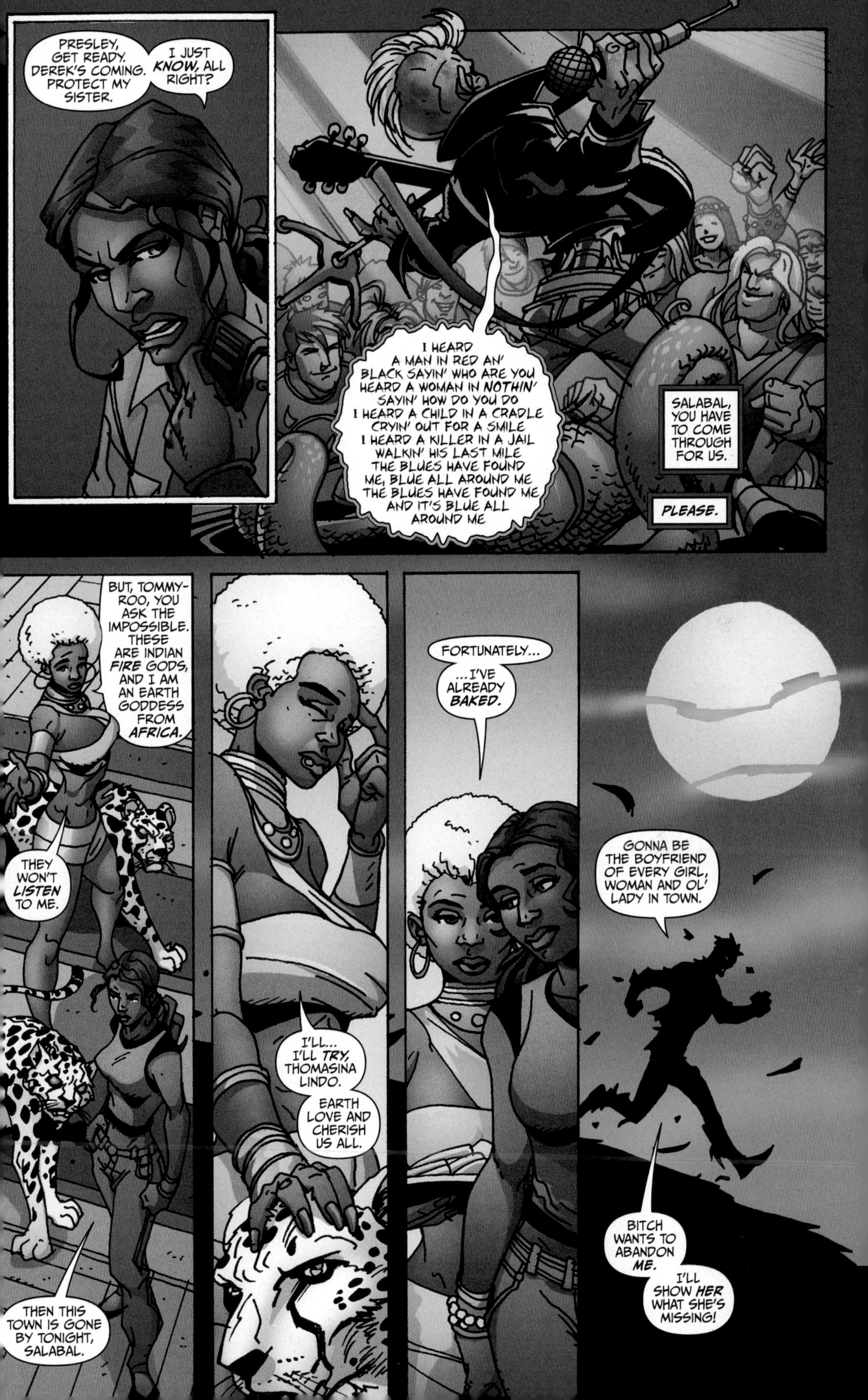
PRESLEY, GET READY. DEREK'S COMING. PROTECT MY SISTER.
I JUST KNOW, ALL RIGHT?
I HEARD A MAN IN RED AN' BLACK SAYIN' WHO ARE YOU HEARD A WOMAN IN NOTHIN' SAYIN' HOW DO YOU DO I HEARD A CHILD IN A CRADLE CRYIN' OUT FOR A SMILE I HEARD A KILLER IN A JAIL WALKIN' HIS LAST MILE THE BLUES HAVE FOUND ME, BLUE ALL AROUND ME THE BLUES HAVE FOUND ME AND IT'S BLUE ALL AROUND ME
SALABAL, YOU HAVE TO COME THROUGH FOR US.
PLEASE.
BUT, TOMMY-ROO, YOU ASK THE IMPOSSIBLE. THESE ARE INDIAN FIRE GODS, AND I AM AN EARTH GODDESS FROM AFRICA.
THEY WON'T LISTEN TO ME.
THEN THIS TOWN IS GONE BY TONIGHT, SALABAL.
I'LL... I'LL TRY, THOMASINA LINDO.
EARTH LOVE AND CHERISH US ALL.
FORTUNATELY...
...I'VE ALREADY BAKED.
GONNA BE THE BOYFRIEND OF EVERY GIRL, WOMAN AND OL' LADY IN TOWN.
BITCH WANTS TO ABANDON ME.
I'LL SHOW HER WHAT SHE'S MISSING!

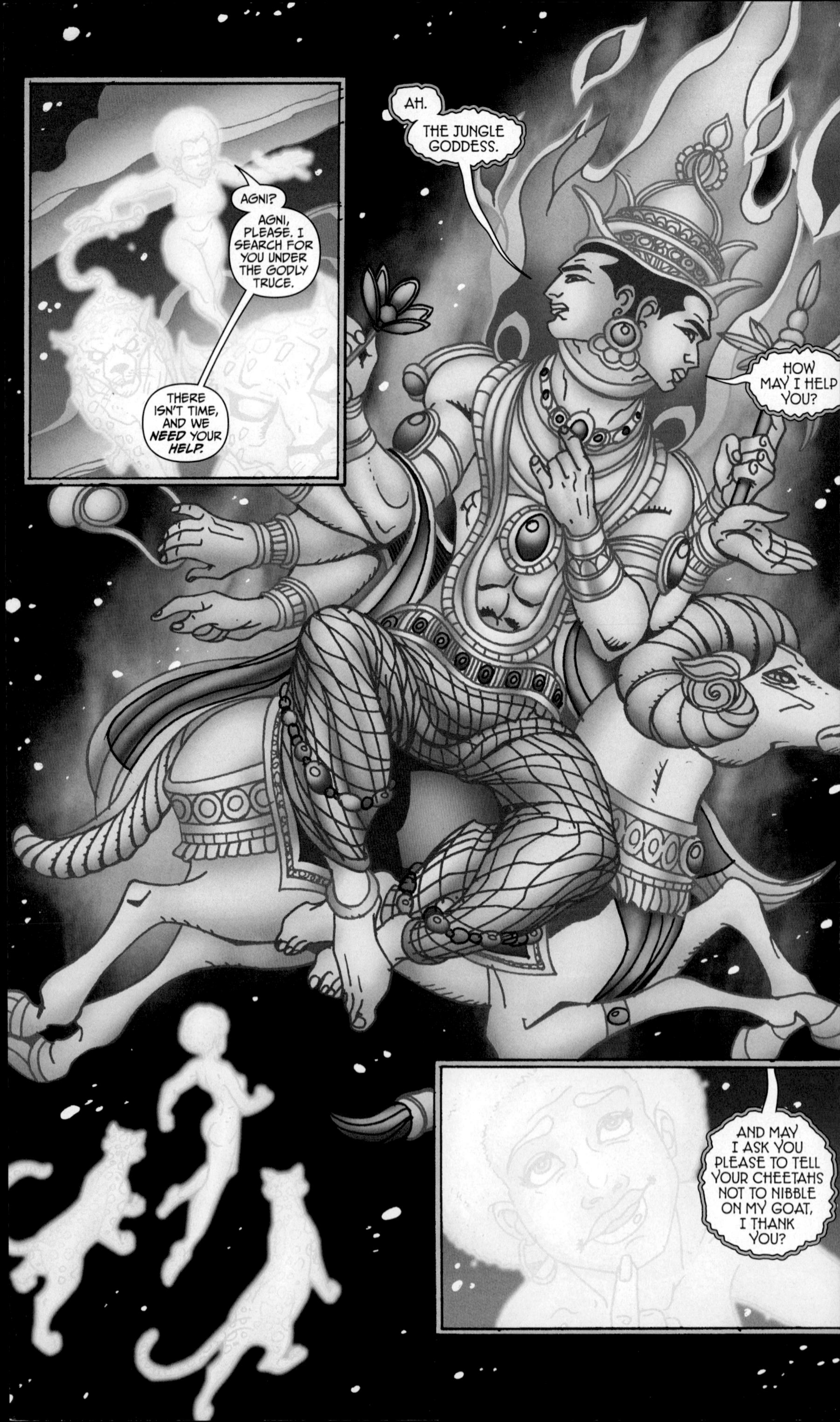
AGNI?
AGNI, PLEASE. I SEARCH FOR YOU UNDER THE GODLY TRUCE.
THERE ISN'T TIME, AND WE ***NEED*** YOUR ***HELP.***
AH.
THE JUNGLE GODDESS.
HOW MAY I HELP YOU?
AND MAY I ASK YOU PLEASE TO TELL YOUR CHEETAHS NOT TO NIBBLE ON MY GOAT, I THANK YOU?

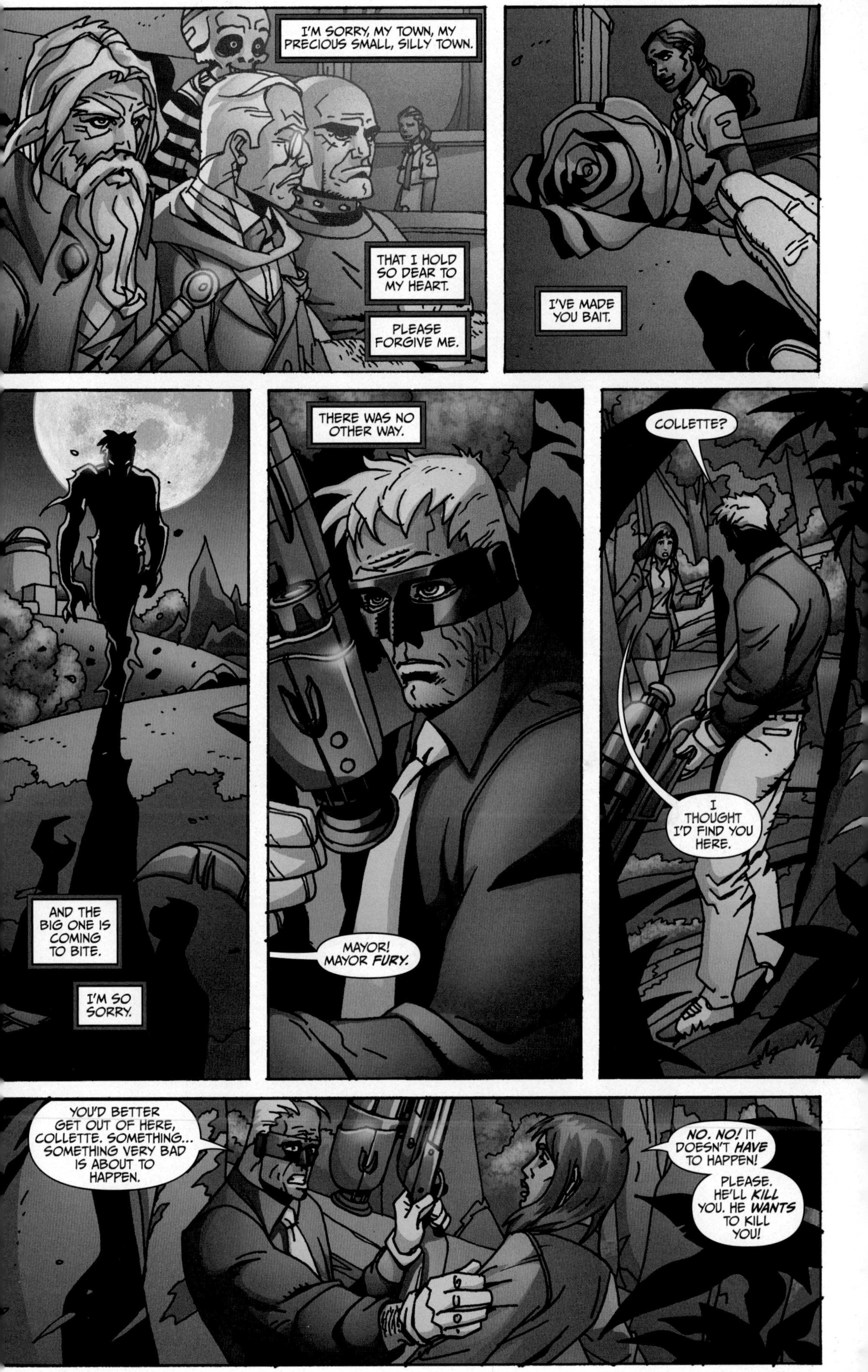

I'M SORRY, MY TOWN, MY PRECIOUS SMALL, SILLY TOWN.
THAT I HOLD SO DEAR TO MY HEART.
PLEASE FORGIVE ME.
I'VE MADE YOU BAIT.
AND THE BIG ONE IS COMING TO BITE.
I'M SO SORRY.
THERE WAS NO OTHER WAY.
MAYOR! MAYOR FURY.
COLLETTE?
I THOUGHT I'D FIND YOU HERE.
YOU'D BETTER GET OUT OF HERE, COLLETTE. SOMETHING... SOMETHING VERY BAD IS ABOUT TO HAPPEN.
NO. NO! IT DOESN'T HAVE TO HAPPEN!
PLEASE. HE'LL KILL YOU. HE WANTS TO KILL YOU!

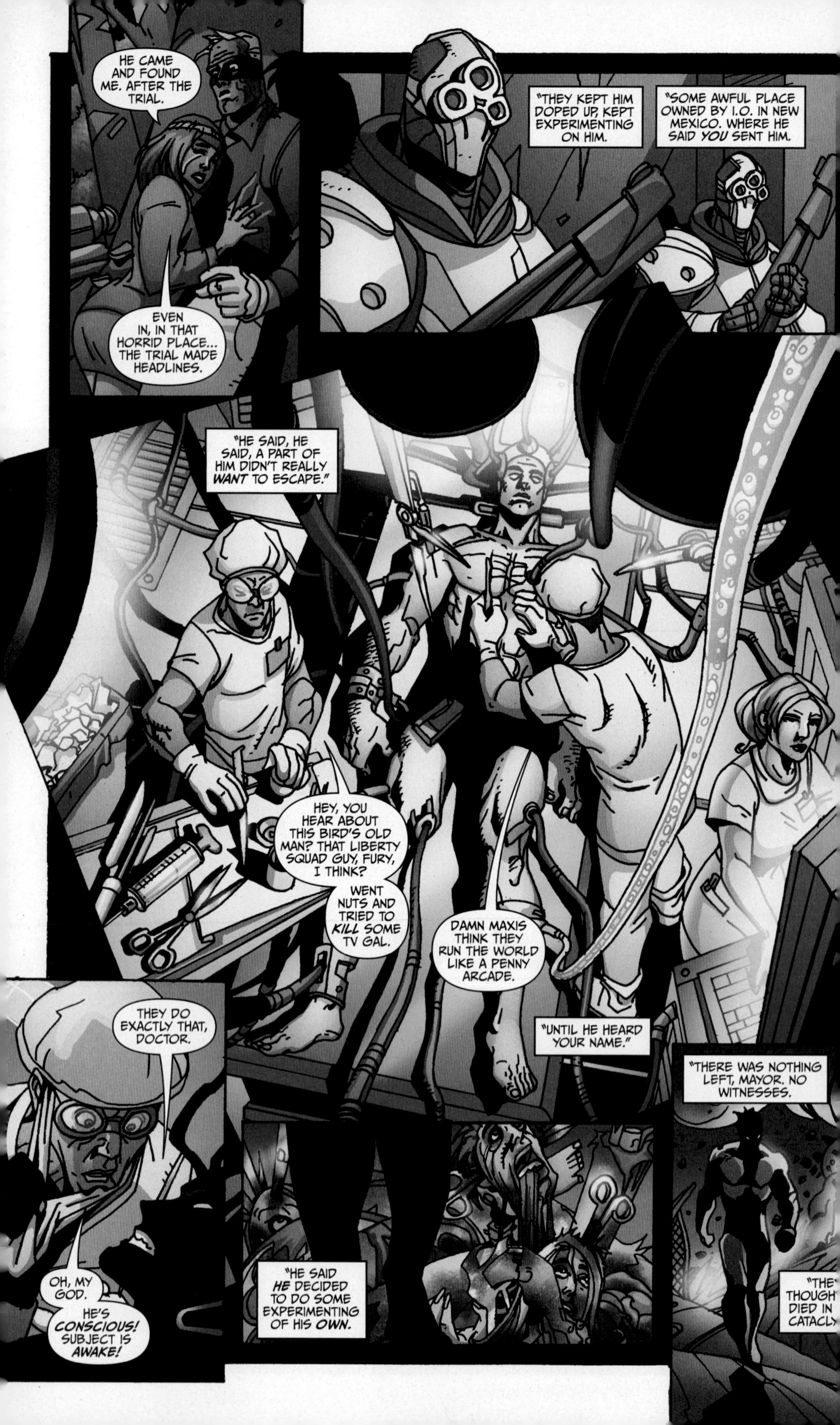
HE CAME AND FOUND ME. AFTER THE TRIAL.
EVEN IN, IN THAT HORRID PLACE... THE TRIAL MADE HEADLINES.
"THEY KEPT HIM DOPED UP, KEPT EXPERIMENTING ON HIM.
"SOME AWFUL PLACE OWNED BY I.O. IN NEW MEXICO. WHERE HE SAID YOU SENT HIM.
"HE SAID, HE SAID, A PART OF HIM DIDN'T REALLY WANT TO ESCAPE."
HEY, YOU HEAR ABOUT THIS BIRD'S OLD MAN? THAT LIBERTY SQUAD GUY, FURY, I THINK?
WENT NUTS AND TRIED TO KILL SOME TV GAL.
DAMN MAXIS THINK THEY RUN THE WORLD LIKE A PENNY ARCADE.
"UNTIL HE HEARD YOUR NAME."
THEY DO EXACTLY THAT, DOCTOR.
OH, MY GOD.
HE'S CONSCIOUS! SUBJECT IS AWAKE!
"HE SAID HE DECIDED TO DO SOME EXPERIMENTING OF HIS OWN.
"THERE WAS NOTHING LEFT, MAYOR. NO WITNESSES.

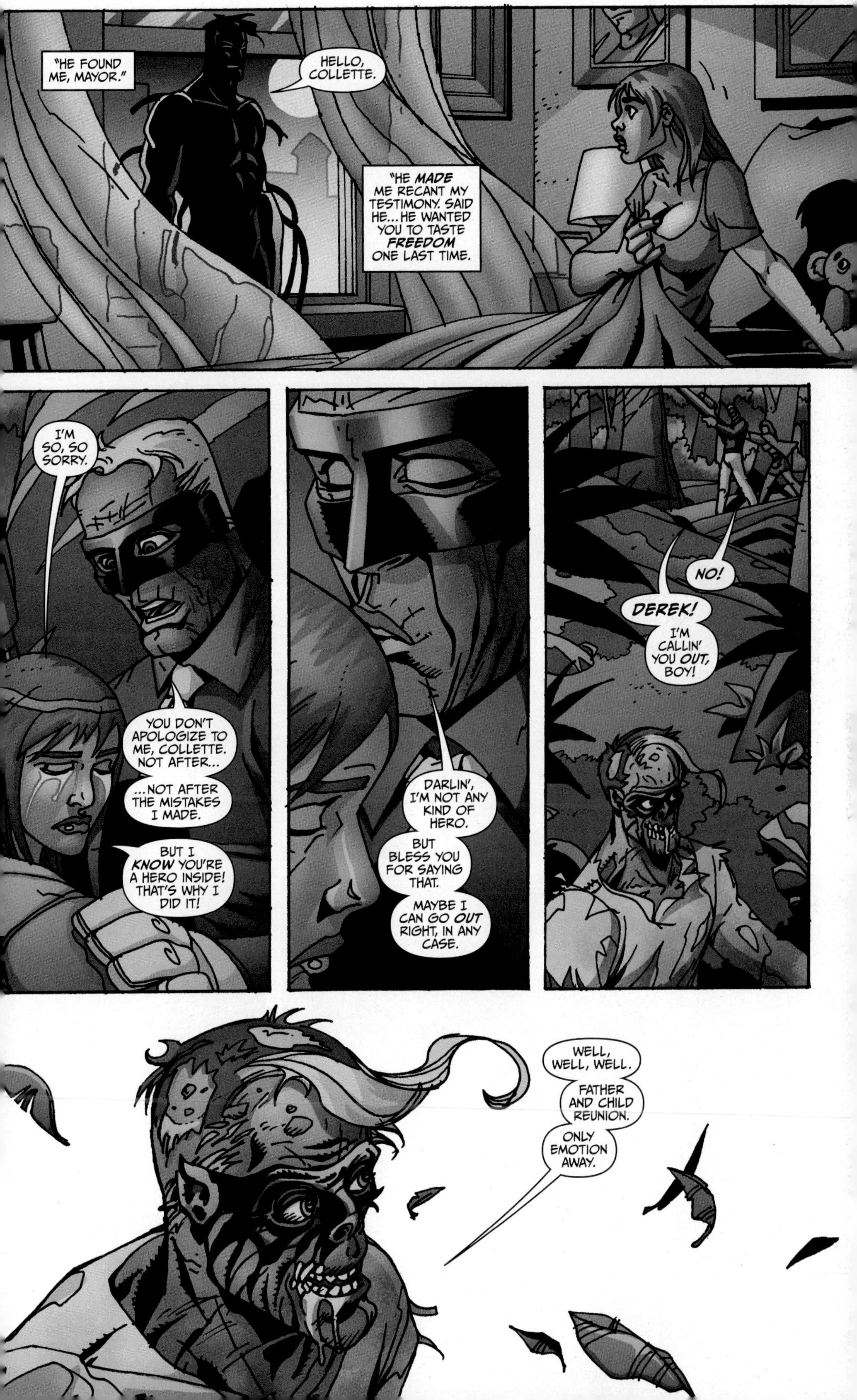
"HE FOUND ME, MAYOR."
HELLO, COLLETTE.
"HE MADE ME RECANT MY TESTIMONY. SAID HE... HE WANTED YOU TO TASTE FREEDOM ONE LAST TIME.
I'M SO, SO SORRY.
YOU DON'T APOLOGIZE TO ME, COLLETTE. NOT AFTER...
...NOT AFTER THE MISTAKES I MADE.
BUT I KNOW YOU'RE A HERO INSIDE! THAT'S WHY I DID IT!
DARLIN', I'M NOT ANY KIND OF HERO.
BUT BLESS YOU FOR SAYING THAT.
MAYBE I CAN GO OUT RIGHT, IN ANY CASE.
NO!
DEREK!
I'M CALLIN' YOU OUT, BOY!
WELL, WELL, WELL.
FATHER AND CHILD REUNION.
ONLY EMOTION AWAY.

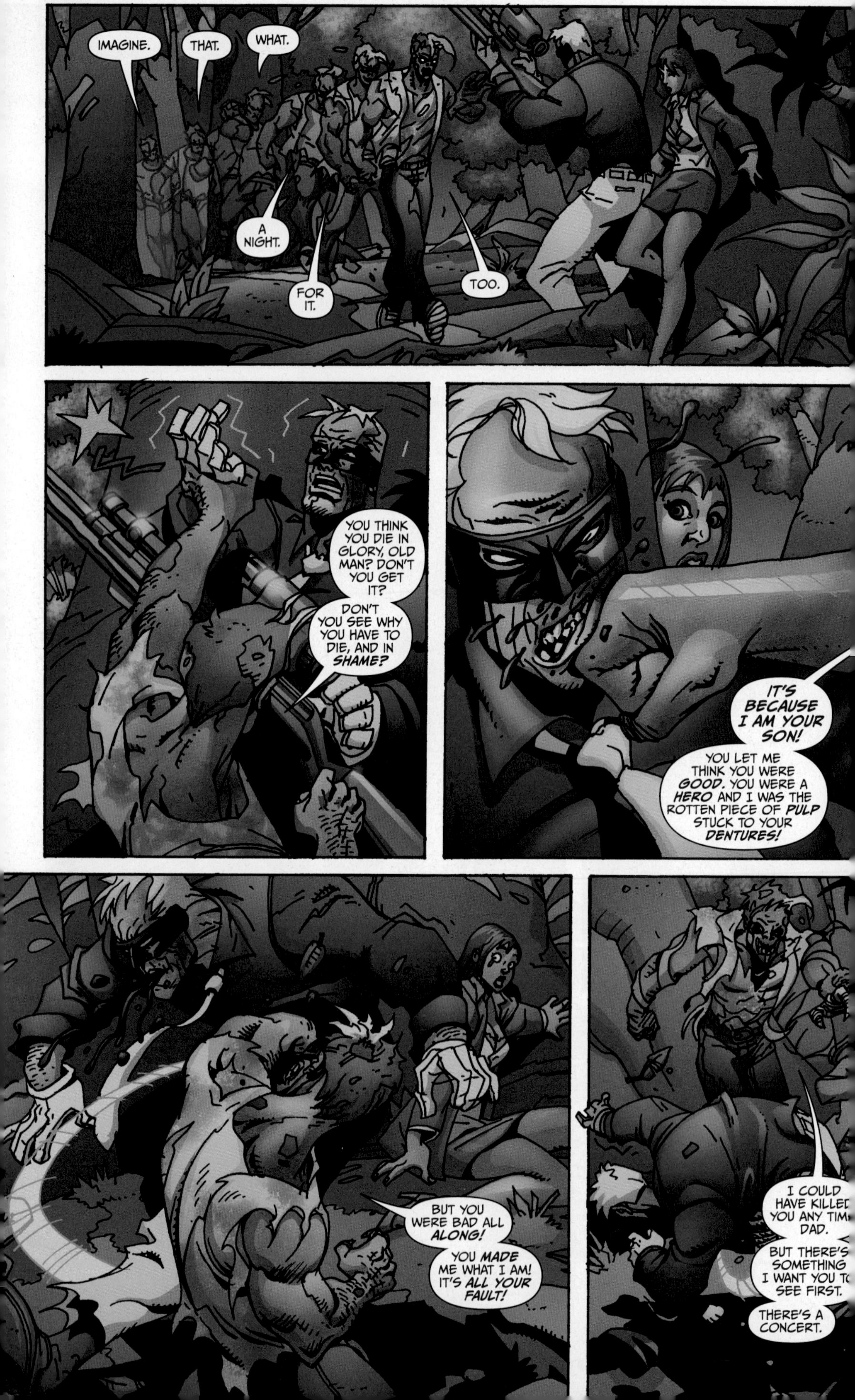
IMAGINE.
THAT.
WHAT.
A NIGHT.
FOR IT.
TOO.
YOU THINK YOU DIE IN GLORY, OLD MAN? DON'T YOU GET IT?
DON'T YOU SEE WHY YOU HAVE TO DIE, AND IN SHAME?
IT'S BECAUSE I AM YOUR SON!
YOU LET ME THINK YOU WERE GOOD. YOU WERE A HERO AND I WAS THE ROTTEN PIECE OF PULP STUCK TO YOUR DENTURES!
BUT YOU WERE BAD ALL ALONG!
YOU MADE ME WHAT I AM! IT'S ALL YOUR FAULT!
I COULD HAVE KILLED YOU ANY TIM DAD.
BUT THERE'S SOMETHING I WANT YOU TO SEE FIRST.
THERE'S A CONCERT.

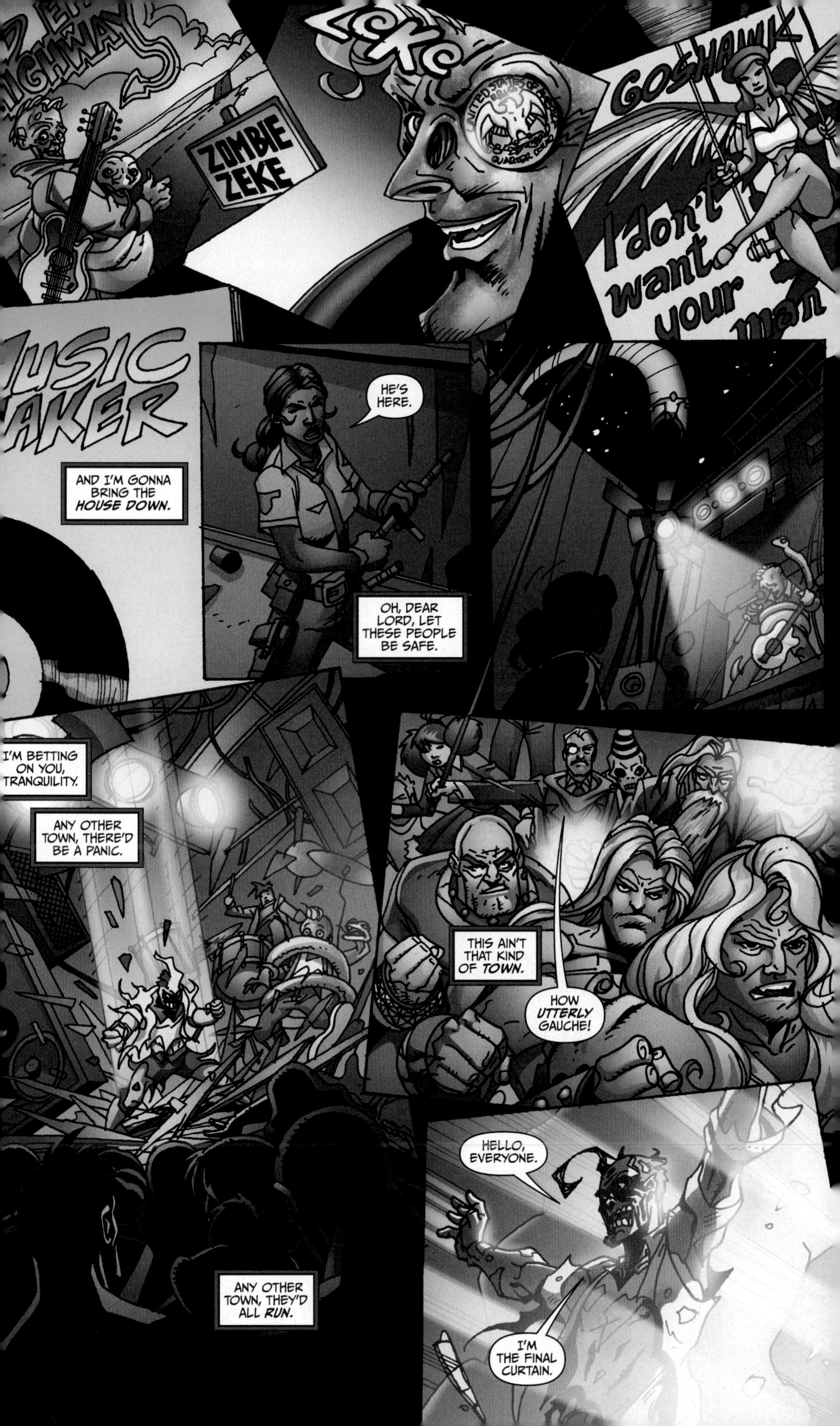

HIGHWAY
ZOMBIE ZEKE
GOSHAWK
I don't want your man
USIC
AKER
AND I'M GONNA BRING THE *HOUSE DOWN.*
HE'S HERE.
OH, DEAR LORD, LET THESE PEOPLE BE SAFE.
I'M BETTING ON YOU, TRANQUILITY.
ANY OTHER TOWN, THERE'D BE A PANIC.
THIS AIN'T THAT KIND OF *TOWN.*
HOW *UTTERLY* GAUCHE!
ANY OTHER TOWN, THEY'D ALL *RUN.*
HELLO, EVERYONE.
I'M THE FINAL CURTAIN.

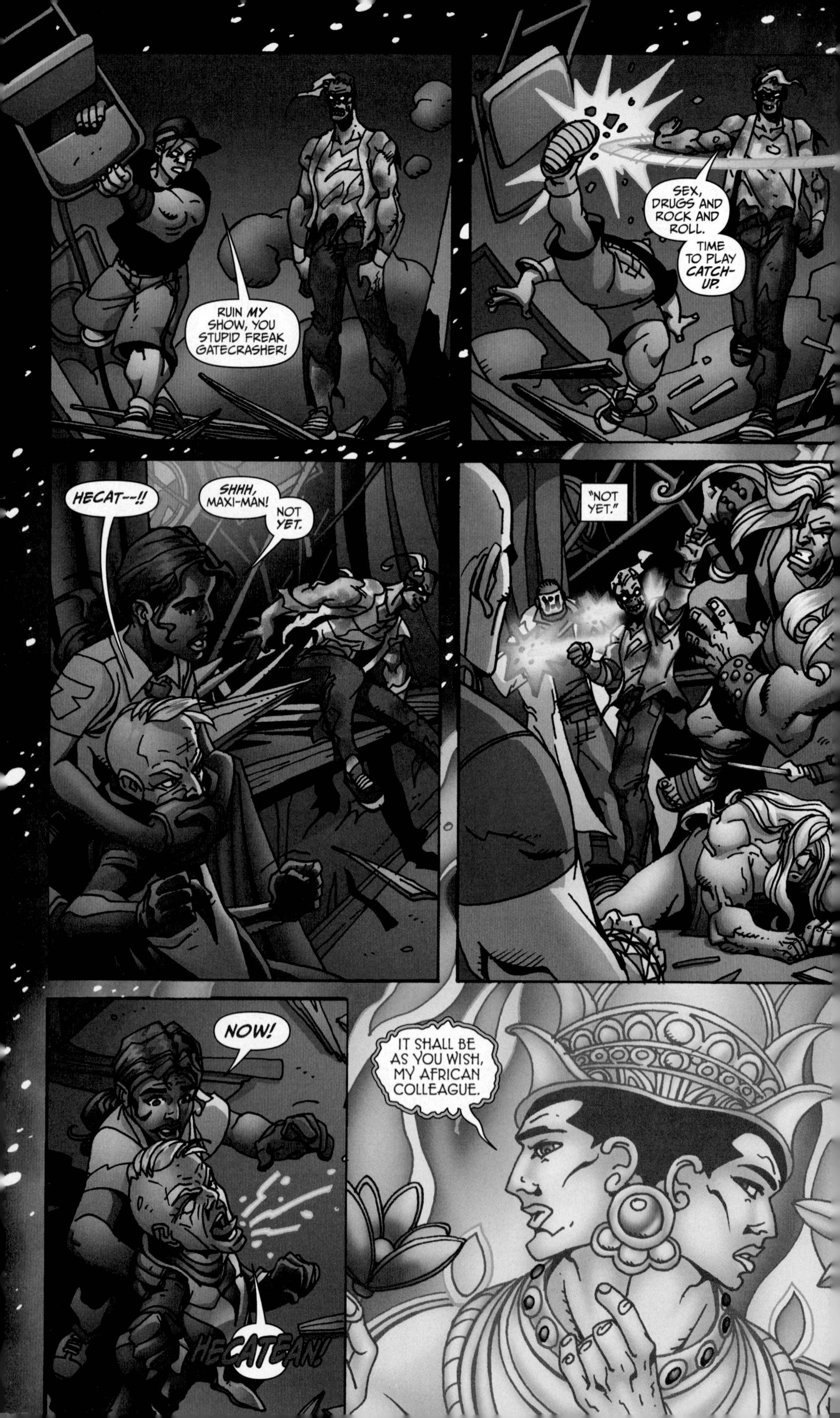
RUIN MY SHOW, YOU STUPID FREAK GATECRASHER!
SEX, DRUGS AND ROCK AND ROLL.
TIME TO PLAY CATCH-UP.
HECAT--!!
SHHH, MAXI-MAN!
NOT YET.
"NOT YET."
NOW!
HECATEAN!
IT SHALL BE AS YOU WISH, MY AFRICAN COLLEAGUE.

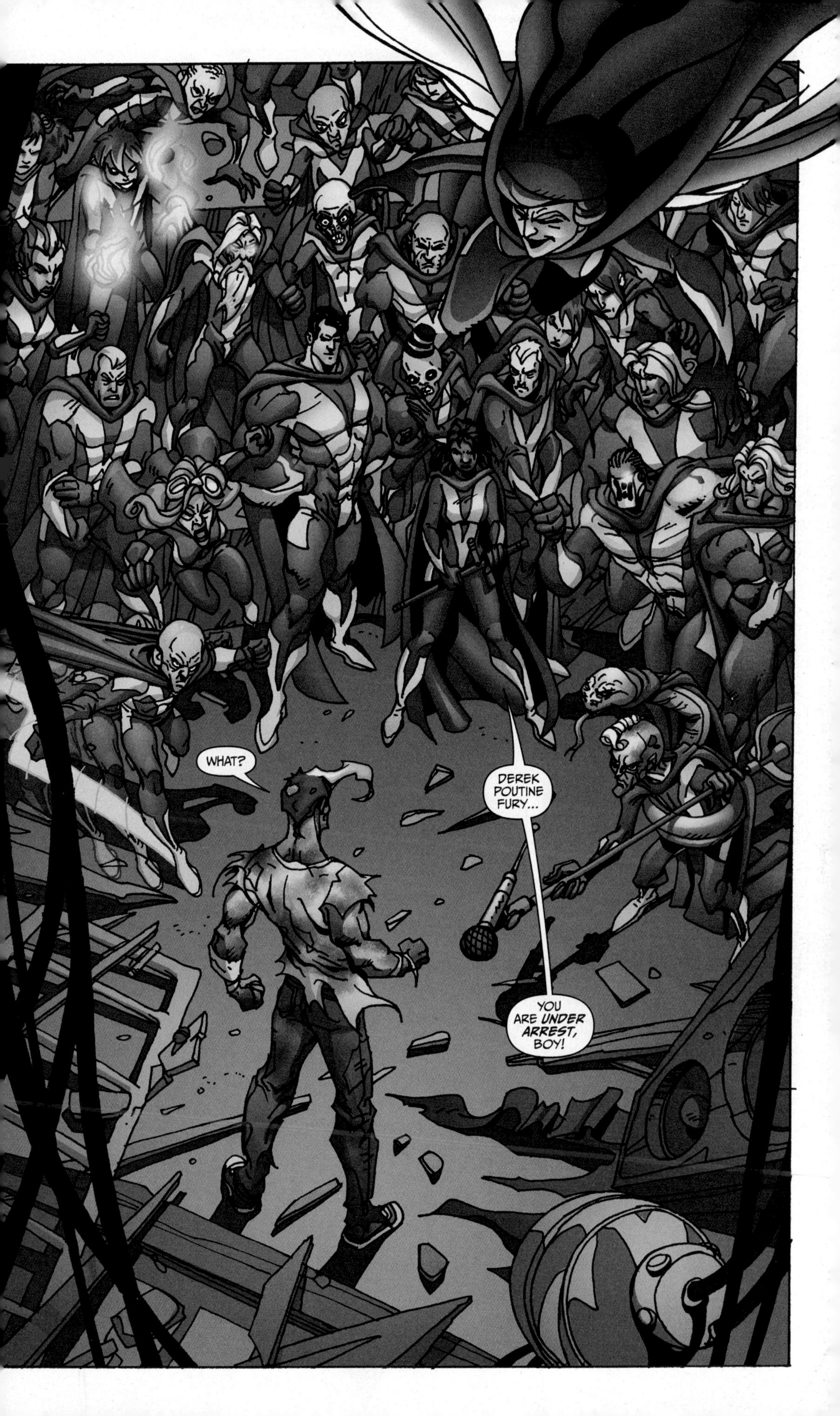
WHAT?
DEREK POUTINE FURY...
YOU ARE UNDER ARREST, BOY!

THIS MAN IS WANTED FOR MULTIPLE COUNTS OF *MURDER*, CITIZENS.

DON'T *HESITATE* TO GIVE HIM A NICE TRANQUILITY *WELCOME!*

WAIT.

YOU CHEATED.

YOU CHEATED!

YOU WERE ALL SUPPOSED TO BE *WEEEAKK!*

GRROOWOOWWLLL.

THIS ISN'T *FAIR.*

QUIT *WHINGING,* EMO BOY!

SERPENT FLAIL CO BANZAI!

IT'S NOT *FAIR!*

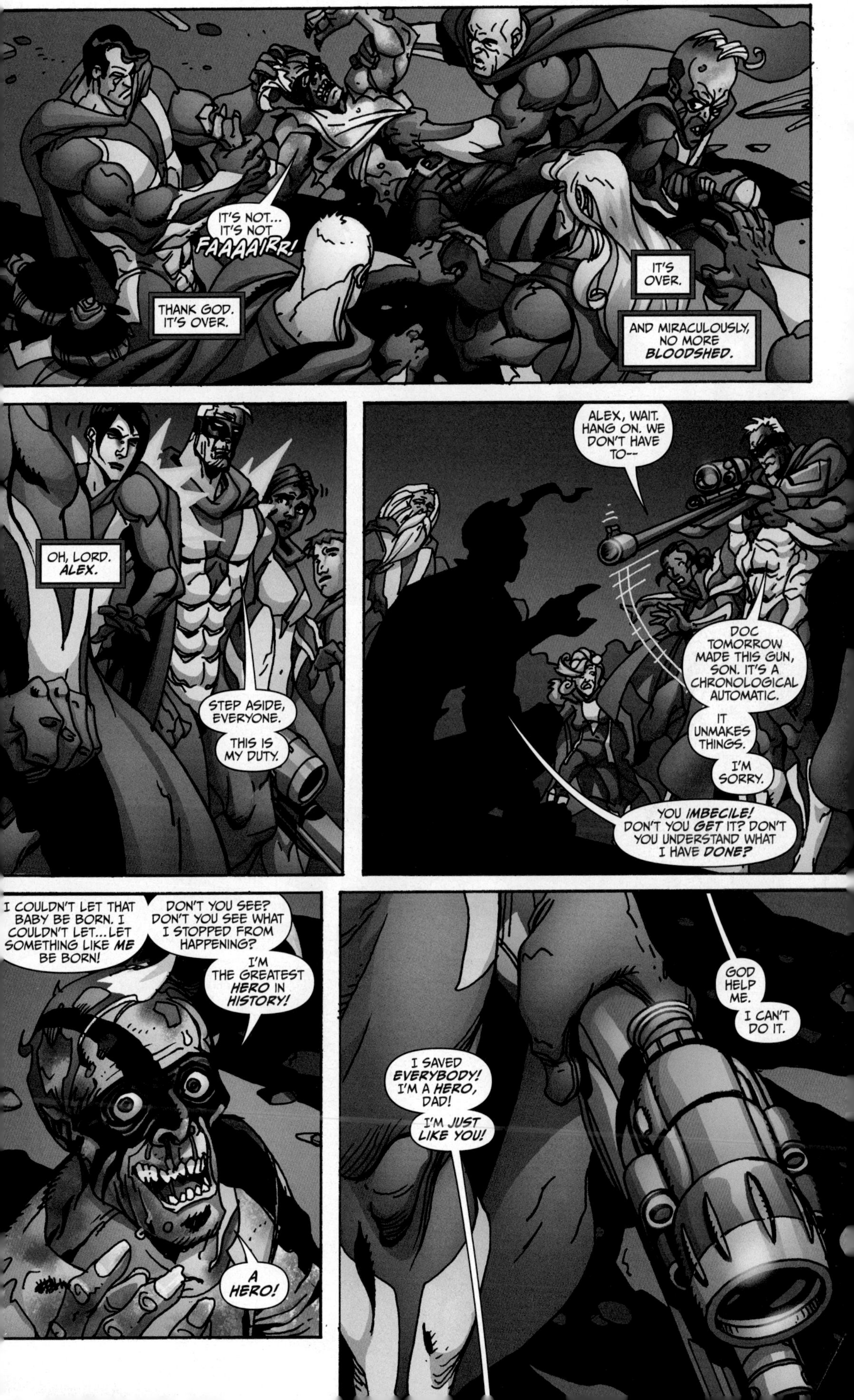
IT'S NOT... IT'S NOT FAAAAIRR!
THANK GOD. IT'S OVER.
IT'S OVER.
AND MIRACULOUSLY, NO MORE BLOODSHED.
OH, LORD. ALEX.
STEP ASIDE, EVERYONE.
THIS IS MY DUTY.
ALEX, WAIT. HANG ON. WE DON'T HAVE TO--
DOC TOMORROW MADE THIS GUN, SON. IT'S A CHRONOLOGICAL AUTOMATIC.
IT UNMAKES THINGS.
I'M SORRY.
YOU IMBECILE! DON'T YOU GET IT? DON'T YOU UNDERSTAND WHAT I HAVE DONE?
I COULDN'T LET THAT BABY BE BORN. I COULDN'T LET...LET SOMETHING LIKE ME BE BORN!
DON'T YOU SEE? DON'T YOU SEE WHAT I STOPPED FROM HAPPENING?
I'M THE GREATEST HERO IN HISTORY!
A HERO!
GOD HELP ME.
I CAN'T DO IT.
I SAVED EVERYBODY! I'M A HERO, DAD!
I'M JUST LIKE YOU!

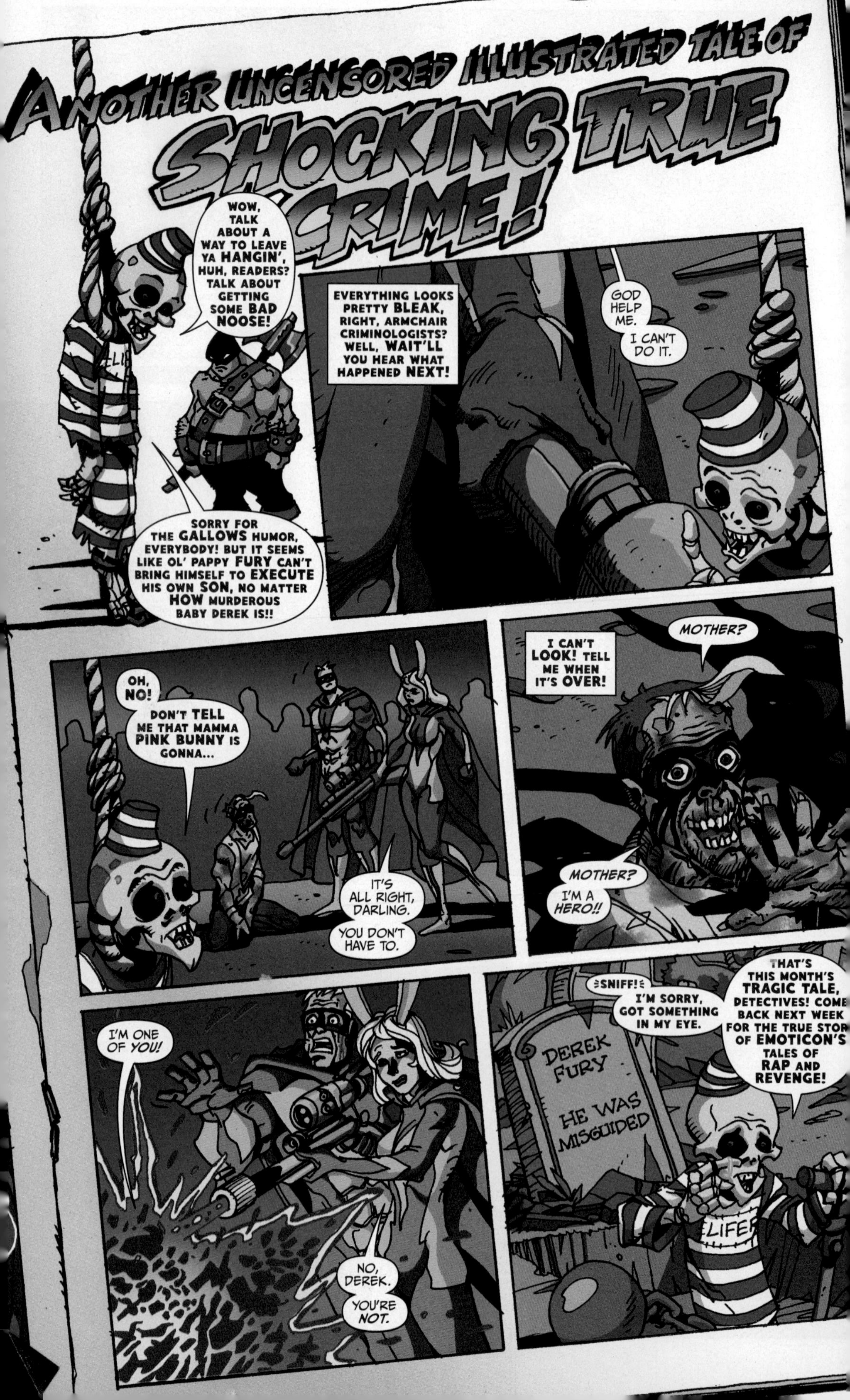
Another Uncensored Illustrated Tale of
Shocking True Crime!
WOW, TALK ABOUT A WAY TO LEAVE YA HANGIN', HUH, READERS? TALK ABOUT GETTING SOME BAD NOOSE!
SORRY FOR THE GALLOWS HUMOR, EVERYBODY! BUT IT SEEMS LIKE OL' PAPPY FURY CAN'T BRING HIMSELF TO EXECUTE HIS OWN SON, NO MATTER HOW MURDEROUS BABY DEREK IS!!
EVERYTHING LOOKS PRETTY BLEAK, RIGHT, ARMCHAIR CRIMINOLOGISTS? WELL, WAIT'LL YOU HEAR WHAT HAPPENED NEXT!
GOD HELP ME.
I CAN'T DO IT.
OH, NO!
DON'T TELL ME THAT MAMMA PINK BUNNY IS GONNA...
IT'S ALL RIGHT, DARLING.
YOU DON'T HAVE TO.
I CAN'T LOOK! TELL ME WHEN IT'S OVER!
MOTHER?
MOTHER?
I'M A HERO!!
I'M ONE OF YOU!
NO, DEREK.
YOU'RE NOT.
SNIFF!
I'M SORRY, GOT SOMETHING IN MY EYE.
THAT'S THIS MONTH'S TRAGIC TALE, DETECTIVES! COME BACK NEXT WEEK FOR THE TRUE STOR OF EMOTICON'S TALES OF RAP AND REVENGE!
DEREK FURY
HE WAS MISGUIDED
LIFER

I WISH, I WISH IT DIDN'T TURN OUT THIS WAY. CONSIDERING WHAT DEREK DID, THERE'S NO QUESTION PINK BUNNY WILL GET OFF WITHOUT SERIOUS CHARGES.

BUT THE FURY NAME IS DONE. WHATEVER GOOD THEY'VE DONE, WHATEVER KINDNESSES... ALL ANYONE ON THE OUTSIDE WILL EVER REMEMBER IS SHE SHOT HER OWN KID.

I'M SORRY, SUZE.

ALEX SAID THAT DEREK COULD BRING THINGS BACK TO LIFE, IF HE CONCENTRATED. SAID IT WAS IMPOSSIBLY HARD, BUT HE COULD DO IT.

DID HE BRING MR. A BACK BECAUSE HE KNEW... KNEW HOW I FELT ABOUT HIM?

WAS THIS A GIFT? A TORMENT? A TEMPTATION?

I DON'T KNOW. BUT MR. A CAME UP AND MADE SURE I WAS OKAY, FIRST THING, WHILE EVERYONE ELSE WAS STILL WONDERING WHAT HAPPENED.

I DON'T KNOW HOW I'M GOING TO EXPLAIN TO MAMA THAT I WANT TO MARRY A SEVENTY-FIVE-YEAR-OLD WHITE MAN WHO MAY OR MAY NOT BE A RE-ANIMATED CORPSE.

BUT I DO.

AND I'M GONNA.

THE HEART WANTS WHAT IT DAMN WANTS.

SHE'S GONNA BE OKAY.

WIN SOME, LOSE SOME, KID.

OREGON

GOT A LITTLE REGULAR CHORE UP THE COAST I HAVE TO DO FIRST.

THEN, OH, YES, THEN.

BECAUSE ALL THINGS CONSIDERED, I WANT TO LIVE.

OH, YES, I DO.

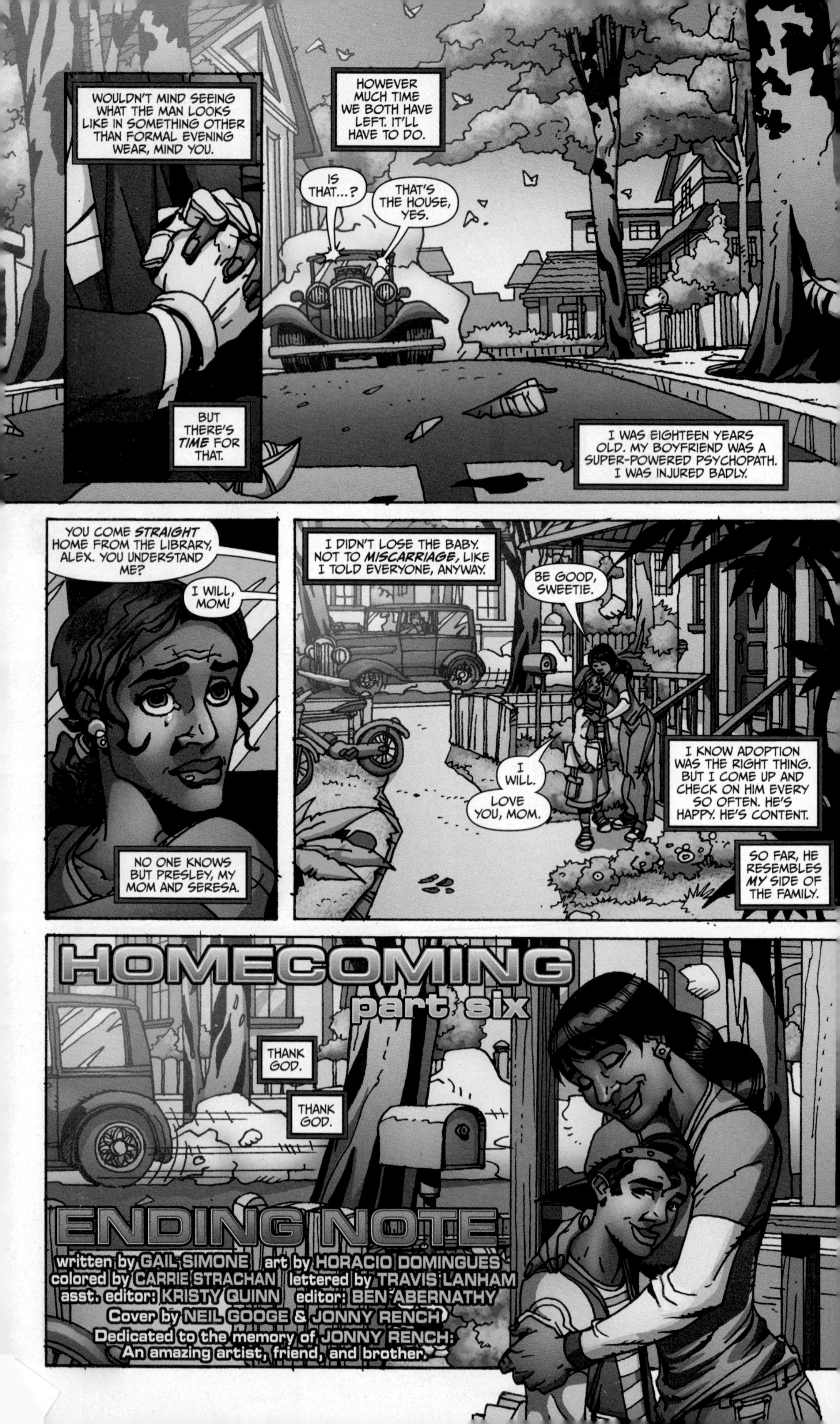
WOULDN'T MIND SEEING WHAT THE MAN LOOKS LIKE IN SOMETHING OTHER THAN FORMAL EVENING WEAR, MIND YOU.
BUT THERE'S *TIME* FOR THAT.
HOWEVER MUCH TIME WE BOTH HAVE LEFT. IT'LL HAVE TO DO.
IS THAT...?
THAT'S THE HOUSE, YES.
I WAS EIGHTEEN YEARS OLD. MY BOYFRIEND WAS A SUPER-POWERED PSYCHOPATH. I WAS INJURED BADLY.
YOU COME *STRAIGHT* HOME FROM THE LIBRARY, ALEX. YOU UNDERSTAND ME?
I WILL, MOM!
NO ONE KNOWS BUT PRESLEY, MY MOM AND SERESA.
I DIDN'T LOSE THE BABY. NOT TO *MISCARRIAGE,* LIKE I TOLD EVERYONE, ANYWAY.
BE GOOD, SWEETIE.
I WILL.
LOVE YOU, MOM.
I KNOW ADOPTION WAS THE RIGHT THING. BUT I COME UP AND CHECK ON HIM EVERY SO OFTEN. HE'S HAPPY. HE'S CONTENT.
SO FAR, HE RESEMBLES *MY* SIDE OF THE FAMILY.
HOMECOMING
part six
THANK GOD.
THANK GOD.
ENDING NOTE
written by GAIL SIMONE art by HORACIO DOMINGUES
colored by CARRIE STRACHAN lettered by TRAVIS LANHAM
asst. editor: KRISTY QUINN editor: BEN ABERNATHY
Cover by NEIL GOOGE & JONNY RENCH
Dedicated to the memory of JONNY RENCH: An amazing artist, friend, and brother.